Photo © Effy Alexakis

Mary Zournazi is a writer and philosopher who lives in Sydney. She has a PhD in cultural theory, philosophy and politics. Her recent books include *Foreign Dialogues* (1998, Pluto Press Australia) and *After the Revolution – On Kristeva* (with John Lechte, 1998, Artspace), and with Lechte she is the co-editor of *The Kristeva Critical Reader* (forthcoming, Edinburgh Press). She also works as a radio producer. *Foreign Dialogues* was made into an eight-part radio series for *Radio Eye*, ABC Radio National, Australia. She has produced a radio feature based on material in *Hope* for the Australian Broadcasting Corporation.

HOPE

new philosophies
for change

mary zournazi

ROUTLEDGE
Taylor & Francis Group

In loving memory of Zara,
who taught me what real hope is:
love, friendship and joy.

'...in impossible times when
one does not know how old one is
or how young one is yet to be'.

FRIEDRICH NIETZSCHE

First published in 2002 by

Pluto Press Australia
Locked Bag 199
Annandale NSW 2038
www.plutoaustralia.com

Published in the U.S.A. and Canada in 2003 by
Routledge
29 West 35th Street
New York, NY 10001
www.routledge-ny.com
Routledge is an imprint of the Taylor & Francis Group.

Published in the U.K in 2002 by
Lawrence & Wishart
99a Wallis Road
London E9 5LN
www.l-w-bks.co.uk

Copyedited by Michael Wall
Designed by Peter Long
Typeset by Hazard Publishing Ltd, Christchurch, New Zealand
Printed and bound by Hyde Park Press, South Australia

Cataloging-in-Publication Data is available from the Library of Congress.

Contents

Acknowledgments

This book came out of an economic and political climate where support for 'ideas', critical or otherwise, is narrowly defined and extremely limited. This is a book about hope – but hope can only come when we live in public and political cultures where there is truly a space for dialogue – that is, a public arena where ideas are allowed and there is a space made possible *for those yet to be heard*. In the light of this, all support for this book, so it could be heard, came from unexpected and independent sources. I am extremely grateful to all who came to my aid, and gave me faith.

I would like to give special thanks to Tony Moore, at Pluto Press, for believing in this book against the backdrop of political conservatism and the concerted destruction of 'independent' publishing. Without his hope, this book would not have taken shape. I would like to also thank Megan Alsop and Antoinette Wilson, at Pluto, for guiding the book through the production phases. Thanks to Michael Wall for his clear-sightedness and editorial suggestions at the copy stage. And, in the latter part of this book's production, thanks to Sally Davison at Lawrence and Wishart for taking up publishing rights in the UK, and William Germano at Routledge, New York.

I would like to thank all my friends who helped make this book what it is; without their kindness and support for me, I could not have continued. And, when and where necessary, for providing me with financial assistance *to continue* and *to believe* in this project – in those moments where I had lost all hope. In particular I thank Alphonso Lingis for his unconditional friendship and generous support for my travelling, Celeste Olalquiaga for a free flat in Paris and teaching me how to be strong and independent, Kirsten Campbell for her generosity and London house, Carolyn Burke for spiritual guidance and friendship, and John Lechte for his ongoing encouragement and financial aid.

I am grateful to the French Embassy in Australia for assistance with translation, and Alliance Française in Sydney for giving me free French lessons. This independent support gave me the strength and resolve that work can be done against the odds. Thanks to Tony Macgregor of ABC Radio National's *Radio Eye* for giving me the space and resources to make a radio feature based on material in this book. Special thanks to Matthew Leonard for his faith in my writing and radio work, and Brent Clough for his continual support of my ideas. I'd also like to thank Cathy Peters for collaborating with me on the *Hope* radio feature and teaching me how to make really good radio.

My sincere appreciation goes to: Anne-Marie Lane, who continues to work with me on my projects and who did the initial transcription work; Peter Cowley for the translation of Julia Kristeva and Michel Serres; and Deidre Gilfedder and Louise Burchell for interpreting for me in Paris. And thanks to the Peter Wall Institute for Advanced Studies, at the University of British Columbia, Canada, for a one-month fellowship that 'saved my life', and gave me great hope.

With gratitude I thank all my collaborators, who, in the spirit of generosity, joined in, and spoke to me about hope. I give special thanks to my family, who continually teach me hope and humility. Finally, throughout the writing of this book, Andrew Metcalfe gave me inspiration, Tonje Akerholt her extremely keen eye, Catherine Campbell her willing ear and, in the final stages, Tania Edwards and Tamara Domicelj the faith to keep going when events in my life made me very sad and despairing.

Prologue

This is a book about hope. To me, 'hope' is about a certain generosity and gratefulness that we all need in life. If life is a series of encounters and chance meetings, events and social relations, then hope lies across all of these. It is a basic human condition that involves belief and trust in the world. It is the stuff of our dreams and desires, our ideas of freedom and justice and how we might conceive life.

In this book, hope is also about a spirit of dialogue, where generosity and laughter break open a space to keep spontaneity and freedom alive – the joyful engagements possible with others. For in any conversation – individual or political, written, spoken or read – there needs to be the ability to hear, listen and give. If we shut down a discussion through resentment, fear or unwillingness – through adversity or polarised individual or political positions – generosity ceases, and the openness of real discussion and debate is diminished. When a dialogue is not permitted there can be no space for exchange – words and ideas become self-enclosed and the exchange becomes a kind of monologue, a type of depression and narcissism where territories are defended and the stakes raised are already known.

Reflections, conversations and dialogues build new social and individual *imaginaries* – visions of the world that create possibilities for change. They lift us out of despair and let us take new risks in our encounters with each other. What I pose here is the ethical and political responsibility we can share in writing and thinking about hope. This is about collaboration – in writing, in thinking, in politics – how working ideas together, across different styles and traditions, can let new ideas, views and expressions emerge. This involves a sense of trust and a 'faith without certitudes' about where hope may lie in thinking about the future. In secular times, when hope has moved out of the religious sphere, the turn towards the future may be found in struggles for individual justice, and in political activity across the globe.

INTRODUCTION

The days of winter

I began to think about hope in the spring of 1999, at the end of winter. Hope and change, it is said, are about 'the end of our winter days', but in the years of writing this book I sometimes felt that my winter had only just begun. This is because we live in a world where our belief, faith and trust in political or individual actions are increasingly being threatened, leading to despair and uncertainty. It is easy to be pessimistic with wars, ecological disasters and increasing social inequalities all around us. New technologies and global economies make our lives less real and more virtual, and lead to increasing individuation – the isolation and loneliness felt in consumerist, market-driven economies. A symptom of the times is the decline in interest in hope as a philosophical and political concept.

So what might a philosophy and politics of hope involve? My initial thoughts and feelings on this were about what it means to live across a range of social realities – as a public intellectual who lives in the midst of cultural despair, and as a daughter of migrants who has not lived out the dreams of economic success in the new country. Hope, then, began to mean many things to me. Standing in dole queues I began to realise that whatever stage of life you are at – young or old, skilled or unskilled – you are always potentially on the social and economic scrap-heap. This led me to consider where hope may lie in social terms, and to reflect on the disconnectedness felt in life and labour. It brought home the real feelings of hopelessness and despair in our identities, in our sense of being in the world. Where is hope when compassion, empathy and dignity are synonymous with self-gratification – getting what you want at the expense of others, whether in the workplace, in our relationships or 'across the board'?

Hope can be what sustains life in the face of despair, and yet it is not simply the desire for things to come, or the betterment of life. It is the drive or energy that embeds us in the world – in the ecology of life, ethics and politics. But it is also to do with power relations – the economic aspirations of what life is 'meant to be'. In late capitalism, our humanness is closely tied to economic definitions of the self, and notions of security and comfort. The search for happiness becomes a search for emotional security based on economic success, and our personal dreams are part of the drive to get more out of life – more success, more money, more hope. But instability at work, at home and in our social relations makes these visions of happiness an *imagined* reality, both individually and nationally. With this comes an increased sense of frustration and insecurity, where feeling 'at home' requires protection against anyone who threatens our comfort. For instance, foreigners may be seen as threatening to us, and to our national security and comfort. In Australia, where I live, we have recently seen this in the treatment of asylum-seekers and refugees.

The success of right-wing governments and sentiments lies in reworking hope in a negative frame. Hope masquerades as a vision, where the passion and insecurity felt by people become part of a call for national unity and identity, part of a community sentiment and future ideal of what we imagine ourselves to be. It is a kind of future nostalgia, a 'fantastic hope' for national unity charged by a static vision of life and the exclusion of difference. When, for the benefit of our security and belonging, we evoke a hope that ignores the suffering of others, we can only create a hope based on fear. This hope lies in the heart of terror, where violence is enacted in literal and figurative ways, such as in the Australian government's response to refugees and the creation of 'border' protection policies, and in the language of public opinion. Hospitality towards other people then becomes conditional and, more often than not, hostile and unforgiving. When public sentiment is fuelled by insecurity, the risks we take with each other, and the potential for public debate, are diminished. The anger, injustice and hopelessness we feel is vented onto 'others' who do not share our 'identity'. We see this tendency worldwide, not just in Australia but also, for instance, in France with Jean-Marie Le Pen and in Austria with Jörg Haider. In each case, populist talk of 'national unity' keeps alive the resentment that accompanies people's insecurity and despair. Empathy and dialogue are denied in the broader public discussion of what it means to belong to a community. In Australia, for instance, can there be a real dialogue with Afghan or Iraqi refugees when generosity towards others is restricted and the provisions for living in a country become ethnically biased?

We could argue, then, that hope cannot be separated from how national debates are framed and from the reality of living in a globalised world. But community insecurity needs to be explored through individual experience as well as national debates. It is easy to take a moral stand and to blame others for their unwillingness to engage in dialogue. But we have to move beyond a politics of blame to one of compassion – a political activity that gives us hope and understands how hope and despair emerge in contemporary life, because when people have no hope to give they also have little space to reflect and engage with others. This is a symptom of the increasing disparities between rich and poor that are produced through national and global economies. The population becomes disenfranchised, giving rise to class divisions, ethnic tensions and poverty. These social conditions produce feelings of despair and anger, and those who feel bereft may call upon the last bastion of dignity – their identity. At the same time the major political parties, and democratic politics in general, are failing to provide other possibilities for hope based on compassion, sensitivity and care.

We must, then, explore hope through the societies we live in: the alienations that affect us in individual and collective ways; the grief, despair and loneliness; and the new social, ethnic and class relations that come out of these alienations. Hope is built on belief and faith, and the trust that there is a life worth living in uncertain times. Without this kind of hope there is a denial of difference and newness, meaning that nothing is possible in personal or political terms. Without hope what is left is *death* – the death of spirit, the death of life – where there is no longer any sense of regeneration and renewal. And in modern concentration and asylum camps, where hope is almost totally diminished, it can be a *living death*.

In the spirit of life and dialogue

What I have set out to explore in this book is a philosophy (in fact, various philosophies) and politics of hope – a hope that comes out of our present lives and struggles. To help me through my ongoing crisis of faith, and since I have an interest in dialogue, I have invited others to come on this journey of hope with me. This book is a collection of ideas and reflections on hope by myself and various Australian and international writers and public intellectuals. Each chapter is a conversation, and each conversation looks at hope in a variety of ways and explores its potential. These conversational journeys are themselves models for dialogues that could emerge in our encounters with different people, approaches and traditions. The aim is to encourage further public dialogue, and to spur readers to engage with these thoughts and feelings on hope. The book doesn't seek to answer questions, merely to pose them, and to allow myself and others to share the ideas that emerge between critical perspectives and public discourse.

I believe there is danger in ratifying systems of thinking and belief – where hope becomes polarised into political terms and rhetoric. Within the three-year period of this book's germination, the world's events have become increasingly less hopeful, and more desperate. The book was conceived and researched before September 11, the escalation of violence in the Middle East, and the Tampa crisis in Australia. Although these events are not directly addressed, there has been space for reflection and revision in some chapters. I continue to believe that we need to re-envisage and imagine hope as a convergence of new agendas, conversations and possibilities in everyday life and political activity. The hope investigated here could shed light on the false hopes and promises that have been sustained over the last several years. It provides a framework to think about 'progressive' politics.

The central questions of the book are about individual experience and political life – what make us who we are. In global terms, what revolutions in thinking and hope can make a difference? I explore what might be important, and indeed useful, in rethinking communal politics and individual agency. I'm interested in what hopeful visions for the future may arise, based on reconsidering what it means to be human, and how we relate to the world around us. For me, this is almost an existential question about our sense of being in the world and our perceptions of it – and about how time, history and living change, in our perceptions and experience. How, that is, can we reflect on the past – to learn and to challenge injustices that have occurred, and to build new sites for contemporary struggles?

We need to take a critical look at ourselves and what we want our lives to be – not in some future or ideal sense (hope is often thought of as future-oriented) but in the act of living, the ordinary elements of everyday life. This requires a 'spark' of hope – a hope that does not narrow our visions of the world but instead allows different histories, memories and experiences to enter into present conversations on revolution, freedom and our cultural senses of belonging. It can allow for the narratives, dreams and hopes both of people within a country and those who travel from afar to belong to it. This moment of crisis in history, and present understandings of it, may enable other ways of documenting how we may live and hope.

I believe a hopeful project for these times is to reflect upon and challenge the way 'progress' and new forms of capitalism lead to false visions of the world. Without a deeper understanding of its meaning, hope can only masquerade as some essential truth for capitalism. For me this involves revisiting some basic tenets of socialist and Marxist ideas of social relations – what it means to be human, our relations to labour, and the alienation experienced in class and social stratification. But we cannot ignore the failures of socialist systems and the turn towards fundamentalism, nor, in critical thinking around this, the dreams of a utopian society – where the future is seen as the end-point to all struggles. Rather, what I am exploring is how certain ideas and visions can be updated in our current economies and lives – rethinking social and economic justice, and principles of equality in a post-Marxist age. Throughout the book I explore the possible convergences and ideas that could provide the Left with new sites for change.

We cannot, however, assume that everyone agrees or understands 'Left' or 'Right' as the standard principles for the political organisation of societies, because to do this is to lose sight of power and *resistance*. In the movement of crowds at the May Day protests over the last several years, for instance, we have seen the links made between global exploitation and community groups who are uniting against economic, environmental and social injustice. In these protests many people who come together may be actively working against global capital and, at the same time, expressing their dissatisfaction with more Leftist traditions of political thought. So how might we consider new calls for freedom and justice, and diverse lines of power and invention? What we need to do is open out a dialogue with the Left to evoke change and find hopeful ways to envisage contemporary political activity and action. Through the conversations in this book, then, I contest various older traditions of revolutionary, socialist and Marxist thought – revisiting the old not to replace it but to think with it, and working through some new tools for a philosophy and politics of hope. I am looking for what might be more global notions of hope, where it may lie, and what human dignity and freedom may now require.

This is not limited to individual or political terms, but engages with wider senses of belonging which relate to our life experiences and how we fit into a 'cosmos' of global concerns – ecological and political questions that emerge in today's world. For me this involves cultivating joy in critical thinking and individual life, for without the experience of joy we cannot move through the desperation that frames contemporary living. A 'joyful hope' is about recognising our hopes in daily ways – the suffering and pain that we encounter – and about the ways we can experience 'happiness' outside of the spirit of capitalism. This allows us to keep asking what risks need to be taken for a hopeful world, what habits of thought need to be changed in our cultures, and what responsibilities and ethical and political acts will make the world a hopeful place.

*

Hope is divided into three parts, or meditations: 'The elements of hope', 'A politics of hope' and 'Revolutionary hope'. The three parts are interconnected conversational journeys which explore the multitude of directions that hope can take. Each of these meditations on hope echoes my broad explorations of where hope may lie in everyday life, experience and politics. Part I provides the framework for the book – various thoughts, ideas and perspectives on hope in personal, philosophical and political terms. Part II develops these ideas of hope, and looks more closely at the social, ethnic and class relations of hope, and the connections with nationalist and political movements. Part III integrates different ideas on the philosophies of hope through scientific, cultural and political questions. It explores the changing face of technologies – our bodies and our relations to ecological and political issues – and, within this, the creative risks we need to take.

In these three 'meditations' and the 'conversations' (chapters) within them, I have chosen certain individual writers and thinkers because of my interest in connecting philosophical ideas on hope with a political framework. Each writer and thinker, whom I will introduce in the course of the book, engages with me about these hopes in very personal ways – through their lives, work and critical perspectives. This provides a space for some visions... What might make us care for our sense of belonging, in social, political and ecological terms? What joys are possible? In uncertain times, what kinds of meaning, trust and diplomacy can move us towards the possibility of peace? What dialogues are necessary in present life, and what are the hopeful possibilities for future generations? And, in all these hopes, what might be new revolutions for our times?

Part I

The Elements of Hope

1
MURMURS OF LIFE
A conversation with Alphonso Lingis

What does hope involve in everyday life and experience? Imagine you have a friend who is sick or a loved one who is dying: there is a trust that situations or events, even in adversity, have an element that could sustain our belief in the world. This hope has no logical or clear definition to it. It may be the hope that things could be different or the cherishing of life, where courage marks the strength to continue, and where aspects of grief, mourning and death become part of life, and the movement is one away from despair. If we can understand hope as composing life as it emerges, there is the possibility of joy and a hopeful vision for the world.

It is this hope that evokes the heroes in everyday life – the experiences of living that are not about success, or aspiring to some greater truth, but about reality itself. This involves a sensitivity towards life and the responsibilities we may have towards ourselves and others. If we introduce responsibility into individual and political discourse, what are these hopes? In this realm, ideas of hospitality and sensitivity to others become part of the critical domain.

It is a sense of the deep connections in life and living, a compassion to and for life that comes out of strength, that can embrace and sustain our hopes. For to live, breathe, think and be composes the truth of what we experience, and what gifts can emerge in societies outside the alienation and disenchantment that shapes daily life. Philosopher Alphonso Lingis and I reflect on this hope: its reality, truth and joy. Lingis is based in the United States but travels extensively throughout the world. His writings are travel meditations and philosophical reflections on everyday life and experience. His philosophy embraces the vitality of living and the ethics of our encounters with others.

Reality, truth and joy

Mary: To begin, I'd like to ask you to reflect on the idea of hope.

Alphonso: The first thought I have about hope is that hope is hope against the evidence. Hope arises in a break with the past. There is a kind of cut and the past is let go of. There is a difference between simple expectation and hope. One could say 'because I see this is the way things are going, this is the way things have developed, I expect this to happen'; expectation is based on the pattern you see in the past. But I think hope is *always* hope against the evidence. I hope she will fall in love with me – there isn't adequate evidence for that. So there is a kind of discontinuity in time, there is a break, and something starts out of nowhere. If you begin to hope you'll get well after this disastrous illness, or that your father will overcome this cancer, you really don't understand where this hope comes from; it just comes. I am always struck with those people who have great hopes and who are in fact no better endowed than anyone else – they are not more beautiful or more gifted or more intelligent or more healthy or more strong. So hope doesn't come out of those things.

I'm thinking about hope in your own life and writing because you have moved across many dimensions of experience. You have travelled through many countries and situations and you have written about so many different facets of hope, suffering and despair...

There was something that struck me when my mother was dying. She was in a small mid-West hospital in the US with other patients who were dying there. These were people who had lived in a small town all their lives – people you wouldn't have thought of as having much guts, since they just stayed in this town and didn't really have any kind of career or anything like that. I remember the very first person my mother told me to go visit; she said she was a neighbour. This woman immediately told me, in a very simple way, that she had leukaemia and it was getting worse and nothing could be done about it. Once she said that, she just pushed it aside and wanted to talk about other things – she wanted to catch up on what she and I had been doing all these years. She in no way wanted any kind of sympathy or pity. I could only think of what she had as *courage*. And I saw this again and again in the hospital. I think that if you and I talked about it or most people talked about it, we would wonder if we would have the courage to endure this end in suffering and hopelessness. Where does this courage come from? It doesn't really come from ideas one forms and attaches oneself to. I began to think that we have much more courage than we realise, and that is the kind of courage that animal species have. We have this *animal courage*. These people didn't whimper, they didn't cling to life, they were lucid and realistic and they had the courage to die. So in the same way it seems to me that hope is something perhaps deep within us. There isn't a kind of explanation of how to become hopeful or what to do to become hopeful. Like that 'animal courage' I saw in the hospital, hope strikes me as somehow natural.

And I think that hope is a kind of birth, as I was saying here – it doesn't come out of what went before, it comes out *in spite of* what went before. Abruptly there's a break and there's an upsurge of hope, something turned to the future. Like the birth of anything new. Occasionally I see a baby bird born in my house and I look with a kind of awe that this little creature is suddenly confronted with the world. Newborn children don't know anything, and then day after day they discover whole fields of reality that are open in front of them to the future. Never again in our life will we have such an overwhelming new moment. So it seems like there is something in being a child that's a movement of hope, and that hope is somehow natural to children. So far in my life I have only once been really sick, and one night I thought I would just die. But when I first detected strength beginning to stir again in me it felt like being a child. I had childlike behaviour but also childlike feeling. You look at the nurses like you looked at your mother when you were a child. Every time hope begins again, however late in life, it is a very childlike moment; it is like being born.

There's a relation between this idea of renewal and joy. For me this involves the joys and hopes that emerge in our everyday life and experience. And there's some discussion of joy in your recent writing and the idea of 'awakenings' to life and living. So how does joy involve something like a hopeful awakening to life?

For me joy always involves a vision. It is an open state in which one's eyes are open to what is outside oneself. One always sees things in joy. It seems to me that there is a very fundamental kind of existential decision we make: do we believe our joy or do we believe our neutral states? In the latter case, the move is always one of prudence – not to make decisions in a time of enthusiasm when one is carried away, but rather to wait until everything cools down. I think one of the most important things there is – I would almost say one could make this a kind of maxim for life – is to always make every important decision in a state of joy. It's an insight I got from Friedrich Nietzsche. For Nietzsche a resentful state of mind is one that rejects a great deal of what there is, whereas a joyous state of mind is able to affirm and accept even the painful, destructive and absurd things. One can conclude from that that a joyous state of mind is open to much more than a resentful state of mind, since it can accept suffering, frustration and grief. I also have the idea that when one reaches the summit of ecstasy one affirms everything that led to it. When you finally perceive the mountain that the imperialists call Everest and the Nepalese call Sagamartha – Sky-Mother – soaring high like a diamond over the clouds of the Himalayas, this ecstatic moment affirms everything that led to it – the long overland trip across the Middle East, all the sleepless nights and the dust and dysentery and so on. At this moment it seems better now that you went that way. Someone who would just want to fly to Everest in a jet aeroplane and see it there without anything prior to it will have a weaker experience. I think the reason that experience is weaker and less meaningful is that one starts with a state of mind which is already closing off a whole range of experience – I don't want discomfort, I don't want bad food, I don't want dysentery, and so on. So a joyous state of mind opens to reality and to more reality than a depressed or resentful state of mind. In this sense it is more veridical; it's more truthful. One should believe one's joy more than one's prudence, or any cautious and fearful state of mind.

Would this 'joy' require a transvaluation of values and what makes us believe in the world? I'm thinking here of Nietzsche, and the transvaluation of values and faith – the idea of a different sense of being, perhaps.

It's a big question. Among the concepts that designate values there are those that open upon a vision of comfort and security and those that open horizons beyond that. I would say that every joy excites values beyond the received values. But what we make contact with in joy that is 'beyond the received values' is not something ideal, but reality itself. Joy makes us cherish reality more than any concept we had of what is ideal.

*

I'd like to return to the break in time or the 'discontinuity' that you talked about earlier and the idea of hope, and how it might connect to suffering and joy. In your writing there is a relationship between joy, grief and the idea of forgetting oneself. For instance, suffering and joy can be linked to a 'void of possibility' rather than a melancholic internalisation of grief – that is, the possibility of overcoming suffering through joy. So I am wondering about that relationship between the discontinuous and time, and this movement of joy...

One thing that struck me a long time ago is that when you are healthy with vibrant vitality and energy to burn you really can't remember what it was like to be sick. The converse is also true. The first time I got really sick one thing that really was in my head was *now I understand*. Now I understand all those other people. But I also think once you are healthy again you no longer remember what it was like to be lethargic, with no energy, headachy and all that. To go further, I think in a moment of exaltation and joy, the joy actually wipes out the neutral state or the bored state that went before. Joy really fills the mind. If you give yourself over to joy with a friend or lover or spectacle or experience, it really disconnects the past. There isn't a shadow of boredom and tedium left. I think the shadow gives place to radiant light. People sometimes say, 'Well, you can't know happiness unless you know sadness', as though you are always comparing, as though a state of happiness is contrasted with a state of sadness, or a state of health is contrasted with a state of sickness. I think that is completely false. There are people who have never been sick and they know what it means to be healthy. I think of all those outdoor people who go for long hikes on the weekend and for whom to be healthy and strong is a feeling of fullness and vibrancy. You are not comparing it with being sick and you are also not comparing yourself with anyone else. If you really feel healthy you are not going round and saying, 'Look: those people are more zippy than those lethargic people'. I don't think there is any comparison at all; it is an inward radiance that you feel. If you've gone for a long drive to see some friends and had trouble with the car and heavy traffic, you're in a state of real irritation and frustration, but when you arrive with your friends in this moment of festivity you laugh at the traffic and the mishaps with the car and turn them into jokes. I think then that happiness can retroactively transform the negative moments that went before it.

So that's almost like the self that was before is forgotten for the experience that is now ...

Yes, I think that is the usual thing. I remember the first time I was pushed into the ocean with scuba gear and saw all the coral reefs – it was a radiant, gorgeous, astonishing spectacle that so fills the soul that there is nothing but the *now*. Neither the past nor the future are there any more. And I think that happiness can actually illuminate the past, as in the happiness of seeing your friend – where you will laugh about all the troubles of the trip. Joy can actually go backwards and transfigure the frustrations of the trip.

I'm thinking how people often cling onto the fear and frustration – so that illumination that you are talking about is a kind of freedom. I think that freedom allows you to be part of the experience, to become and be *in the experience. But what about that hanging onto or clinging to the past?*

I think that I have never really understood that. It is really very bizarre. I remember the exact moment when it hit me: I was in Paris staying on the Île Saint-Louis during summer. There were only one or two shops on the island and they were closed in August, so to do anything – to find food, go to the post office – you had to cross the river. So every day that I left the apartment I went across the bridge and saw on the next island, the Île de la Cité, the back end of Notre Dame Cathedral with all those flying buttresses and the old buildings of the Latin bank; it is one of the most beautiful spectacles ever built in the world. And Paris has this patchy light – it's damp and low and the skies are never really completely clear, and never or rarely overcast. So this light is different every day. After a month or two, one day I stopped and I suddenly realised that every day I spontaneously paused halfway across the bridge to contemplate this magnificent view and I had a moment of happiness. But these moments don't build up, you know; they pass. The next day it's like it had never happened, and there's a moment of surprise and delight all over again. So you don't cling onto those moments, and they also don't build, they don't stick to one another. They are free like birds who take flight. And then I thought how many moments and hours did I brood over some little slight, some little humiliation, hurt or setback! It is so strange how we cling to those moments and somehow can't let them go. Sometimes we say to ourselves, 'Drop it', or we say to a friend, 'Quit thinking about it, quit talking about it', but it is hard to do. I think it is wonderful that we don't cling to the joy because I think surprise is an integral part of joy. Every joy is a surprise and a moment of hope.

I want to move somewhere else in a moment, but I am just thinking about pain – whether it's a physical pain or it's pain that you hold onto because of being hurt by someone or something. And the idea of courage – there is a way that you have to overcome that pain and there is a courage needed to overcome it or to forget it. The notion of overcoming comes from Nietzsche, and you have talked about it as well – when there is a very deep-seated pain, like somebody is suffering or dying, it is a really intense experience and trivial things become amplified. So when you are right in that moment of pain it's often difficult not to cling to or intensify the hurt...

I don't think I've thought nearly enough about it. On the one hand, there is often the situation that one wants so much to share suffering. I remember when my mother was dying I had all kinds of psychosomatic stomach aches and so on. I was also doing things like smoking cigarettes, you know; it was compulsive – there was a whole part of me that just had to suffer too. And then I think of cultures like the Papuans: when a woman loses a child or lover or husband, she chops off a finger. I have a photograph of an older Papuan woman walking with a child in her hand, and it was only after I had developed and studied it that I realised that the woman had only two thumbs left. So she had lost eight of her family. I could really understand that. But, on the other hand, there is this Nietzschean thing that there is no virtue whatever in pity. You are doing nobody any good to commiserate. I think that we also realise that: when we go to the hospital we put on a cheerful face. We try to bring some cheer and the sick person wants that. So there are these two things and somehow we have to put them together. I think you can't get away from both these elements. And then there is the third aspect that Jacques Derrida talks about: that in grief we *cherish* the one we've lost, so we want to grieve. When a mother has lost her child she doesn't want to be cheered up by her friends and go out to a movie. She wants to mourn. This mourning is a way of affirming all the joy and the marvel of the person that she has loved. The mourning becomes a way to continue to love the one who's gone and to bring that love into one's heart.

That makes me think that the mourning and the memory allows that love, but with memory you also have to forget it at some point, too. Otherwise you are continually mourning and you don't allow the memory to be truly kept alive.

Yes, I think so. Recently an older colleague of mine died and he was cremated. There was a meeting one day and I went with some trepidation. But when I arrived his wife was very joyous, very happy to see us; she didn't take on a gloomy face at all. I realised that's what he would have wanted. Certainly they loved one another and without the least doubt he wanted her to live and not to shut herself down when he died. Sometimes the very best way to remember the love of the person you've lost *is* to live.

Somewhere in there is the idea of hope – in the fullness of life or cherishing mourning – where you do have to continually be reborn. But I am also thinking about laughter here as well, in the sense that laughter often breaks open a moment of pain or grief. You write about how laughter dissolves boundaries between people and the way it kind of breaks open another time. So I think the importance of laughter involves how we experience life and our connections to other people – which is hopeful...

The thought I had just now, and I hadn't thought about this before, is that laughter also marks a discontinuity. Something broke down, something collapsed, a train of sentences may end up in absurdity, and there's an outbreak of laughter. There is a process that can't go on, that suddenly broke down, but the laughter greets it joyously. There is almost a structure of hope in that. If you can see that something broke down and you laugh, already then there's a space opened for *something else to begin*. There may be a very real connection between laughter and hope. But there are also so many kinds of laughter. There is cynical or bitter laughter and that would be a different process.

But laughter that is spontaneous isn't that. Bitter laughter is a more premeditated thing, don't you think?... But you are always laughing with somebody – even if you are laughing at yourself; it always has to be in relation to something else. For instance, the pleasure a baby gets laughing would be in the sense of touch connected to the mother, or maybe it isn't always, but there is some exterior or surface outside of oneself that enables it...

Babies laugh before they speak. I think as adults we usually think that we produce laughter by telling jokes, using words in complex ambiguous ways. We tend to connect laughter with meaning, but it is very striking that babies have the capacity for laughter. Another astonishing fact is that you don't laugh alone. As soon as there is somebody else there are things that you would never laugh at yourself, very tiny jokes, which provoke a really vocal laughter more than just a bemused smile.

Ethics, responsibility and action
This makes me return to courage again, and the like, and to the idea of heroes that you have written about. There are the great heroes we admire, like Nelson Mandela, but there are also heroes in everyday life. And that's a site of hope, you know, the ordinary things that inspire us to have a faith

and trust in the world. One point you've made is that it's not always success that makes the hero – but maybe it's when they don't succeed and they can 'laugh at death'. Laughing in the face of adversity – when things seem impossible... What do you think about this relationship between courage, hope and the laughter at death?

It's something I haven't thought through. There's an ambiguous line when a leader, through some kind of continuous process, turns into a dictator if he or she seizes power – where that heroism closes up into itself. In the end, he is just pursuing his own dream, his own vision or will. And there are those heroes whom we all kind of instinctually admire. For instance, in Nicaragua during the Sandinista period the leaders went every weekend to villages and had meetings with the people and listened to their criticisms and complaints. But they were also very human: they ate and drank, sometimes too much, they had lovers and so on. I think too of Nelson Mandela, who breaks out dancing with crowds. One of my ideas is that we recognise someone of our own kind in laughter. When we see someone with whom we do not laugh, that person seems to us to be an alien or from another species. I think that before we understand anyone there is this laughter. When you are in a country where you don't understand anyone because you don't know the language and they don't know your language, there are moments when you laugh together, when the eyes meet over some amusing incident and you feel like one of them. We always think of the real hero as someone who has grown up in a country and we say he loves this country, these people, these slum-dwellers, and is really one with them. But it seems to me that the most fundamental fact of a hero is not that he has some kind of idealistic ideology that these slum-dwellers deserve justice or they are the proletariat and he should fight for them. It is that he genuinely enjoys being with them, would prefer to sit on the stoop and have a glass of rum with the slum-dwellers and tell jokes than to sit in an office and plan strategies.

What you are saying reminded me of one part in your book Sensation *where you make a brief reference to revolution. There is a very beautiful moment where you talk about guerrilla fighters who, after a day out, come into a peasant's hut to share some rum and they don't speak about ideology; they don't speak at all. It's silent and there's no thanks, there is only the interchange of sharing the rum. And it is this silent moment, this relation between humans, that you suggest is a utopia or a revolution that is possible... It seems to me that revolution or hope is often tied up with the idea of a future dream, vision or struggle – for example, in the traditional Marxist struggles of the working class. There is something really significant in that image for me, those silent moments of human exchange and this other idea of revolution and hope...*

What I may have been thinking of is the *home* – the place of hospitality and intimacy – and the kind of silence that Emmanuel Levinas talks about, which is the murmur of hospitality. There is a certain kind of language of hospitality, you know: 'Come in, how are you? Sit down', and so on. This is not really an exchange of messages at all; it's a kind of murmur, a kind of warmth, a kind of spreading and resonance across a space. In the struggle, everything depended on whether the guerrillas were sheltered by the people or not – the fish in the water that Mao Tse-Tung talked about. When people have gone through a struggle they very often speak of that time when they lived amongst the peasants in the high mountains, sharing their food and their shelter, having to trust them completely not to betray them. It is probably then that they began to feel in the deepest way the land as their home, these peoples' homes as their homes. Nicaragua is a kind of classic case because the guerrilla struggle occurred in the mountains and only at the very end did they really seriously infiltrate the cities. There is a beautiful book by Omar Cabesas. He was one of the great fighters of the revolution, but the formative period of his sensibility was those years when they weren't fighting, they were hiding out in the mountains surviving and gradually coming to know the mountains and the people who lived there.

The murmur of hospitality is linked to some kind of 'alterity' or otherness and, of course, there are moments when that hospitality is denied. For instance, if you are in a crisis or war, and you are seen as a foreigner infiltrating the country or the home. But this murmur seems fundamental at the level of hospitality but also at the level of community, or the bonds between people.

In Martin Heidegger there's a kind of moral opposition between resolute, truthful speech and what he calls 'idle talk' – 'idle talk' is very pejorative. But, as Levinas suggests, so much of language doesn't have as its purpose 'the formulation of truth'. Nietzsche once said that it is bad taste to formulate rational arguments in polite society. And he's right! We feel this all the time with our friends because most of what we say is nonsense. This language of hospitality is really spreading warmth around a place, it's a rhythm. I mean there's that kind of earnestness in people getting together to plan something. But we should think more about rhythm. When you open your home to someone you keep saying things, keep talking, and often it doesn't make any real sense; there is always a sort of periodicity to the conversation. The time of nature is periodic and rhythmic. So the language of hospitality is a kind of connection with nature. And I think hospitality is often around natural things. For instance, people gathering around fireplaces – even suburbanites often want to have a live fire – because since the beginning of time people have gathered around the fire, and that was a moment of being together and being at home with one another, being in a kind of intimacy. Now we go out to the garden or bring the garden inside the apartment by plants. So there's this suggestion of nature in the place where we meet friends.

I'm thinking about a related idea – that of responsibility and the time of action. Because in this murmur of life lies another time of action and responsibility to others. This is an ethical issue that involves bonds between people, but it is also about the responsibilities we have in the writing and work that we do...

I haven't gone anywhere with this, but now as we speak, it seems to me that there is room really to rethink a lot of these ideas of action. Most of the discussion of action gives us an image of someone wilful, someone who takes an initiative. There is this idea of 'resoluteness', to use Heidegger's term – a fixing of a will and then, of course, having a plan. Whenever any kind of enterprise or education is underway all the emphasis is on that: set up a plan, mark your goals, and then develop it and discipline the will. There is pride in being wilful and having one's own will. In that way the discourse about action becomes disconnected from other things – for instance, laughter, sensuality and hospitality. I think that in real life we understand that very well. For instance, if we set out to do something with someone – even if it is to start a business – you don't just find somebody who is wilful, has plans and a managerial mind and that's it: there is a development of a different kind of bond with your partner... After some time we realise that we have met our wives, spent evenings together, gone to the movies together, suffered together. There's a relationship of intimacy, of hospitality, of peace, of a kind of withdrawal from action. Life is not a matter of one initiative after another. So that if the action is successful – let's say if you have a really good partnership in your workshop – the initiatives and plans that will come arise out of a broader, deeper and more complex partnership.

Do you mean a different kind of bond and sense of commitment?... I think it's a bond between people, but it is also a different sense of communal bond to others. That's why I'm thinking of this responsibility to otherness, you know, because this responsibility has to be outside your own narcissism and individual projections. Hope is one element of this but the possibility of joy and sharing, as opposed to the fear, resistance and denial of all those things, is important – for instance, in a political sense to those who are different, and in an everyday sense to those who upset you.

I would like to connect responsibility very much to sensitivity. Responsibility is commonly connected with verbal principles. I'm thinking of my friend who just broke up with his business partner and accuses him of irresponsibility. There is a certain accusation that to run a business you have to follow principles – you have to be reliable, on time, keep your word and things like that. But there is this other issue – that was quite clearly bugging him – that his partner was *not sensitive to him*. He was not sensitive to the fact that he was doing an inordinate amount of the work, and also that his life was unhappy. What he wanted was a friendship, a relationship of trust. To be sensitive to the other person is to be responsive. Responsibility is connected with the notion of answering to the other, responding to the other's moves and to the other's sensibility. It's too weak to say that the other person is not responsive to my feelings. It is much more than that. It is more to do with a kind of sensibility – the way I perceive things, the way I make sense of the whole environment about me.

Yes, I think it's about the responsibility to life really – life in its many forms. A responsibility to life, a responsibility to others which is unconditional to a certain extent. In a concrete sense, there is always a kind of conditionality that is placed on relationships with others, or relationships in a community, which is a premeditation about how people should behave or act – that's where action comes in, I think. If you constantly pursue that type of 'action' then it is almost like those plans will be impossible – they don't have the sort of sensitivity that you are talking about. But it is the responsibility towards life, the hopefulness towards life, the hopefulness towards community that does have or can have that sensitivity. And this idea of responsibility is fundamentally ethical. So that the responsibility to nature, the responsibility to others, the responsibility to the earth or whatever, has to break open the discontinuance of time that we spoke of earlier, and a different sense of action.

I am really struck with this word 'unconditional' that you use. The people we think are sensitive and responsible tend to respond completely to an extreme situation that comes upon them: they don't put limits. I am thinking of Joe Kane's book *Savages*, where he gets involved in the struggle of a small tribe of rainforest Indians in Ecuador. Suddenly he is thrust into disasters and there are extreme things happening beyond his control. And then of course he involves his wife and children in it. But that is the case of every person, and a family. If you have a child there may come a moment – for most people happily it doesn't happen – when you would give your life for that child, you would give everything. But ever since Aristotle the problem has been that responsibility has always involved a kind of legal discussion. Before the courts I am responsible for what I foresaw, what I planned, what I was in control of. Unfortunately that language tends to dominate ethical discourse. But, as Levinas said, 'I answer for what I didn't do'. For example, on an expedition in the high Himalayas with a Sherpa guide, if he gets sun-blindness because he goes to altitudes where he has never gone before and no one has told him about the possibility of blinding, this is due to the fact that two hundred years ago the British took over this subcontinent and subjugated these people, putting them into a second-class political and economic existence. I didn't do any of this, I'm not even British, but when I'm there *I answer for it*. To give another example, if my child is born with a genetic defect, perhaps that is because my grandparents two or three generations back married and their genes combined in some defective way – or maybe it was just an accident of biochemistry. I didn't do that to the kid but I answer for it.

Following from this discussion of Levinas – 'I answer for what I didn't do' – as writers and intellectuals, how does that involve a responsibility towards life and others?

The idea that I am responsible for what I myself chose to do and whose development I conducted or managed is completely incompatible to writers and intellectuals. We answer for what others have said – others who may well have died long ago. And if we publish what we write, we address readers who may read what we write after we are dead. When we write seriously, we are sensitive to and responsive to the lives they are leading. We write out of sensitivity to their lives when our own life will be long gone. The expression '*my* work', referring to the body of writing one does, is misleading. But this is true of any kind of work. There are few works we undertake entirely of our own initiative; most of the works we undertake continue, build on, or join with the works of others before us. And there are very few works that we conduct or manage until they come to an end. We build a house our children will inherit, plant trees that will bear fruit after we are dead, invent a vaccine others will use long after we are dead. So most of our works are in response to the needs or wants of others. Even if we ourselves put an end to a work we have initiated, the work leaves a residue, or an empty space others will deal with. We are aware of that when we empty our belongings out of an apartment we have rented, or get rid of a car.

Political hopes

The importance of having to answer for what's gone before, in that example you gave of British colonialism, is connected to hope – the responsibility we have to situations that are not of our making or doing. No doubt this has resonance across a broad spectrum of social and political situations. And I'm thinking that often in the development of the industrial and capitalist world – and more so now in the more global and technological world – hope is often linked, I would say, to some kind of monetary or material exchange. So responsibility is not tied to some form of unconditionality; it is linked to what can be gained or can be taken from people. So, in a different way, I'm thinking about the relation of hope and the idea of the 'gift' – which you have written about – the responsibility and unconditionality that the notion of giving could take on if it is not tied to some capitalist claim or an exploitative relationship between people. In that sense, how does the possibility of the unconditional, responsibility, giving and exchange, take on another form in the very basic act of giving between people, but also in a political sense? What if 'exchange' wasn't about appropriation – what possibilities are there in conceiving gifts and hope. Is that too huge?

Well, I see two dimensions and one is different to what I have written about. On the one hand, it seems to me that a real gift is always a kind of liberation. A liberation towards something grand and something more grand. The most beautiful recent case I can think of is: a friend of mine in Japan called me and said, 'I've just turned 50'. To give himself a birthday present he gave a round-the-world ticket to two of his students. He freed himself from this money and wants nothing in return. He freed his soul from the kind of anxiety that everybody feels when you turn 50 and you want to hold onto your own life and you realise life is beginning to decline. And of course the students in question were free to travel around the planet and to open their sensibility, their hearts, their minds to all kinds of new things.

It's a completely liberating gift, a gift of freedom for everyone. But the other thing is the political dimension – and here I have hardly been able to say anything useful about it. Surely political hope is always somehow utopian; it is a hope that we will set up a better world and set it up to endure. That must be true of every kind of political hope: that the situation could be different for *good*. I did think a long time ago that you have this kind of pattern of discourse: here was a revolution, and here is what it was seven years later when it became ossified into a bureaucracy. It's a process that people follow about every revolution: the French revolution, the American, the Cuban. And that led me to think that we really have to free the notion of liberation and revolution from the idea of permanently setting up some other kind of society. The revolution is not something that is done 'once and for all'. Well, it does seem like there are contradictory ideas here. On the one hand, every revolution, every political hope is for setting up a better world, but on the other hand, there is this other very difficult problem of understanding that the revolutionary fervour and act is of its nature ephemeral. Just because it doesn't endure doesn't mean it was a failure. But one of the great intoxications of revolution and the reason that it does continually recur is that those who fight the revolution find it a kind of moment of effervescence, of transfiguration. Even if it fails, it was a summit experience for people in common.

*

I'm thinking about a different but related idea around inequality and injustice. For example, you've written about Nietzsche and his ideas about justice and mercy. What struck me is that when people have suffered an immense amount of injustice there is the possibility of mercy or compassion, and even in the worst situations, there may be the possibility of hope within it. It seems to me that real freedom or liberation, even under oppressive regimes or systems, has to have that relation of justice and mercy from the point of view of those who have experienced the inequality...

Nietzsche's idea is that justice is the work of the noble and the strong. He has this wonderful image of a lion who is covered with parasites and laughs, 'What are parasites to me? May they live and prosper; I am strong enough for that!' So in a strong and bold moment of society and history – I wonder what the word is; 'tolerance' is not really the right word – there is a kind of pleasure that you are strong enough for all kinds of things that are parasitical in a society. I think of the proud cities like Paris: these are not places of extreme conformism, law and order. You take pleasure in the fact that there are hoboes and street people, street musicians and all kinds of illegal foreigners in the city. There's that part of it. But, you know, there is something I haven't thought about before and that has to be rethought: that the Nietzschean compulsion of a compassion that comes out of strength – 'May they live and prosper' – may be like hope itself. I am thinking of situations when a nation has gone through periods of absolute horror. I was in South Africa when they were doing the Truth Commission. When you listened to it, you finally came to wonder: how could this society be reconciled after that many horrors? There probably isn't a family in South Africa that hasn't been either victim or executioner. How can these people begin to live in a rainbow nation? The same thing about Vietnam; the Vietnamese suffered so hideously from America. I don't know if anyone knows how many people really died – at least two million – yet when Americans go there they are not treated with hatred and vindictiveness. Of course a lot of people think, well, in the end what's basic in humans is the fast buck, and the people after the war just want to make a buck. But I don't think that is the case. It does seem to me there is this strange fact that again and again people who have suffered terrible injustices from another group are able to, I was about to say, forgive...

That's not quite right, is it?

It's not quite right. It's not right but one could think, of course, of something you know so much more than I do, about Aborigines, or the black people in this country, or slaves! And yet there is this power to somehow overcome this, to overcome this fact that you have suffered a terrible injustice from this other person, this other party. I don't think we've thought about this very well.

I don't think so either. That's why I was posing the question. Which makes me think about what we spoke about earlier – having to answer for what I didn't do is part of this overcoming and compassion. And, in Australia, the indigenous politics – I mean there has to be hope there for some form of reconciliation. It's important not to deny the past and the suffering because that's lived – the memory of that is lived in the very body of people. But I suppose without hopefulness you couldn't come and meet at the table, so to speak. The problem is when the other party doesn't want to hear what you are saying, which is then a denial or taking away of hope...

Individual time of belonging...

Coming back to the idea of hope and compassion, the way of overcoming also involves the discontinuity in time...

Well, to go back to a very individual level – and again it is something that just came up with a visiting friend who said, 'You can't run away from problems'. I have always believed the exact opposite: the thing to do is to run away and get a different perspective. Sometimes you can actually confront the person you've got a conflict with and work it out, but very often you can't. What therapists and pop psychologists want you to do is go to your spouse or friend and talk it out – and sometimes this works. But I have found with friends when you actually start talking it out you are really fixing and solidifying the conflicts: marking them. But if you were to go away for a couple of weeks or months, other things may have started in your life, and you are not quite the same person any more. And maybe you could just put aside your quarrel without ever having really resolved it, because now you are both somewhat different people. That is connected to what we were saying: you establish a discontinuity, in which something new gets born. Very often when you have quarrelled with your friend or spouse or lover and you have hurt one another, you really can't eliminate the hurt. You can't reverse it, but you can let time, nature, heal it. Especially if you give the other person freedom from you for a while.

And allow the spirit to come back?

In fact I was just thinking of the line by Nietzsche in *The Will to Power* – the beautiful end of a sentence is: ' ...in impossible times when one does not know how old one is or how young one is yet to be'. I love this line. Because hope is to hope that things can be born in your life. I think that every new friend is a birth in your life. You know, when you pick up a hitchhiker, here is someone who came from nowhere in your life, with nothing in your life prepared for him. So every new situation or friend can bring this moment of hope.

2
CARNIVAL OF THE SENSES
A conversation with Michael Taussig

What if hope was like another human 'sense' – like some kind of anatomical part of us, not physically but allegorically? Hope as a sense that is visceral and ever-present, much like the kaleidoscopic experience of a fair. What would a 'carnival of the senses' involve in individual and political terms? How does this get played out when, in western cultures, hope is closely tied to the material definitions of living, and in these times capitalist economies link our cultural senses and dreams to economic imperatives of the self? 'The American dream' is often cited as the promise and aspiration of a free-market economy. So, if these hopes and dreams can be the vehicle of the free market and culture, what gambling does this involve? It could be linked to envy and resentment, which in political terms leaves very little room to move.

It has often been the case that resentment, melancholia and lack of hope produce a vehicle for political enterprise and creative work. However, hope in cultural expression is more than this. If we evoke the capacity for joy which every moment of hope can embody, then creativity – in intellectual, political, personal terms – takes on a new meaning. This is a real carnival of possibility and revolutionary spirit, where hope can be a dialogue about gifts and exchange in another sense – the spirit of generosity – which is often lacking in western living and critical thinking. And what if hope and despair mean different things in different cultures – how do we then begin to define the spirit of things? What 'islands of hope' are possible – the acts of giving that open a gateway to the imagination and possibility in the midst of individual and political uncertainty?

Anthropologist and writer Michael Taussig and I reflect on these hopes and a 'carnival of the senses'. Taussig is based in New York, and his anthropological work encompasses aspects of myth, magic and carnival in contemporary Western and Latin American countries. His writing is about transforming reality: our dreams, beliefs and particular understandings of the senses.

Dialogue, carnival and the senses

Mary: Let's begin with hope and the idea of the 'senses' – how might we understand individual perception and political action, and where hope may lie?

Michael: I was somewhat floored by your topic when you first announced it on the email many months ago, because hope would seem something ever-present and ubiquitous, and crucially important – something like the very air people breathe. But rarely is it speculated on or philosophised about. When I first came across this as a philosophical or political issue it was with that book of Ernst Bloch's, *The Principle of Hope*, and I was not that impressed by it. But I was very impressed by his conviction that here was something that was part of the warp and woof of everyday life – speaking as a West European in the twentieth century – and that it had not been given its political or philosophical due. In a way, it has been talked about a lot politically, right? People are always supposed to be positive – the use of motifs from the Bible, in civil rights movements in the US, and so on – I mean, 'We shall overcome' is the motif, really, of political struggle. But that type of – how shall I put it? – desperation, the mixture of desperation and hope, I don't think I ever came across that much in England or Australia – that is, certainly not in the form of sublime rhetoric in verse and song. So I have been mulling it over ever since you raised it as a theme worth pondering further...

What I would want to do is start talking about hope as a type of sense or something like a sense. A sense which we are not very conscious of – unlike seeing or smelling or hearing, where there are anatomical sense organs and receptors and things like that. The way I think you would do justice to your question would not be to refer hope to spring or lack of hope to winter, which is fair enough – gloom and despair and how people in different places survive spiritually. But rather, I would want to take the notion of the senses more metaphorically and say, 'Well, there might be a hope sense'. Now I do *insist* that this is metaphorical and allegorical and in no way under the sun would I ever want this to be truly thought of as biological, because I think most of sociobiology is really bad science and reactionary political stuff. But I *do* think it would fun and intellectually stimulating to say there is a sort of subliminal hope sense. Walter Benjamin talks about a mimetic faculty and so we could borrow from that and maybe talk about a hope faculty and see where that might take us...

So hope would have a kind of visceral evocation... And I suppose if you were to talk about a hope faculty, then, in that sort of mimetic sense, we're not talking about something that is necessarily intellectual. I think we are talking about something that exists outside reason and rationality. So what you are alluding to is that hope has to be much more primal, in a sense – is that what you are getting at?

I wasn't, but I would wholeheartedly agree. And I mean you have extended the logic of what I was saying, or the direction I think that idea of mine should be propelled in. In fact it cuts across the rational/irrational split. It's in a different sphere. It's a different game altogether. I think it would be wrong to try and locate something like hope immediately or maybe at all in clinical psychology, or in terms of depression or its opposite, happiness. I don't think it belongs in those compartments or systems of classification of what constitutes human being or well-being. I'm not quite sure where I would put it at this moment... But I do have the suspicion that a lot of intellectual activity, at least in the twentieth-century Western cultural orbit, correlates lack of hope with being smart, or lack of hope with profundity. I am thinking of someone whose work I admire immensely and who has been very dominant in guiding me, and that's to say Walter Benjamin. I mean you don't have to look further than him or Susan Sontag's essay on him as 'the saturnine genius'. It seems melancholy goes along with, or is even necessary for, giving oneself *over* to the other, giving oneself over to the 'thing' world, in particular. And Benjamin has a huge amount to say on that via astrology and Baroque theatre in his famous book on German tragic drama. But then there is always this glimmer of hope, you know, in his theses on the philosophy of history, which were written in the last four years of his life. And you can't relate to that history – he was writing in 1936 with Western Europe faced with Fascism and catastrophic upheavals – if you don't have a belief in hope. He calls it the Messiah. But it's a weak hope and you always wonder why the weak hope? First of all, the

Marxists say, 'Well why the Messiah? Get rid of all of that stuff', and second, if you've got the Messiah in there I suppose the religiously-minded would say, 'Why not the full load – why not a weak hope or a weak possibility that the Messiah would return?'

But, by and large, what I would hear when I was a kid in Australia was about Kafka and this Central European investment in melancholy or the dark side of things, you know. There's surrealism in Paris and there's sort of black surrealism in Eastern Europe and so it goes. There does seem to be at the level of popular culture, *within* intellectual culture, this strong temptation to bind lack of hope to being profound, and that might be worth opening up and talking a little bit more about between you and me right now... or a little later. And certainly we could reflect on the place of the Messiah in Benjamin because that is a good way of talking about hope and its relationship to political philosophy and practical politics in this new century too.

Yes.

In thinking about this relationship between pessimism and being intellectual there was always, at least in the 70s, people who were very optimistic. They would get together and have their meetings, academic meetings or political meetings or both at the same time, and a certain type of depression would enter almost by necessity as one enlarged upon the forces of opposition. And then you would always remember, or some wisecrack would always come out with, this saying of Antonio Gramsci: 'pessimism of the intellect and optimism of the will' – and this was an almost eternal, essential mantra which one had to work with. So how do you combine those two apparently opposed forces which were so important?

I'm interested in what you are saying about melancholy and the intellect – that there is the relationship that the more melancholic, the more profound you are. But what if you didn't begin with the negative, but with another sense – something like joy. Where might that take the possibility or the relationship between intellectual practice and some kind of idea of revolution?

Well, I think a huge amount of this is culture-bound. For instance, I think of people I know who live in difficult circumstances in Colombia and I can't imagine them ever wanting to entertain disillusion and depression. I'm not talking about middle-class people and I'm not talking about people who spend a large number of years at school either. I am thinking about people in the midst of agribusiness, on the peripheries of cities or on the frontier. And I keep thinking about the cultural and mental field that they live in – it's like a completely different orbit... But I would be impressed by the sort of equation you are drawing attention to and tentatively establishing between joy and revolution. I think there would definitely be a constant correlation. What I was immediately thinking about when you were finished was 'carnival' and the relationship of carnival to revolt. And the work of Mikhail Bakhtin put this back on the agenda in a very imaginative way for a lot of people (although it seems that interest is dying away a little bit).

I remember in the late 60s someone mentioned that Lenin, of all people, had said that 'revolution is the carnival of the oppressed'. Well, we accept that is something that he had said and it seemed so out of character for Lenin, but I had often thought that the anarchists and the certain ultra-Left dimensions of modern politics may try and enforce that, or try to keep that spirit alive between carnival and revolt. So that work on carnival is where one could first start looking for the ideas you were talking about. I'm no expert, but some people take exactly the opposite point of view – that carnivals existed in Western Europe in the last 2000 years or whatever to appease misery, and as a holiday from reality... the sort of argument that suggests that this would allow people to better adapt to reality. But Bakhtin's argument always seemed to suggest that carnival was not simply a safety-valve, and it was not something that functioned to allow people to have some joy in an otherwise mean life. He was particularly thinking about living in the Soviet Union in the 30s, and I've always felt he was suggesting that carnival was open-ended, and that it could extend into something else. So that the spirit of laughter, which was very important to him, combined with this yearning for freedom, was kept alive through carnival. I think that is considerably different to using the functionalist language of a 'safety-valve' or 'cybernetic feedback' and so forth.

There's another idea that's close to this, that I came across in the work of Peter Lamborn Wilson, who is an anarchist writer in the New York area. He has this concept of 'temporary autonomous zones' (or 'TAZ', which my students love). The idea is that there are moments, hours, weeks, months or even years whereby groups of people get it together to test freedom (which we will leave vague and undefined). And then it collapses – so these experiments, these temporary autonomous zones, are *bound* to fail. You enter into them with the notion that it is like carnival – that it is temporary – and these are expressed in all sorts of different ways: through history, actual revolts, marginal people who have been able to find some autonomy away from their families or communities or the state or whatever it might be. So how hope fits into that is interesting, because it is a type of controlled pessimism or it's a mix of pessimism and optimism, because you need the optimism to be carnivalesque or the carnival stimulates that optimistic stance in the world. It seems to me that this is done in a very sophisticated way and that one realises one is living in an 'artificial kingdom'. It's like going to the theatre where you suspend disbelief and you become full of hope, but there's another part of you which says it can't last forever. So that seems to me what human beings are about – that level of complexity, the ability to hold opposite ideas at once – and I think that is where I would really be most comfortable talking about hope – in a field where hope and lack of hope are organised into a sort of dynamic mix.

A spark of hope: ethics and the space of writing

The sphere of hope and lack of hope in the same kind of place-holder invites, I think, a different of sense of time and of memory – the hope of filling in the gaps of history that can be so easily elided when talking about revolution and freedom – other peoples' histories, our own, and the telling of stories about political struggles. I think the 'spark' of hope resides in a moment of danger and crisis in history, rather than a kind of documentation of the real: you know, simply recording an event and hoping it speaks the 'reality' of a situation. So it is that crisis, that spark, that moment, which I think you are also talking about in terms of revolution and so on, that opens out history and the ways of understanding it. So the question I'm really putting forward here is about this dimension of time and memory...

You're right. I mean you could certainly fit that in beautifully with Walter Benjamin's theses on the philosophy of history, where he has two types of time going, and two types of realities. There's the homogenous, empty time and then there's the *jetztzeit* or the 'now time'. The now time is where everything collapses into an incandescent present and the past and future are juxtaposed. It could almost be seen as a space of no time, a cessation of happening. He refers to it at one moment as the 'Messianic cessation of happening', which he says is the moment of a revolutionary chance to fight for an oppressed past. So he is certainly working with these two time dimensions: one which is chronological and flows like a river and the other which does weird stuff – leap-frogs, stops, creates holes and vacuums like Swiss cheese, and then charges in another direction. In fact he has notions of the archaic and prehistory suddenly emerging through fossil-like forms into a present which, now charged with this *jetztzeit* in thoroughly anarchic destructive images, can dismantle the institutions of the present and then presumably build them anew. So they are monstrously powerful images of different senses of the real and different understandings of what time could be. I need to do justice to your interest and to your point, to then try to kind of rework the place of hope into this...

Well, I think hope would link to the idea of practical politics inspired by Benjamin that we raised earlier, and the now time – the possibility of dismantling and finding another language to build politics and visions anew. For instance, hope would lie in re-envisaging political discourses and how we define reality. Rethinking politics and the machinations of political rhetoric – that takes us outside of adversarial and polemic positions and moves into more sustained and concrete actions (finding ways to 'mourn' the loss of certain notions of human dignity and activism, and working through what might be effective for the Left now). And this would be about finding a 'politics of hope'...

But I am thinking specifically about your own work in the US, Colombia and other Latin American countries, where you have been working across different times. I would say different times in terms of the world – I don't mean in the sense of underdeveloped or developed worlds, but in the sense of other notions of the real or reality. You've written about the terror and fear and colonisation that occurs in Latin American countries, and the healing practices that have been part of dealing with those histories. I want to address the very concrete nature of that work in moving between the holes or gaps in time yourself. Or, to put it another way, I'm interested in the different sense of time that emerges in the contacts and interchanges you have had in those countries, and how those are bringing forward into the present different senses of the real – in the same way that we have been discussing the spark of hope – the idea of other histories being brought into the present.

I'm intrigued by your interpretation or reaction. I don't feel that there is a different sense of time. Remoteness in space I could understand, but I'm not confident or sure about this being a different time. I mean obviously there are different parts of my work, like hallucinogenic healing, that have come straight out of historical work in the eighteenth and nineteenth centuries. But, otherwise, where the sense of reality/time as a complex might be pertinent is in the mannered or staged style of presentation. I think maybe there are changes, not so much of voice, but rather the slippage and deliberate slips in time. For example, where the author – that is oneself – is playing with the distance between the writer, the reader and the material which the text is evoking. I think I have tried to keep that uppermost as a writer. Perhaps there the issues of time are significantly about *coming close* and *going far away*, which might be the most powerful way of putting this. So that's where the question would lead and how one writes about foreign material.

Yes, that's what I am thinking about. The different enactment of time. In the sense of being a writer and putting the material together in some form, and that's what writing is about – an extension of life or some life activity. I think there are those relationships to writing and reading but also to the gathering of material and the sensibility that you are engaged in the world that you are writing about. So that's one aspect of it, but the other is time not as just chronological, but as sensation. Like in Marcel Proust, for example, where he has the notion of involuntary memory – those memories and sensations that unexpectedly appear in a moment and exist on another plane or dimension. And I think the way to relate to or understand different senses of being human involves those other dimensions, rather than being simply a narrative of time – you know, telling a story about another culture or producing some orthodoxy about it. So the connection I want to explore is how your own practice and responsibility to writing about otherness and other cultures might be this question of time...

If one is striving for what I call a mimetic form of writing, it does involve the visceral evocation of what is being spoken or written about. For instance, the way Theodor Adorno talked about Walter Benjamin's style of writing as: 'Thoughts press close to its object, seek to touch it, smell it, taste it, and thereby transform itself'. This magical sense of the means of representation, the magical capacity of words to become one with what they are about – this is the disillusion of the fearsome division between subject and object, and that sort of thing. Now if one is trying to write like that and one is not doing it in the sort of conventional form of, say, *The New Yorker* writing, or lots of writing where you are told you have to be concrete – that is, you have to talk about the way the light falls on the window pane or the shape of a person's smile and so on – then you've got that sense of the real and that form of evocation of particularity and concreteness. However, because of its conventionality, its clichédness, it gets in the way – as it's seen as a formula even though it's not consciously understood in that way. Leaving all that to one side, I would think that this mimetic evocation – as I've tried to describe it – just as it dissolves subject to object and requires recourse to some sort of word like 'magic', so it would obviously play havoc with time as well.

And presumably that's what Proust talks about in the miracles of involuntary memory. By the way, I will tell you one thing which is very interesting in regard to this. I've never experienced these flashes of involuntary memory as much as when I was doing what we call field work – in the context of being deliberately out of place. It's when I am working and driven by some sort of demonic thing that I just keep bumping into my childhood in Sydney. Here I am just over 60 years old and it has been going on for the past 30 years. In the countries I work in, which still seem to me distinctly foreign and sometimes quite dangerous (especially in the last ten years), I constantly have these amazing flashes of *mémoire involontaire*. So this is quite apart from sophisticated discussions about mimesis and writing and so forth. It's a comment on the psychology or the reality of field work or certain types of field work. I would presume if one is capable and fortunate enough to be able to export or import something about that frequency of involuntary memory into the text that one is later creating, it should certainly illuminate one's field notes. So you've got a point there, you really have!

What I want to discuss is the relationship between hope, everyday life and violence. Your writing deals with the articulation of violence and terror in cultural and political situations – namely in Latin American countries but also in the US. It seems to me that your writing is getting at different levels of violence – the ethical position that you put yourself in when writing, and the articulation of violence that is often hard to express…

In regards to writing about or talking about ethics and the representation of violence, and what place does hope have to play in that, I guess one of the things that I've noticed in my work between First and Third Worlds, US and Latin America in particular, is the temptation to pick up on the theme of resistance. For instance, this was notable for me as a student reading very inspiring works, hope-filled works of someone like E.P. Thompson. His book *The Making of the English Working Class* and other writings on late eighteenth-century England have a type of optimism or controlled optimism. On the one hand, there is this sense that incredibly important movements and people have been left out of history and therefore made amnesiac. And at the same time, there's hope in the future if these holes in history could be filled in and indeed foregrounded. But, I guess, in a primitive sort of way, writing about other people's resistance – people in the past or contemporary situations, Third World peasantry and, when I was younger, the Vietnam War… that identifies the writer with those events, with those people, and therefore includes the reader into that identificatory bond – creates hope for everybody. Looking back now, I think that was enormously wrong-headed. I'm not saying Thompson did that, but I think as a way of reading his work – and certainly anthropologists of my own age in their frustration felt that, by doing that, they could generate hope. But it was too much of a substitute, and where I felt the mistake was – and this is getting closer to the ethical dimension of your point – was that it was too easy and too quick to put the burden on the people you were writing about, rather than install it in the way you were writing. The crucial political and hopeful point of all of this is that if the writing itself wasn't challenging conventions of how words work – the mischievous, unexpected, rethinking image and text and so forth – if the message was different but the way of telling it was the same, nothing *was* gained. So instead of putting the politics on someone else in another place or another time, the politics had to be there in the writing itself, and that is how matters of taste, of discrimination and so forth actually emerge in one's work – that is where the struggle should be. And, of course, that doesn't happen.

Another example, now, might be post-modernity, because you find very few people – especially in my field, and more so in that crossover of literature and philosophy – who actually put their money where their mouth is. That is, who actually do put into practice what their philosophy is about. There is Jacques Derrida and a few other people who actually do that, and their work is in synchrony with what they are talking about. But usually in my field, especially the 'social sciences' as they're called, there's a big gap between the content of the critique on the one hand, and the way the critique is expressed on the other. We could talk in more detail about violence *per se* and ethics of writing about violence or representing violence, but I've sketched out a quasi-historical synchronic platform from which we could extend further.

Awakenings

I want to address something that we said earlier about the idea of revolution, and Walter Benjamin's idea of the 'wake up' of consciousness.

There is a link between Benjamin and Marx's ideas that we have to wake up from the dream that we've made about ourselves or the society has made of itself. We were talking about Benjamin writing through a period of Fascism, and that was happening in his life and in his experience, and we are now living in a time that is not Fascist – it' s not the same history, but there are other complexities around power and terror. At times, the mobilisation of power emerges in a kind of vacuum... So where might something like the wake up of consciousness come in the culture or the imagined realities that we continually cite, narrate and construct now?

One of the things that upsets you most in the US is the frequency with which 'the American dream' is cited by mainstream politicians. I laughed at it when I first moved here, but I didn't realise how ubiquitous it was as a concept. It is almost like a serious philosophical concept. You will hear people of all walks of life believing this, not just the President. So you have people from poor communities saying 'We've been deprived of the American dream', and so on. The whole vocabulary of dream and magic in countries in more sober times, and political lexicons, would not have used it as such, or it would have been frowned upon. In this country it seems you have been mightily cheated upon if you don't espouse it. Adorno said after Auschwitz, 'There can be no poetry' – it is almost like after they have phrased 'the American dream' there can be *no more dreaming*.

Yes, the dreaming loses its dream-like qualities.

There is something really terrible in the way that the universe of dream and hope has been gutted, and it is a miserable state of affairs. So there is a vacuum and it is hard to know how to handle it. But the awakening is a difficult thing for me to understand – and Benjamin takes the phrase from the very young Marx in a letter to Arnold Rouge in the late 1830s. Here is Marx boiling over with romance and optimism – there is no doubt about it. He's not ironic or cynical. And 'awakening' is a word that would be seen by most people today as equivalent to demystification: shedding light on obscure fields of knowledge, separating myth from reality, lies from truth, and so on. I think that is quite wrong. In terms of what Benjamin was doing, and more importantly how the world is put together in my opinion, it seems to me that awakening means piggy-backing, *moving* with the dream world. It is not a clarion call through the enlightenment to separate myth from reality. It is to enjoin myth to reality. It is not an awakening from a period of inertia to one of action. It is not an awakening from a period of despair to one of hope, or from error to truth. So I've always understood his work as demystification and re-enchantment, in which that spark of hope you talk about presumably has an electrifying role to play. And I would see the awakening in that sense too.

Also I notice something funny with Benjamin too. He has this notion, in *One Way Street*, about waking – that in waking one has to be very careful, because there are minutes or even hours after waking where one is still in the wake of this dream/sleep world, like a ship has a wake. This is when all sorts of fantastic things can happen to you. Especially if you are a writer and you depend on your miserable living for your writing – that is, your ideas and your creativity. In a sense this is a very physio-economic idea and he's very physiological, like Nietzsche is. So the body plays a big role here. For instance, he has various notions about what you should eat and not eat, and whether you should go outside or not when writing. I take some of that to heart. I think a lot of people do. If I'm working I don't like to get out of the house until the afternoon, and stuff like that. There's a private relationship between the night, the body at night, and the body in the day.

Another thing that is important here, and I don't know how hope works in but I can try it out: it seems to me little attention has been paid to the half-awake world – and call it what we will – this world of daydreaming, the world of reverie and, more complicated still, the world of free-floating attention that Freud wanted from his patients. This free-floating attention is what I understand Benjamin to mean when he talks about the 'spectator' in films.

That suspension of reality where you enter another state and connect with other thoughts and feelings...

And, it also seems to me, it is that state of mind that many people get in ritual – healing rituals, religious rituals, the sort of experience of being *in* and *out* of a situation at the same time. Now this state of mind just fascinates me. We call it trance... And, you know, since the beginning of time and across all human cultures there's this capacity to, I would say, live a huge amount of one's life in this in-between state. For one reason or another in the West we've been pretty bad at either taking advantage of it or giving it a name. It may be that the movies have filled up that space for modern people. In other cultures – many, many, cultures... perhaps the majority of the world's population, although it's the poorest people in the world – spirit possession fills that, trance and spirits come into that space. Now hope: if we started off this conversation with 'Where is hope?' 'What status are we going to give it?' 'Is it rational or irrational?' 'What's its role in the every day?' 'Is it a faculty?' and so forth... perhaps thinking about hope in terms of spirit possession would be a shoe-horn into thinking about hope and healing, hope and miracle, or hope and metamorphosis. As I understand it, spirit possession often implies being possessed with the power of grace, the transformation of a bad situation into a good situation. It might be interesting to contemplate a place of hope in this in-between consciousness...

Yes, and as you were saying that, I was thinking how we live most of our lives in this in-between way, or in a half-awake state. But the 'spirit possession' in the capitalist world we live in has been filled by certain kinds of fetishisations around commodities, or spiritual meanings get filled up with material worth or whatever. So the spirit seems to be filled by some relationship to money, power or objects, and reality is there to be consumed (which is obvious in the media and the representation of politics). I think there is a movement away from the 'power of grace' to transform life, and there is a movement towards the future or progress, which takes away that ambiguity or freedom to occupy that half-awake space or spirit. I'm trying to find the right word, or some sense of spirit which isn't about relations to material well-being, but a fundamental and essential existence that can connect to more compassionate, dignified and hopeful relations to the world...

I think you're right. The businessman or businesswoman has to be fully awake, not half-awake, and so forth. The existence you posit seems diametrically opposed to the spirit of utility, which is really what guides so much of common sense and intellectual reasoning. For example, in what I do in the social sciences, I mean 99 per cent of it is deliberately and directly marshalled, corralled, bullied by utilitarian reasoning. For instance, rational choice theory and its various modulations are all driven by the model of profit maximisation, and so forth. There are two things I want to say in case I forget them: I want to follow this line of thought which is to relate hope to profit, and the other is to think about being half-awake – that in-betweenness and the relation to drugs. But taking up the first one, I wanted to flip around what I was saying and think about how much of the market and market entrepreneurial activity is dependent upon hope, not revolution. Let's change the topic: let's not talk about the relationship of revolution to hope, let's talk about the everyday dependence on hope in keeping the market active, whether it's buying or selling stock – and there we enter into the world of the gambler, which presumably hope is exquisitely addressed to. And perhaps there must be a great deal of optimism and hope necessary in the more generalised behaviour of whatever it is that makes entrepreneurs *entrepreneurial*. Hence you get in the US, and probably other countries, guru-like characters such as Dale Carnegie and so on who talk about positive thinking and all that bullshit.

As you're suggesting, we cannot underestimate the role of hope in driving this amazing machine called a capitalist or free market. Now that's a very sobering equation to think about, and maybe we will want to put it in the same compartment as the American dream, and the use of the words 'dream' and 'magic'. And on the other hand – changing gears completely here – this in-between state is being explored by kids every day for good and for bad and it seems to me to be unstoppable, you know, this interest in altered states of consciousness. This is very political in many ways, not the least of which is the vested interest in the US and other states in declaring a war – that is, a 'war on drugs'. It is probably more pronounced in this country than any other Western country, and the amazing fallout from that is that you'll find a full-page ad every other day about it, and people do say that the war against drugs has done more damage than the drugs themselves, and so on and so forth. I agree with that wholeheartedly. But this is a dimension of hope and/or hopelessness. And we need to accurately work through these issues so as to inhabit more fully, explore and understand the world of reverie and half-awakeness.

The politics of envy – *ressentiment*

I have a question that is really taking us away from what you've just said but it does link in some ways and has to do with the idea of the 'public secret' and 'knowing what not to know', which you have written about. The question is driven by the complex field of inequality and injustice that exists in countries like the US. Coming to New York to visit you and walking the streets heightened my sense of how this city is emblematic of capitalist progress and consumerism, but on the other hand you have this layer of people walking the streets collecting cans to make money, or people living on the streets. There's the sense that in everyday life these opposed relationships exist – the stark distinctions between wealth and poverty. What do you think about the public secret in a cultural sense, because we all know that this exists but we live our lives in such a way and with certain systems of belief as if 'we know what not to know'...

So you would like me to meditate a little on the relationships between hope and that sense of the public secret?

Yes.

In relationship to polarisation of wealth and the feeling you have of this amazingly commodity-driven, dependent culture?

It's also about a relationship between Marx's ideas on class and struggle, and the need to recognise new forms of disadvantage and inequality. And the reason I gave that example is that I think there is something in the idea of the public secret and inequality, or the complexity of class relations and experiences, that has now arisen. So, yes, it is a meditation on all of that...

What you make me think of – and this is perhaps a reflex on my part – is *ressentiment* and envy in hierarchy and class polarisation. By *ressentiment* I'm referring to Friedrich Nietzsche's concept of a 'transformation' of the soul from a sort of reckless *joie de vivre* to a mean-minded, calculating, secretive, envy-riddled personality that he typified in the good Christian and healthy bourgeois of his time. In this case – in a class-, colour- and gender-polarised place which, according to what I read, has undergone amazing polarisation of wealth in the past 10 or 20 years – as we see when the welfare state gets dismantled and neo-liberalism is given free reign. It is really a cause of bewilderment and astonishment to me just how fast this has proceeded, and how come there are no signs of protest. Now remember that the society of the US is ideologically grounded on the notion that everybody gets a fair deal. In other words, everybody is a player and in this game some are going to end up winners and some are going to end up losers. Let's not really specify what proportion of each, but the argument is given this ethos and there's not much complaint because that's the nature of the game and so it proceeds at that pace. But I would think that a lot of people are holding their breath and wondering what has happened to those old-fashioned attitudes of resentment, or *ressentiment*, and envy. I ask this because I have lived in places in Colombia in the Putumayo, where people are *exquisitely* concerned with envy. This envy is interesting because it is not just a question of having more money, it is a question of having intangible things as well. For instance, it could be about children who help or it could be the beauty of one's children. It is not simply something that can be measured by a bank balance or amount of money or the amount of land or all the signs of wealth that we associate with. I wonder whether the issue of hope has a linkage with the medieval spectrum – speaking of European cultures – of the seven deadly sins, of which envy is one, gluttony and sloth and so forth. If I was more of a scholar on that it would be interesting to pick up on your comment about where the terms of hope lay in medieval theology and in everyday life – particularly in relation to envy and how that seems to have disappeared in this 'most advanced capitalist country in the world', where it *seems* that the discourse, the rules of the game, is that there are winners and losers, and the losers just have to shut up or they are bad sports...

But – perhaps I am naïve – there does seem to be a really serious commitment to notions of fair play and types of equality enshrined in the American experiment – call it the American constitution, the type of republic that was forged here in the late eighteenth century. I mean, it is easy to scoff, laugh and dismiss things like that, but I think that would be very wrong-minded and wrong-headed. This is a project that does go wrong a lot of the time, but there is something distinctive about the American political experiment which makes it quite different to Britain, Australia, France, Germany, Zimbabwe, etc. And it cannot be thought of simply as a crude imperialist and capitalist society. There is a commitment here to a certain notion of justice and fair play which is extraordinarily commendable. So one wonders to what degree the imbalance you talk about is compatible with those sorts of preoccupations. I would like to work on it in relationship to your interest in hope, and the perversions or distortions that happen to envy in a society which is based so heavily on the free-market principle, and ask 'Where does envy go in a situation like that?' I can't believe it disappears. For instance, I would go so far as to say that, in universities and closed-off corporate settings, envy is not only alive and well, but it is the motor behind most of the social psychology of the institution. I guess the idea of hope would be that pessimism or lack of hope can be undone by figuring out the network of resentment and envy and doing something about it.

I am also thinking about how Nietzsche might have answered this in terms of his interest in *ressentiment* and the so-called slave mentality. The story you get about Nietzsche – at least I get – is that once upon a time there was this cynical Nietzsche who dismantled everything, and then he saw the light and became a sort of positive thinker and wrote *Thus Spoke Zarathustra*. But this is a not a switch from hopelessness to hopefulness; it is more like a switch from cynicism to hopefulness, and that is interesting given the degree to which he emphasised resentment or envy as the mark of the bourgeois ethos.

And ressentiment *is about a 'weak' culture, and, as Nietzsche says, this weak character gives rise to envy – which does not allow a reckless soul or the spirit to live.*

I can't answer how he exactly hoped to pull that off – to move from the state of envy to positive thinking. But it is almost a cliché to think about Nietzsche's work as moving from despair – I don't know if despair is the right word, maybe intellectual despair – or from a high-spirited cynicism, to hope. Now thinking about his life, the hope which comes with the works like *Thus Spoke Zarathustra* is the hope that is actually mingled with despair. It is like the hope of a drowning person, or something which goes back to our 'optimism of the will, pessimism of the intellect'. And what I love about the beginning of that book is the use of the sun, and its relationship to giving for the sake of giving – this spirit of the pot brimming over and exaltation in going further than is necessary, you might say, beyond utility and the need for that – which, I think, is also a central problem for Georges Bataille and his notion of visions of excess, and his drawing attention to this spirit of expenditure.

The point I would take from *Thus Spoke Zarathustra*, let's say for argument's sake and your interest in hope, is about this overflowing exchange between people, and here we come back to your class issues – such that generosity and hope would be mingled with unleashing the spirit of the gift, alongside or in place of the spirit of the commodity. Zarathustra says something like, 'Every day I am in the mountains, every day I see the sun come up, pouring light into my cave, the warmth and the energy of the sun that keeps overflowing from my cupped hands – now I want to go with the people and I want to fill up people's hands with this energy, refill, and refill and refill'. It is a sort of constant giving over... It sounds very moralistic or religious or something, but it's a very thoughtful way of trying to replace the commodified world with this replenishing gift-giving – the generosity of exchange which has very different sorts of implications. And that's how I think you would connect up hope and life. This is the image that he had, at least in moving from his attack on categories of thought to taking the bit between his teeth and espousing a philosophy for living – as opposed, you might say, to a philosophy of attack.

Islands of hope
Here I suppose you could argue that the idea of replenishing is the ethical

dimension for living... a generosity and gift-giving which isn't based on commodification but is about a replenishing of the soul which is life-affirming. That's what is interesting about Nietzsche and his concept of the human – how replenishing or generosity could change what it means to be human...

I have a concrete example, and it will probably appear to people as predictable and mundane. I was thinking about the experience of some journalists I know in Colombia who have been there for, like, 30 years, and really know the place inside out – people who have covered the war in El Salvador and Central America at close quarters, as only photographers and TV people do. They're the ones who get blown to bits as well as the combatants, or almost as much, and I know one person in particular who is on top of everything and constantly in the middle of everything. A couple of years back, I got the greatest surprise when I discovered that this person had basically given up being on top of factual details, the latest crisis or political scandal – of which there are so many in a country like Colombia, where the US is so deeply invested. For instance, the drug enforcement agency is corrupt to the hilt and everybody is framing everybody else, and then you've got layer upon layer of Colombian military and police, all deeply corrupt, saying they are fighting drugs while living off it, etc. And you have the language of human rights circulating through all of this, and you can imagine it's like a world with 10 dimensions at any particular second. Anyway, he has given up any claim to getting the real story or any story. He has sold all his cameras and has completely given up photography, on the grounds that the camera got between him and people. And what he did was create a tiny foundation to help kids in the immediate four blocks around where he lived – kids who are prostitutes and drug addicts. He goes down every night with a bag full of syringes, condoms and vitamins and puts up posters in the neighbourhood giving instructions on what to do in emergencies and so on. I just found this so-called band-aid treatment extremely important: this attention to immediate crisis as opposed to the macro concern with international politics, the war against drugs, 'Plan Colombia', and so on. I felt it should not be put in terms of someone being burnt out or even frightened of recrimination – because it's got to the stage now where that type of intervention has to be thought about.

To me, it was particularly interesting in terms of *Thus Spoke Zarathustra* and the idea of giving and generosity. Of course it can be easy to be cynical and dismiss something like that and say, you know, 'That's not dealing with the reality of the problem'. But I have been very struck by that in terms of, say, academia and other walks of middle-class life, where people I see are completely unable to relate to that aspect of their being with other people. And it doesn't mean giving beggars in the street a dollar instead of 10 cents, or a dollar instead of nothing. It seems to me it is a way of life, or generates a way of life, which is a completely different calculus of hope.

So let me try and put it this way – there is the hope of the person who works as the news photographer or the TV photographer, who is meant to capture the minds or the eye of millions, right? – the BBC and CBS and all this sort of stuff. And what does it mean to shrink from that world of the international media to working four blocks around from your house and in this, one might think, hopeless way – these totally destroyed kids of whom there are so many – and, you know, night after night go out and do this thing with the age difference, the colour difference, the class difference. But, at the same time, getting to know everyone by their first name, and all the jocularity in getting to know each other and building up a sense of what it is to have another type of community. Let's say that this is an 'island of hope', and it's totally unconventional, I think. There, obviously, the world has to be composed of these islands of hope. This is not the missionary, this is not the Mother Teresa type of thing, this is *ad hoc* and done in the terms of a personal style that I find one of the few convincing – how shall I put it? – politics of hope that I have seen in a long time. Another rather different example of this would be the highly spirited, much more collective operation of the Zapatistas in the south of Mexico. And why do I bring hope in there? I bring it in because of the humour, poetry, writings and emails of Subcomandante Marcos and his mischievous, original wordplay which take the notion of revolution and carnival back to their real meaning. That degree of spirit combined with the sort of physical daring of taking on the

Mexican state and combining violence with wit – very minimal violence, I must say – there's an astonishing politics of hope. This is quite different to the first example I gave of a solitary individual, the photographer, which to me is a fascinating and amazing image. But if you took those two examples – and one can come up now with many more, because I think I have opened up a gate to the imagination – you could extend the possibilities of the politics of early twenty-first century hope.

3
JOYFUL REVOLT
A conversation with Julia Kristeva

How might we create a dialogue where ideas of faith, love and care can enter into our individual and political vocabularies? Imagine a world where this is possible – a space to invent other kinds of love and care, to transform the misery, alienation and despair felt in individual and political life. But love is often expressed in the media and popular culture as a romantic escape from our own lives and our responsibility towards others. And other kinds of love that involve hope, as a notion of faith and care – which are about a concern for others – are often difficult to sustain. Yet these feelings and concerns are important issues in how we live and connect with others, and in the urgent need for care and sensitivity in national and global debates.

French-based writer and psychoanalyst Julia Kristeva engages with me in a dialogue of love, faith and care, and where the possibility of revolution may lie in politics and individual life – the kinds of revolt that can transform us and create new acts of critical thinking. At a political level, in the traditions of the Left and progressive politics, this requires a faith to overcome the limitations of the past and imagine a hopeful future. It is about what it means to be human – a rebirth in aesthetic, cultural and individual terms which involves the creative risks we can take to invent other ways of living. Kristeva's work as a psychoanalyst and teacher informs her philosophical ideas and her writings on the importance of love in therapeutic and cultural practices, and the need to examine the 'new maladies of the soul' that we witness in contemporary life, such as the destruction of the psyche and the imagination in contemporary media-oriented and performance-driven cultures. In this context, Kristeva embraces a caring hope *for the new kinds of narratives and reflections that are necessary for individual and political revolt in an increasingly desensitised world.*

Love, faith and care

Mary: I'd like to ask about your ideas on hope as part of the human condition, and how it can transform the 'new maladies of the soul' – the conflicts and despair that we experience in daily life...

Julia: Hope is a question which holds some significance for me, and which reassures me a little as well. To my ear the word 'hope' has a religious connotation, so when you first told me what this conversation would be about I wondered what I could possibly say, given that I'm not a religious person, and that I've even lost hope in ideological structures. As a psychoanalyst, a woman and a writer I have for some time now been aware of what I call the destruction of the psychic space, or at the very least the threat which hangs over that space. What I mean is that the idea of the soul, or introspection, or the psychic (internal) representation of our conflicts – all essentially Western inventions – have long been a way for human beings to protect themselves from either biological or environmental aggression. By representing biological and social aggressions to ourselves in our psyche, we manage to get over them. We metabolise the aggression, and we survive. In the modern world, however, this *camera obscura*, this psychic space, is being threatened on several levels: by the crisis of family breakdowns, by the ever more aggressive world around us (whether we're talking about the social environment, wars, or about natural, biological events), and also by the world of images – media and televisual. These three factors have unsettled that psychic space, and as a result our ability to deal with conflict. If in the face of this there is to be any hope for us, to use your term, it resides in what I would call *care*. I'm convinced of our ability to restore that psychic space to well-being, in particular through psychoanalysis. That may seem minimal, but it's all we can do and it is in fact a form of hope.

What is this idea of care – is it psychoanalytic therapy, the idea of a 'talking cure'? Is that what you mean?

Yes, absolutely, by care I mean the psychoanalytic cure, but also any other kinds of care, which can take the form of therapy, or the way we welcome new students to university, or the way we are mindful of older people in the street, or the disabled on public transport. There are many different kinds of attentiveness and courtesy which are frequently forgotten in a society more concerned with performance and productivity... So we can think of it this way: the notion of 'care' implies a concern for others, and a consideration for their 'ill-being'. This would be a somewhat disenchanted kind of love, without the romantic, enthusiastic dimensions which cause us to distrust love. These days, however, we've forgotten how to attend to the suffering of others and ensure that they get the chance to start over. This is less about cure or resurrection than it is about renewal. We no longer think in ways that favour this kind of renewal. On the other hand, the process of transference and counter-transference involved in the psychoanalytic cure is an example of the economy of care.

We could say that this transference involves another kind of love – a love that is the care and trust that is allowed within analysis, where the speaking of 'unconscious' thoughts gives them a space to be heard and can be a form of renewal. So that does make me think about love. Across many of your writings you have talked about love and its importance in the capacity to be a subject in this world. The relationship or the necessity of love, and the relationship to something like faith, is essential, but not in the religious sense of the word. I'm wondering where hope may lie between this love and faith...

We're all part of a religious tradition, and we have to situate ourselves within it. But for a couple of exceptions, I think it's impossible to move beyond this tradition. At the moment I'm working on book which is on the French writer Colette.[1] What I'm noticing is how much this woman, who is taken to be a great, if not the greatest, lover – she who allowed herself every possible kind of love, with men, with women, with cats, with flowers – was in fact quite dismissive of love. She says that love is the most banal thing in existence. And I think I understand why she would write it off like that, because it isn't just that a lot of crimes have been committed in the name of love – a lot of truly stupid things have been done too. It can turn into a form of repressed idealism – quite regressive – and it can lead to submission and masochism. On the other hand, I believe that the best way of transvaluating both love and faith, which you mentioned, was invented by Freud. Nietzsche, as you know, used to say that we need a transvaluation of values, and the way of transvaluating love and faith is via transference – transference and counter-transference. How does it work? Imagine someone who isn't going too well, and who goes to see an analyst to relate the history of their suffering. This is a narrative act, which is itself a kind of love, or at the very least an expression of confidence in the therapist to whom this person is connected. And in this tale of love, which is what the analysand's discourse actually is, an older love is revisited, remedied, left behind – not so that it can be reconstituted, but in order to burn it down and find release from it. Yet the result is neither a desert, nor solitude, nor nihilism, but the possibility of connecting with others again. This connection is not necessarily love. It can be friendship, or creativity. It can also be a form of love, but with all the disillusionment and caution that memory brings. And so you see that it's all about transvaluating faith and love, which is possible if we take our past experiences seriously and don't cut ourselves off from other people.

Acts of solitude

I am thinking about the crimes in the act of love, or crimes that can occur out of it, like the love for a country or love for one's nation, and the many crimes that can occur there. For instance, you've written about depression in the nation, how people can experience a loss of identity. And this loss can often fall into fundamentalism... What might be a love that is more hopeful – one that doesn't enact a crime or that does allow a certain care or empathy for others, rather than depression?

This puts in my mind something which is happening in France at the moment. We are trying to preserve the nation-state, the Republic, while at the same time we are trying to decentralise by giving a degree of autonomy back to the regions, especially Corsica. Many people feel that if you tinker with the Republic, or with national unity, you lose the touchstones of your identity. People feel wronged, they feel hurt, they feel as though they've been orphaned and can even feel quite depressed. As an analyst I find this attitude quite understandable. It reminds me of that book I wrote a couple of years ago about nation-wide depression. I wrote that when a community (whether it be a family or even just one person, but predominantly if it's a family, or a social group, or a nation) goes through some kind of crisis, for instance, an economic crisis (high unemployment, inflation, the price of petrol is rising, etc), or perhaps there is an influx of foreigners and so on, then it's very difficult to get through this crisis of identity without clinging to an ideal identity. In a crisis this ideal identity is relied upon like a crutch, but almost fanatically – 'I don't know who I am, I'm broke, unemployed and I've lost my identity, but I belong'. Belonging is a way of staving off this identity crisis. We can criticise it and see its limitations, but it's inescapable: at this point in time humanity needs to belong in order to survive. Where we belong, whether we're talking about family, religion, ethnicity or nationality, is like a safety-belt we can't go without. The question is whether we can undo that safety-belt. I don't think we can yet; the time isn't right. If I did, I'd feel naked! But do we need it to be quite so tight, or can we loosen it a little? I think we can, but not without a huge effort on the part of the individual, and not without rethinking how we understand democracy.

I'd like to give two examples of how an individual can loosen this structure of identity, this safety-belt. At the moment we're in the middle of the new literary season in France. There are a lot of new novels coming out, and most of them, as is always the case, are love stories. A patient of mine said to me recently, 'It's all very well for these famous writers to go on about love, but they don't know how to be alone'. I was quite struck by what she said, because she didn't mean that everyone should stay at home in complete solitude. What she saw in the pathetic and extravagant public demand for the love stories of these media-hyped writers was in fact an *inability* to be alone. Not solitude, but *esseulement* (I'm not sure what that might be in English). The psychoanalyst D.W. Winnicott talks about 'at-one-ment', the ability to unify oneself, to constitute for oneself an autonomous space, which is a form of solitude, the ability to be alone.

Of course Winnicott believes that when we are born we already possess a primitive autonomy, and, for example, without this autonomy a foetus could never leave the uterus... Obviously this is a fragile thing, because as everyone knows a baby needs its mother, and this at-one-ment, or 'ego-relatedness', continues to develop for our entire lives, passing through the different phases (oral, anal, phallic) which psychoanalysis recognises. Ideally we reach the point where we can tolerate solitude, and it may be that this capacity to tolerate solitude is where creativity comes from.

The creativity to learn how to be alone?

Yes. So I need to be able to have a relationship with myself, both biologically and intellectually, which is a way of partaking of solitude and not relying exclusively on the outside world. The important thing to note is that someone who is capable of solitude is also capable of connecting to others, in the sense of caring for others, without which one remains in a state of constant need – one is consumed, the way that love can be all-consuming. As far as the individual is concerned, then, there is still a lot of work to be done, both through education and through psychoanalysis, to establish this sense of at-one-ment, which is a kind of primitive independence, as a value of contemporary civilisation. It will be important because it will teach people to relate to others without demands and expectations. We're forever asking things of the state, of schools, of our family, but what do we give back, how independent are we? This is something we need to educate people about, and we're getting there, in part through psychoanalysis.

As for larger groups, the idea of democracy still needs some work. To return to the French situation – but you may have other examples from Australia or New Zealand – we have always tended to rely too heavily on a collective, such as the monarchy, or the Republic, which we treat as a kind of divinity we can depend on, and which takes care of us. The idea is that we experience the Republic, or a monarchy, as all-giving, omnipresent structures we can depend upon for our very salvation, notwithstanding their repressive, dogmatic side. Democracy, on the other hand, is more supple, is open to new questions, takes differences into account, continually manages conflict – this is what today's society wants, with the development of new technologies, the ever-greater consideration of the place of the individual in society. But this kind of democracy frightens us, because a dogmatic republican (or monarchical) regime goes a long way towards protecting us from certain risks, and keeps us lazy.

And this laziness makes people surrender their individual agency and passion for political issues. So this keeps us from taking risks and asking questions...

I think the question is how to preserve our sense of security while at the same time opening ourselves up to the democratic dangers which guarantee our freedom. This is much less easy; it implies risk... Democracy is based on a network of independent individuals, and on continual dialogue. That is the democracy we have yet to build.

Principles of justice

This idea of democracy raises the question of how we form new democracies with the fall of communism, the experience in Eastern Europe, and so on. How do we construct the democracy you suggest? – even, to stretch it further, an imaginary or imagination so that we can exist in collectivities with some sense of the principles that were useful in many of the Marxist ideas that have fallen apart with history. It seems to me there needs to be a relationship between democracy and senses of justice, equality and so on, that would continue to take into account some of these socialist principles...

The people's democracies gave us a false image of democracy, and disastrously so, because they were all about equality of the lowest common denominator, and the deprivation of liberty. As far as I'm concerned this is not democracy. When we talk about new forms of democracy, here in the West where we've experienced the limitations of bourgeois democracy, the first word you hear is decentralisation, in other words handing power over to smaller, localised groups – regions, ethnic groups, religions, gays and lesbians, and so on – while at the same time trying to safeguard the general interest. It's all about balancing the general and the particular, the centre and the periphery. It also gives a much greater importance to the individual, who was always neglected in the people's democracies, especially under communism, where the role of the individual as an absolute value was completely abolished. I've examined this problem through Hannah Arendt's work, which I think makes two points relevant to our discussion. First of all, the false democracies of the old Eastern bloc, especially Stalinism, which degenerated into the gulags, destroyed all respect for individual thought. This was the first step on the road to the gulags. It's when there is no respect for what you think as Mary Zournazi, or for what I think, that one thing leads to another and you lose your freedom of expression, your freedom of movement, the right to choose your neighbour, your clothes, your food, and finally you lose your life. We must be mindful of this denial of individual freedom, which leads to the destruction of free thought and of life itself, whenever we think about the so-called democracies of the communist regimes. However – and I think this is where you're coming from – there was always a sense of the need for equality, the demand that everyone have an equal chance, associated with the communist ideal. If that's how we're to understand it, then I'm all for it. But if we're to understand it as crushing everything and everyone down to the lowest common denominator, then we're setting ourselves back on the road to the concentration camps. Nonetheless, giving everyone an equal chance remains a problem of the utmost importance, which is why I think that the French motto 'Liberty, Equality, Fraternity' is more important now than ever. It simply needs to be adapted to the modern world.

The second point from Arendt which I think is relevant here is about how we might value the individual, give everyone an equal chance, and still manage to connect these individuals as a community. The answer to that problem lies in imagining a society made up of relations between very different individuals – something no democracy has yet managed. There was the aristocratic democracy imagined by Plato, but it was based on a caste system. We've had the repressive, levelling democracy of communism. And now we need a democracy where everyone has equal rights and an equal chance. This is a utopia. We don't yet know how to achieve this, but we're lucky in that we're able to imagine it, and work towards it, so that we can come to value the individuality of each person more than we do now, but without falling back on forms of elitism. And this calls for a great deal of tolerance towards others, while at the same time a heterogeneous, differentiated understanding of the general good.

Hope itself?

Yes, this involves sharing differences – taking differences into account, a sort of democracy of singularities, if you will. That's very difficult these days. For instance everyone says, 'We respect homosexuals', but when it comes down to putting that into practice they take a step back, they won't compromise themselves. Or else they say, 'We're listening to what the regions want', but get cold feet as soon as Corsica demands independence. As you can see, this is not the right time. We believe in the principle, but it still isn't easy to recognise and accept difference, and live with it on a daily basis.

*

For me this raises the question of how we define the 'human subject' within this framework, because we often understand the human or being in relation to production and capital. That's one of the problems of trying to find another sense of what it means to be human... How can we redefine a sense of 'being' that's not caught within a capitalist system or capitalist production. In fact, you talked about that right at the beginning, how 'mediatised' images and the aggressions of the world onto us create a threat to the self, as today we are more concerned with productivity and performance...

We're inextricably caught up in the capitalist system. I'm not one of these daydreamers who think that you can avoid globalisation. Whether we're talking about the economy (after all, our salaries are paid by a capitalist society) or the media, we're constantly being caught up in the networks of information which the media deploy. Moreover, we depend upon these networks to communicate our ideas, all the more so if you're an intellectual. But I think people understand now that the kind of revolt that I've been trying to imagine is neither about rejection, nor opposition, nor simply sitting around and doing nothing, which is a form of nihilism. Let me give you an example. Here in Europe, in France and in Belgium in particular, we protested quite loudly against Jörg Haider, but then the European Community decided that there was no cause for sanctions against Austria. The initial revolt was quickly followed by a certain embarrassment. People were saying, 'Did we do the right thing by protesting? What are we going to do now? Should we remain vigilant? How?' I have an answer which may seem a bit weak, but which is, I think, emblematic.

The other day I read about a CD-ROM production company in Austria – in Vienna, in fact – which is run by a cosmopolitan group of young people: Austrians of Hungarian background, Italians, Belgians, Canadians. These young people spent a lot of their time last year protesting against Haider, while at the same time producing a CD-ROM about Freud. What they produced is in fact the only CD-ROM that you can use to trace the development of psychoanalytic thought, as you might through a web, jumping from one idea to the next. My uptake of this is to say that it is no longer sufficient to demonstrate in the streets if you want to protest against something. These people tried that, and realised that it wasn't enough. Real revolt is an effort of memory and analysis, which may appear insignificant but which in the long term alters our way of thinking. And where does it lead us? Neither to simple opposition (going to demonstrations), nor to sitting at home doing nothing, but to the development of critical thought. What is most interesting about it is that it's the first and the only such CD-ROM, and that it happened in Vienna. It didn't happen in Australia or in London or France or Germany, but in Vienna.[2] And at the same time they were demonstrating against Haider. It was their way of continuing to demonstrate in a way which appears totally unrelated, but which is fact deeply connected to revolt.

Joy, memory and revolt

Your notion of revolt is about engaging in a political way, but also engaging with the etymological sense of the word – revolt is about a turning back or a revolving, bringing forward a different sense of memory and of time. How might this revolt connect to hope and the idea of joy? You've written about Marcel Proust's notion of embodied time and enjoyment – the little moments of joy, both experiential and memory-evoking, that he tried to create in his writing. This notion of joy is about the sensations and experiences that can provide another kind of psychic imagination and revolt in writing and in life. So how might that joy transform our reality and perceptions?

At the moment I'm doing little radio programs, a few minutes every Wednesday morning, and last week I spoke about two religious images which struck me during the summer. The first was from Russia, either Moscow or Saint Petersburg. It was during the terrible drama of the *Kursk*, with all those submariners trapped under water and so on, and the Russian Church was weeping and making martyrs of them. This lamentation, which of course is understandable given the tragic history of the Russian people, is somehow essential to orthodox religion. The second image came from Rome, during the celebrations of the international Catholic youth organisations who were there to see the Pope; they were all extremely festive, very much in a party mood. These are two quite different faces of religion, one lamenting, one joyous, and I thought once again of Nietzsche, for whom God is dead but who also said that if he ever had to believe in a God it would be a dancing God, which goes a little towards answering your question about Proust.

In other words we know perfectly well that it's up to us to transform reality, but the transformation depends on our mental state, on the forms of discourse we adopt, and if our symbolic disposition leans more towards that of the dance, and of optimism, we have a stronger hold on reality than if our disposition is that of lamentation and melancholy. It's for that reason that I'm interested in Colette, whom I spoke of earlier, who in spite of the disasters of the twentieth century tried to find within herself and around her the resources for joyfulness – in her pagan and stylistic jubilation. This is something which we must try to cultivate, both through memory and, as I said before, through the best possible relations with our environment and other spaces of freedom which we've yet to invent. What is absolutely imperative is to underline the possibility of joy. It isn't necessarily voluntarism to rely on joy like this. You don't just decide to be joyous. But psychoanalysis has taught us that joy is a way of mourning our grief. Or, to put it another way, it is only by traversing our grief that there can be any possibility of hope.

Postscript

On September 11, 2001 I met with Julia Kristeva again in Paris, to follow up Hope *and to further discuss her ideas of revolution and revolt, from her historical and critical perspectives, and the essential link between them for new ideas of change. While we were talking the first plane hit the World Trade Center. At that moment we were both unaware of it. In the light of this, and on reflection, there is an essential need to assess the role of hope in social and political life – how to move beyond lament and into a space of hope, and where this may lie for contemporary politics and the Left.*

I think that I've had the idea of revolution since I was a child, because I was born in a communist country [Bulgaria] and experienced first-hand the limitations of social revolution. This social revolution, driven by the most generous of goals, would get bogged down in totalitarianism and hindered not only economic evolution, social progress and material comfort, but also and quite fundamentally spiritual and symbolic evolution and the freedom of individuals. So I very soon came to ask myself questions about the conditions and the logic of symbolic change, since that was precisely what was missing from the communist revolution. And I think that the idea of revolt as a return to the past, and innovation, renewal of the self – in other words a process of re-evaluation of the psyche, a questioning of identities and values – this idea of revolt, as opposed to that of political contestation itself, was always present in my theoretical work. For example, *Revolution in Poetic Language* is a book concerned primarily with the rhetorical logic and the psychoanalytic bases of the experiences of the late nineteenth-century French *avant-garde*, in particular Mallarmé and Lautréamont, and only secondarily with specifically political problems. Because when I arrived in France I became interested in these experiences, particularly in contemporary art, which seemed to me to be a secular link to religious or mystical questioning, in the sense that these aesthetic experiences sought to alter the language of individuals while at the same time, far from shutting themselves off in solipsism, aiming to effect social change. So my primary interest was with the symbolic mutations, which I associated with socio-historical mutations, but it was the symbolic ones that I stressed above all. Now it's quite true that afterwards, also due to the rapid disintegration of communism, the fall of the Berlin Wall – what has been called the end of ideologies – the exclusively political problematic seems to me even more limited, if not impossible. And so after that I became interested in emphasising the idea which had already taken root, namely the necessity of the symbolic deconstruction, the symbolic renewal, which comes from creation – psychic creation, aesthetic creation, rebirth of the individual – or what I call revolt.

The second part of your question, on hopeful visions for the Left, is an extremely complicated one – I don't think anyone really has the solution. At the moment, in France, we're witnessing the difficulty the Left is confronting. More than elsewhere it has reality, because the Left is in power. The French Left is perhaps also the most realistic, and the most diverse. For instance, in England the Left has had great success, but it has also cut itself off from its extremes, whereas the French Left, which is currently in government, embraces a plurality which is inclusive of some of its fringes, even some of the more extreme ones, such as the Greens and the Communists. But this is not unproblematic. I think that it's very important, in the world we live in, to take account of misery and social inequalities, and in the light of that there is something still valid about the Marxist position. I'm not talking about the Marxist *solution*, but the Marxist view of the class struggle and exploitation of human beings by technical development. These phenomena remain extremely widespread, perhaps in more dramatic and underhanded ways. That is why the goal of the Left is the necessary taking into account of this *ill-being*. I think that there is still a distinction to be drawn along party lines here. I'm not one of those who simply note that the Left and the Right are drawing closer together. There is a tendency to say of this *rapprochement* that there's no longer any difference between the Left and the Right. But I think that the difference remains, in particular because one part of public opinion is more sensitive to exploitation, exclusion and misery, and develops ways of counteracting these evils, the difficulties, these dead-ends. Now the problem with this politics of the Left is firstly that, while dealing generously with exclusion, it must also take into account technical and market imperatives, or in other words not isolate itself from the evolution of technical and market developments. And secondly, it must take into account the necessity of constant symbolic re-evaluation – in other words stay in touch with intellectual energies (spiritual forces, the forces of education, the forces of aesthetic creation) and not get locked into a mentality of dogmatic managerialism.

Which is what has tended to happen...

Yes, and as it turns out, at least in the European tradition, a certain number of left-wing movements are open to these preoccupations. It's therefore a question of remaining faithful to this tradition, and being prepared to adapt it as necessary to new forms of exclusion and new forms of aesthetic expression. I think that this is the vocation of the European Left, which thereby perpetuates a certain generosity from our spiritual tradition. And when one speaks of a Europe with a moral and spiritual heritage to which we ought to remain faithful, it's that generosity that I think of, and that's why I'm convinced that our future lies in a social and socialist Europe.

Translation during conversation by Deidre Gilfedder; translation of written transcript by Peter Cowley.

Notes

[1] This is the third volume of Julia Kristeva's *Génie Féminin* series.

[2] It would be significant to add to Julia Kristeva's point here. Freud was forced out of Vienna in 1938. As a Jew and intellectual, he was directly threatened by the Nazi hatred of this time and suffered the consequences of this hostility. In essence, then, the CD-ROM can be seen as a form of historical revolt against right-wing movements.

4
Faith Without Certitudes
A conversation with Nikos Papastergiadis

Empathy, faith and dialogue are words and experiences that are not often understood in political environments. There is a language that is needed, and a faith and belief in the struggles to define personal relationships, and the relationship between hope and the journeys one makes in life. It is in these narratives of hope that empathy and compassion are necessary to understanding the turbulent processes of cultural and political change. And this condition is no more prominent than in the exiles, migrations and displacements which could define the experience of contemporary life. For in leaving home to go elsewhere, or if you are an exile in your own country, the narratives of hope and despair are closely linked. The movement across and between cultures creates new forms of alienation and despair – of which the experiences of labour, economic and political disenfranchisement require a re-evaluation of the ethics and politics of social justice.

What this involves is a 'faith without certitudes' – the love, trust and belief that can sustain one's life and struggles for justice. Writer and critic Nikos Papastergiadis and I explore these ideas of hope and exile as a lived experience – through his own life and relations to others, as well as through methodological practice – in the space of writing itself. Here we explore the inspirations and hopes that can travel across words on a page, or enact a space of dialogue and surrender to ourselves and others.

Papastergiadis' own writing reflects these theoretical and critical movements, and his travels between different cultures and experiences. His philosophy provides insight into the turbulence of the modern world, and how we might affirm the journeys that we make throughout life. Papastergiadis is currently based in Australia, but has lived and worked extensively in the UK.

Journeys

Mary: There is a relationship between hope and exile as an experience as well as a methodology – exile as a metaphor for modern life and philosophy – and the hopeful connections that can be made in our perceptions and experience. So to begin, what are your thoughts on these connections?

Nikos: Hope and exile, of course, are often thought of as polar conditions. Sometimes they are connected in the sense that you leave a country with the hope for something better, and sometimes they are the opposite – you leave because you've lost hope at home. I guess that through exile you realise how necessary but elusive hope is – necessary for living and elusive because you never quite get what you thought you would get at the end of the journey. And, at the end of the journey, you realise that the journey continues and that it is one of the many journeys you will be doing in the rest of your life. So hope and exile are inextricably linked but are also so far apart that they can't even touch. In terms of my own work I never thought of them in that relationship and it's something that has just come to mind. In fact I realise that it is a deep relationship and that's not just a flippant or 'off-the-cuff' comment. And, for me, the relationship was more about the limits of self, of language, of culture that are exposed through exile. That is, how exile and migration and displacement and estrangement in one form or another expose certain taken-for-granted practices that otherwise have been seen as natural and no longer visible, because they are already placed in the armour of someone's mind and culture.

So for me, at first, the fascination with exile and migration was quite a personal feature because my parents, like yours, were Greek migrants to this country. So those words and those stories and those experiences were something that I grew up with, and I wanted to arrive at some deeper level of understanding of that. Initially I did a lot of work on artists who had migrated to Australia, and how the relationship between their journeys and their art had been changed as a consequence of their displacements or migrations or exile, and this was also a way of thinking about *living* in the modern world. And when I looked more closely at one person's writing over a long period of time – that's John Berger's work – I saw the methodological link that you point out and the sort of metaphor of exile being more closely tied to perception and experience. Because I realised that – although John Berger often wrote about migrants as artists or as peasants leaving their villages to go and work in cities, or the children of peasants, like us – he not only wrote about these people, but his way of seeing the world was very much informed by that perspective as well. So there is a fascinating connection between experience and perception, between subject and methodology, and so I thought more deeply on how the experience of exile was a trope that goes right across modern culture and philosophy.

I mean, this sounds quite straightforward, but it is a connection that has not often been made. The experience and theme of exile appears right across twentieth-century literature, art, philosophy, cultural and critical theory. So you can see Novalis' quotation, 'Philosophy is home-sickness of the mind', has become the slogan for critical theory. You could argue that the work of the Frankfurt school was very much informed by exile. And even certain concepts, like Karl Marx's 'alienation' or Max Weber's notion of the disenchantment in modern life, or Georg Simmel's idea of the stranger, are fundamental motifs for thinking about the exilic conditions of modern culture.

So exile actually enabled me to think in more assertive, and – what could be seen in the light of your interest in hope, more 'hopeful' – terms about the experience of migrants, rather than thinking about them always through the paradigm of a 'sociology of migration', because this sociology has often thought about them as trauma victims or a subset of greater forces – economic production and other political forces. So I got to see how exile and migration are *constitutive* features and not just the consequential parts of modernity – constituent in the sense that modernity as a phenomenon is about change. It is about transformation. Modernity is a turbulent process of change – and migrants are part of that process, for good and for bad. So this doesn't elevate them to be the great victims of the twentieth century, which in some cases they are, nor does it create them as the great criminals of the twentieth century, which, of course, in some cases they are. But it enables you to think about them in more dynamic and in more focused ways. So I think there are two aspects to this. One is to think about how the experience and the mode of perception are interlinked – that is, how one informs and shapes the other. And the other is to think about it in terms of how change is understood in the modern period, and how that relates in fundamental ways to the broader understandings and dynamics of culture, history and society in the modern period. And only lately have political economists and urban sociologists recognised that migrants are constituent agents in the modern period. So much of the early literature, as I've suggested, tended to relegate them to that victim status...

Or simply as outside...

...and not significant parts of the twentieth-century narrative.

I want to go to back to the relationship between perception and experience, and how language has a relationship there – for instance, the way perception and experience is expressed through language, or how writing can enable experiences that have been silenced to take some form. I see language and imagination as a critical element in expressing hope, or the possibility of changing entrenched modes of thought...

Tell me a little bit more about how you think about hope and its expression and its relationship to language.

Well I think there has to be, in order to exist at a certain level, the possibility of being able to communicate in language – so words have that basic element of being hopeful, of being able to communicate something through language. And I think Martin Heidegger said that hope is in language. Perhaps this hope might be about the state of being – in the broadest sense – as a gift, or the possibility to communicate that constitutes itself through language and thought. I'm trying to open out what hope might mean – not thinking about it as a future thing – but in people's everyday language and experience.

Yes, I think hope is a powerful force within us and it is also a principle that drives us to want to do things. Obviously you can think about hope in very crude ways: I hope to have X or Y, abstract quality or material commodity. But that's not what hope is about because that sort of hope is so easily disappointed. What is more important about hope is this sort of generalised state of being, which is an alluring state where you hope and you work and you dream and you yearn and you live in these states simultaneously, and these layers of feeling and energy and labour are so tightly linked that it is often difficult to distinguish them. Just like in a beautiful piece of music where there is a sense of hope. And it's not clear whether it is the oboe that conveys that, or it is a little rustling of bells, or it is that very subtle or sudden introduction of a bit of guitar that came and went, or may be even that tambourine that came for one second. So hope is like music because its quality is not really confined to one particular thing. It is the combination of elements that gives it its alluring quality. In that way you can say hope and language are connected. Heidegger is right to say that hope is in language, but only insofar as it is the part of language you often don't reach – in words at least. It's that part of language that words strive for and sentences try to reach but only get there through their mixture, again, rather than their individual components. So hope can only be seen between the lines, so to speak...

And when it comes to thinking about hope, language and migration, I guess there is the obvious point to make, which is, first of all, that the migrant encounters a sense of dissatisfaction and frustration with language. Things aren't as they are meant to be. The word for door is not what it is meant to be...

That's right!

And you keep bumping into them, or they don't let you in when you want them to, or you are always going out the wrong one... And so there is that frustration and disappointment and that can lead to despair, or it can lead to laughter, as we've almost done. But that is also important in terms of hope, because of course hope is the other side of despair – and being closer to one in fact reminds you of the need for the other. And it also reminds you that language itself is not complete, as the desire for communication is never destroyed by the frustration of words. That's why migrants flap their arms a lot more, because they are trying to open those doors without those words.

Physically, yes.

They gesticulate. In a sense we could say that, for the migrant, the hope is in the body of their language rather than just the words. Hope is more powerfully felt in their expressions of gesticulation.

It makes me think about body movements and how migrants flap their arms, but also what you are saying about hope not necessarily being in the words articulated but it being somewhere in the space between... So hope lies in the rhythms and the sounds that come to mind when you hear a word or a phrase – it's the possibility offered...

Yes, that's important. It's rhythm – isn't it? – that generates hope more than the actual word itself.

Faith without certitudes

There is a certain amount of faith that is required in language or in living in general to survive. But you've written about a notion of faith which isn't about certainty. How can you have faith without a certain sense of certainty? What's the potential in that?

Well, 'faith without certitudes' is an expression of love. Because only when you feel real love can you have trust, and trust is not dependent on guarantees. I guess what I am trying to communicate there is the love for life – which encounters so many frustrations, so many disappointments, so many kicks – and yet it produces a sense of energy that is a form of resilience and is an energy that comes from wanting to keep on struggling and to keep on trying to do something. In my case one of the most inspiring features of observing and following and thinking about another person's life and their work is to see the number of times they return to their first principle, and to see the number of times in their life they have repeated themselves. For instance, when I went looking for all of John Berger's work I started with his journalism and I found a two-or-three-sentence notice that he had written for the *New Statesman* in 1950. Immediately, when I read it, I recognised it as a piece of his writing, and it was the way in which he turned the metaphor, his use of voice and the demanding presence of that text. This is evident in every sentence, and it was as evident in that first sentence he published in 1950 as it is evident today, 50 years later. This is not to say that in 50 years he hasn't learnt to write better or worse, but rather to notice a certain quality of meaning which is there from the beginning – it's like a thumb-print. This is how it links to faith: that quality is one of endurance and of conviction and of belief. And those beliefs are sometimes sustained because they're aimed at particular things, or sometimes they don't need those particular things to drive them, but they are generated by more abstract general principles like hope.

So I believe that there is a connection between the expression 'faith without certitudes' and the principle of hope that your project is asking us to think about. To have real hope doesn't mean that you'll ever be satisfied, and it doesn't mean that you are aiming for one particular thing in this world and once you get that then everything else will be fine. It doesn't mean that once you achieve wealth, or even a revolution, that the struggle is over. But rather, one has to be constantly fighting to develop and push and make things the way you want them to be. Of course, in a writer like John Berger's case, part of that struggle is about questions of human justice and, if anything, you've got all the more to struggle for in this period of history than ever before. So that faith has to be constantly replenished – and that hope which is crushed by history and experience. Yet people do get up and fight again, and they often do that despite any promises of success.

What I'm interested in is this faith and your own relationship to writing. I think people and situations that inspire us are part of a principle of hope. As intellectuals, writing itself is about that, and the ethical issues and responsibilities that emerge when engaging with some sense of human justice.

Well, it is not so clear in yourself perhaps as it is with others. But I can see a pattern that has unfolded in my own writing and I can see the common struggles. So my relationship to people like John Berger is one of alignment in finding positive ways and examples to deal with issues of social justice. My books are all closely connected with the issues of exile, modernity, and migration processes. So for me, my books on these themes are in a trilogy. It took me three steps – the hop, the skip and the jump – to express and discover something that I felt was fundamental to my own personal experience, and I needed to track it through the life of others (which is what *Modernity as Exile* and *Dialogues in the Diasporas* are about). I also needed to think about the issues in a broader sense – that is what *The Turbulence of Migration* does. This is to try and present this whole story in a theoretical and global context, to see if there is a framework or system of sorts that is adequate to that task. This trilogy was in some sense a personal quest, but it was also an attempt to respond to certain social and historical questions which are much larger than the self. It is by trying to forge a connection between these spheres that the ethical and the political aspects of writing become apparent.

*

Your last book in the trilogy brings together a lot of the work you've done, but it is specifically around globalisation and migration and you introduce the metaphor of turbulence itself – not as a closed framework but as some sort of guiding principle. For me the idea of turbulence evokes a bumpy ride, like being thrown about in an aeroplane. And often when you're in that state you don't necessarily feel a beginning or an end to it. Obviously it is triggered by something but it's about a change to the conditions of one's life and movement. What it raises is the changes that can happen to perception and experience and how these are related to time and place, which is also a question about hope – the way we think and perceive history and the turbulence of migration... the turbulence, perhaps, of being modern?

It is a metaphor in the broad sense of word, but it also a reality for many people. So obviously we shouldn't trivialise it. But, on a trivial level, everybody's life is turbulent. You always think, or you've heard the expression a thousand times, 'When things settle down I'll be able to see my friends, you know, cook dinner etc, have a regular routine where I swim twice a week or something'. But you never get to that stage because something always disrupts you, and just as you feel you are getting to that point something even more disruptive will happen. We've become almost blasé about this process of disruption and we think it's the norm now. My ideas on turbulence focus on more aggressive and more challenging forms of disruption. So what I try to do is think about energy as a field and as a particular force. And to think about how through that combination of disruptive pushes and shoves and pulls there is a certain pattern that forms which is always changing, and as a consequence of being changed, new elements come into play. Taking into account your idea, when an aeroplane goes into a turbulent field it isn't just *rocked around* by that turbulent field and the air pressures, but its presence in that sphere actually distracts, diverts, diffracts, etc, the flows of energies around it. It too is changed – it goes off course but it also changes, whether in significant or insignificant ways, the actual forces that it is interacting with. So, in a way, I wanted a metaphor about the complexity of energy levels of the modern world – intellectual, social, economic, political, and also one that gives credit to the agency of individuals.

It seems to me that the concept of turbulence moves in that direction because it shows that as a consequence of leaving home, taking your culture with you – whether you do so willingly or unwillingly, consciously or unconsciously – you are not a blank sheet on arrival at another place. You are not a passive or neutral or invisible presence in that place, because everybody affects the other place and everybody affects *this* place through their otherness in some form or other. I think to try and define these levels of interaction, according to more classical forms of sociological or theoretical mapping which have grid-like structures or bipolar axioms or centre-periphery models, does an injustice to the energy levels which exist in the present which are both good and bad, both hopeful and despairing. It also underestimates the active presence of the stranger and the citizen as they interact with each other. So the concept of turbulence is a way of trying to rethink the process of interaction as it affects individual and social relationships.

So it is a process because you are talking about the interactions between experience and the conditions that shape history and life. But it has to be temporal, doesn't it? If you are talking about the forces that occur in a place, in a given locale, and if you are talking about individual agency and interaction, there has to be some other notion of time in operation here. You know, how relationships are formed in social life and the way change does occur, which is an opening out of the present and the past.

Yes, the relationship between time and space has to be dynamic as well. In the past there has been a tendency to privilege one over the other. That is, to try and think of migration as a story of leaving one place to go to another, or the migrant as trapped in a particular timeframe and therefore incapable of entering the modern world – because they are always nostalgic, always traditional, always mired in their own atavistic practices, etc. And there is the grand narrative of the migrant who left the past to march forward into the present and the future. So there has been the tendency to see that migration in terms of a linear movement from one place or time *to* another place or time. Now by definition turbulence as a model or metaphor or the system of interaction I am talking about is both temporal and spatial – it is multi-temporal and multi-spatial. In a sense, the migrant will arrive with many senses of time, one layering on the other or interacting or spliced or fragmented by the other. There will be a constant juxtaposition of temporal experiences and perceptions, memory lags and belatedness, and certain nostalgic phases. But, you know, everybody has this kind of experience where you suddenly get caught in a trance and whether that lasts for a minute or a week is not the point.

Or years...

Or years, yes. And you get caught in that moment of the past overtaking the present and sometimes you look like a stunned mullet – and your friends, neighbours, lovers think of you as someone that needs to be shaken and brought back to the present. But that's part of the process. And that happens in significant or insignificant ways. So the question of time is a complex one and perhaps we need to think of it in a more concrete way...

Well, yes. I suppose I was thinking about time when you were making the link between turbulence and individual agency. I don't know whether this is going to be more concrete, but this is the way I am putting it together for the moment. There has to be a relationship, say, of an individual to a community and/or a moment in time, perhaps taking a dog for a walk or something... There's got to be a relationship between you and something else and I think that the experience of turbulence does involve multiple layers of time. But that time is activated by the person walking the dog or being there in a particular relationship to something else... For instance, walking the dog through a park is about a spatial movement through time, because where you walk – along the grass or path, with people or other dogs, etc – is part of that experience, which is the encounter of time, movement and agency.

That's true, that's true... Well, I can add to it, but I think you've said it.

I guess I'm thinking of the importance of agency, which is a recurring theme in your writing on exile and migration – how individual agency is constituted through interactions in time and space, and I wonder there, are you thinking about it in terms of a sense of freedom as well?

That's a good way of putting it. For me, part of it is this frustration and general sense of 'pissed-offness' with the way migrants were portrayed in the past as stereotypes – either clowns or victims. You know, real go-getters or real exploited types, and I want not so much to develop another character or present other sorts of personality types or even highlight different modalities, but I really want to explore and put forward the centrality of the migrant's presence in the world and the fact that this is not a passive thing. I want to explore this presence as an active part of culture and history, and whether that is acknowledged or not is a different story. It is a story of ideology then. The ways in which it is acknowledged or repressed, as it is now, are of fundamental importance – as we are discovering with this present Liberal government in Australia. Because recognition now is the hardest concept of all in terms of what is acceptable to both sides at least. So that debate about recognition which occurs in philosophy is not an abstract one for us, it is a very real one, especially for Aboriginal people and migrants; who feel that the way in which their histories are being appropriated in the mainstream are so folkloric and so ridiculed and so traumatised that it has no bearing on the actual energy they have for living.

I mean, I feel quite energised and positive about certain parts of my daily experience in Melbourne, when I encounter the way people make ends meet. For instance, the way they express themselves through their own architecture or the way they arrange their gardens. I always get a kick out of watching my father prepare his garden at the end of every winter, and the way he plots certain vegetables next to certain kinds of flowers, and that gives me a great sense of what multiculturalism could be about.

Narratives of hope

There are two parts to what you were just saying, and one aspect of this is to find other ways to document what I would like to call 'narratives of hope' – the historical and contemporary processes of migration and of colonisation, and how you could represent Australian culture. I mean, your father's garden is about living a history in the present – his flowers and vegetables would no doubt reflect a deep relationship to Greece and also to Australia. But the other part of it is the idea of class experience – and the relationship between the new forms of capital and globalisation that complicate these processes now. You've written about 'disorganised' labour as one of the new experiences of alienation today. In that context there is a necessity to reinvent the ways of looking at labour and alienation in relation to capital. I am very much interested in addressing the relationship between the experiences of migration, the kinds of agencies you're talking about, and the complexities of class itself and labour.

I'll never forget that time when *perestroika* crumbled, in a sense, and the Soviet Union came crashing down. And my mother, who's by no means a communist, turned to me and said, 'Oh, I'm glad I am retired now; I wouldn't want to be a worker for the next 50 years'. And she said that in a flash, and she was right. It was the end of a certain form of organised labour, and she always used to say the reason why capital conceded some rights to the unions was the greater fear of communism. So, in her mind at least, the bosses and the factories that she worked in would give the workers some small concessions for fear of a revolution. Well, that says more about her background and experience than I think it says about Australian political history. But there is a certain point there about the stability and strength of working-class communities, and the way they were organised and gained both *symbolic* and *real* political power. So you can see how the fear of communism added symbolic power at the bargaining table when the trade unions sat before the capitalist owners. This was a strong memory and experience for me as I was growing up, and I had other uncles on my father's side who were perhaps much more left-wing than my mother was, who would talk about the civil war in Greece and the fight for socialism. So from quite a young age, you know, I developed a gut feeling against the power of the Right.

But now there is this transition that we are all going through in terms of the shift towards disorganised labour, and I think that has profoundly changed the way we understand alienation and estrangement. Alienation as Marx tried to explain it was the alienation through labour and estrangement – and is often accounted for or thought about in more anthropological terms – in terms of estrangement from a particular type of community. Now you seem to have both at once: the community fragmented and the relationship to labour more complex, because everyone in a sense is a member of the 'reserve army'. Everyone is potentially on the scrap-heap at any point in their career. And so the anxiety levels are more ambient and more jagged at the same time, and they cut deeper. They push people to more competitive and individualist practices. The idea of solidarity and communal forms of resistance appear now, at least, as more distant. So there is a lot less to feel hopeful about... The avenues of struggle seem to be foreclosed in some areas, and people are isolated and feel less capable of joining together to struggle against things.

And there is something important we ought to bear in mind – there is a sort of illusion of equality and egalitarianism in Australia which I think is even more crippling. There is a denial about class in Australia, and I think that is one of the most disabling features of our political and cultural climate – because we are not a classless society. And this denial ends up asserting itself in very insidious ways, and in a very covert fashion. For instance, people often talk about culture in positive terms – like folkloric symbols, through modes of recreation and sport and expressions of dance and music – but one of the surest ways in which a culture is defined, and its boundaries are perpetuated, is through corruption. Australia is a profoundly corrupt country, as many other countries are, and its preferred mode of corruption is not overt clientalism – where one climbs up the social ladder by making an ingratiating network of influence – but through covert cronyism. And cronyism is rife in Australia. What is interesting to see is the ethnic bias through which cronyism operates. And you see it all across the spectrum in Melbourne and, in particular, the art world I operate in. It's rampant. In that sense class is not an invisible or irrelevant feature. In fact it's a central feature in the way certain rewards are distributed. And the way in which those rewards are distributed is never to do with merit. I can think of a good number of people who have been recently appointed as directors of galleries and who haven't 'earned' their position in any sense of the word. They have been awarded a position in the hope or in the belief they have what is necessary to take on the task. Now that act of generosity to recognise the potential of the *other* is unevenly distributed and, I would add, ethnically biased.

In a way, this is a lack of generosity and hope that reinforces already entrenched attitudes and social bias. I guess that is also reflected in the more 'positive' definitions of Australian culture – like sport, where class and ethnicity are covered over in the belief that we live in an egalitarian society.

Well we hear of people like the tennis players Mark Philippoussis and Patrick Rafter time and time again, having their little public exchanges and attacks on each other. I'm not one of these people who want to say, 'poor Mark Philippoussis, he's the sort-of exploited wog in all of this', but I don't think Patrick Rafter knows the meaning of the word 'being jerked around'. I'm sure he's never been jerked around in his life and he has no right to say such things on global media as far as I'm concerned. Rafter has become 'our Australian of the Year' and, as the media pointed out, he had come home to pick up this honour. What sort of exile is he returning from – his tax haven in Bermuda? Whereas Philippoussis, who is a resident of Australia, but whom the media often portray as 'un-Australian', I guess because he prefers a Ferrari over a Holden. I wonder what they would have done to him if he single-handedly lost the Davis Cup out of sheer hubris like Rafter did.

*

The direction I would like to take now is how migrant cultures themselves negotiate the transitions of class. Many foreigners, as you know, come to a country as working-class people, but their children may become more middle-class through education and opportunity, or vice versa. In my experience there is a huge cultural and educational difference, as I'm the next generation and I have an education which enables or gives me more access to class mobility than my parents. The point I want to make is around the complex nature or the networks that emerge around class which aren't just structural. There is a need to look at the movement of class, or how it's experienced, which can no longer be defined in the old categories. I think that this 'class' experience can be felt in the most intimate of relationships between parents and their children, and the tensions and conflicts that can arise from that.

Oh yes, this is not an abstract thing. We have to be clear that when we talk about class today it doesn't repeat itself in the way it did in the nineteenth century or even in the early twentieth century, and within my own biography that's obvious. My father was a peasant. He grew up in a peasant community and for the first 20 years of his life he had no access to any of the resources of the modern twentieth century, and he didn't get to wear shoes until he joined the army, but his son went to Cambridge. That's a huge leap in history. And when I think about what my father was doing when he was 18 and what I was doing when I was 18 I say, 'We can't be related, can we?' Yet there is nobody closer to me than my father and mother. And so on the one hand, through my own biography I could think about the opportunity that was afforded to me through education that was never afforded to him. But at the same time, as much as I can reflect on how those opportunities allow you to leap-frog through history, in a sense, there is always this close relation and difficulty of moving through and defining those elements of class experience.

Affinity – empathy, hope, surrender

I want to explore how collective forms of struggle seem more distant now, and how the ideas of change and revolution are losing sway because of the effects of more individualised and less communal practices. Or, to put it another way, there is a need to reimagine forms of communication and solidarity. You have this notion of how 'clusters' can form communities – clusters being a positive way of people getting together around the idea of community or communal belonging. What is the relationship between this idea of cluster and the necessity of dialogue for you, as an active and hopeful process of collective life?

That's a very important concept for me and it's an experience that I constantly yearn for, and when it does happen it surprises and enthuses me to such an extent that it keeps me going for a long time. I'll give you a little example of it. The concept of cluster comes out of certain kinds of experiences that I had particularly in London, and I have more regularly now in Melbourne. For instance, when I worked for the journal *Third Text* I would constantly be in contact with people from elsewhere. Everybody was from elsewhere. Being Greek-Australian was the least exotic thing you could be in the company of friends I had in London. On one occasion I can remember sitting around the dinner table with Jimmie Durham, who is Cherokee, Zia Sadar, Rasheed Araeen and Ashish Nandy, who are from India and Pakistan, Jean Fisher, who was from England but had spent most of her time in New York, and Mona Hatoum, who is Palestinian. So there was this group of people who would meet to discuss the journal or what we should be doing about debates on contemporary art, what multiculturalism is, or other political issues.

There was an energy there and it came out of working with people who had such different backgrounds but with whom you perhaps share similar goals – but it is not as simple as that. I mean you have an affinity with them rather than necessarily having things in common. In that sense the cluster was like, 'Wow, here we are, people from remote parts of the world. We are living, thinking and working together in our different ways and also trying to find ways of being in parallel with each other' – and that gave me tremendous 'hope' in your sense of the word. It also made me think: What is it that you need to create a community? What is the bare minimum? And the bare minimum isn't kith and kin – you don't have to be related to these people to feel close to them. And what is it that you feel? It's an admirable feeling towards them and also a contestatory feeling in working towards something, whether it be political or creative. And I think that it is important because the slogan 'living with difference' that Zygmunt Bauman put forward was a reality for us. So the cluster was the term for thinking about how you arrange a meeting or grouping of people without imposing a structure and common identity on that group, because the moment you try to do that you have created a hierarchy or you have already defined the identity rather than *allowing the identity* to be created out of the experience. So what I think is interesting about clusters is the way they lead towards identification and projection in dynamic forms of expression, rather than towards some identity in the clear, fixed, and political sense of the word.

One of the reasons why clusters never survive is because they are not about committee formations and delegations – for instance, setting up leaders and vice-presidents and therefore potential oppositional leaders. Those sorts of political formations do not excite me. They are obviously necessary at different points in time. But Alberto Melucci uses a different term to describe this political formation; he calls it 'nomads of the present'. But I think it is similar – how these political formations do not require a common origin but require perhaps common tendencies, and in a sense they are more ephemeral, more specific, fragmentary and complex, because they might have in their membership people from a diverse range of backgrounds, class positions and affiliations, and what drives them forward is certain beliefs or goals.

There is a vital link between the idea of affinity and empathy... I'm just forming this from what you said, because you've written about how empathy is something that's very human and important in understanding otherness and foreign experience, and at the same time, empathy itself is a useful critical tool in understanding a whole range of social and political experience. So affinity and empathy may bring us closer to the truth in our perception of ourselves and others...

Yes, that's true. In a way, empathy and affinity are obviously parallel concepts. For me, empathy is important, especially when I tried to understand how exile operates as a method and perspectival concept as well. In this regard, exile clearly refers to that process of going away, and you also need a counter-force – the process of coming close again. And one of the qualities that I observed when I first got to meet and become close friends with John Berger was that he had phenomenal empathic qualities. He had an uncanny ability to get inside you – to see inside you, to see how you see the world, to be like you – and to have figured out what you have tried to express even before you have articulated it to him. I've seen him write passages about aspects of my life where I have only given him the barest of details, and yet he has expressed them in terms which are both more succinct and abstract, more concrete and more precise, than I could ever. For instance, he wrote about a Greek dance at wedding which I had described to him. I had given him a few Rembetika CDs and on the basis of a few conversations he described the effect of Rembetika on your soul as a tattoo. And, for me, there is no better metaphor for the sense of confinement and liberation that Rembetika expresses.

But what this also taught me – and he says it all the time – is that you need to get *closer* to get to the truth. You need to get inside things and then you need to pull out as well. So there is this constant tension of going to and fro – the metaphor of the shuttlecock that he uses – and through this process of surrendering to something there is also a catching of yourself before you totally fall into it. So empathy shouldn't be confused with a completely mindless or uniform absorption into the other because it *isn't* a non-critical adoption of the other. It isn't simply seeing the world purely as another person sees the world and trying to be at one with the other. Empathy is a much more dynamic process: of going closer to be able to see, but also never forgetting where you are coming from, and how that process of coming and going actually alters both where you came from and where you have arrived. For me, empathy is about that process of *surrender* to the other and to learn with the other, but also the *catch* that transforms your perception.

Part II

A Politics of Hope

5
ON BELIEVING
A conversation with Christos Tsiolkas

What 'believing' is possible in secular times? What dreams can we evoke? Without dreams and a belief in the future there is a shattering of hope and the will to live. But in the dreams of contemporary life, cultural aspirations and hopes are often linked to social mobility. Indeed, this has been actively pursued by political commentators in Australia, for instance, who see justice as part of the aspirations to a better life – in economic and material ways. Social inequality can be overcome by the drive to invest in capital and property relations. But what if, because of poverty, you are outside these hopeful aspirations? How do we conceive a space to understand the dreams and necessities of life when the reality of unemployment and lack of access to basic tools of social exchange are denied? In the language of public life, this reality is often framed as an individual's failing to benefit from what society has to offer. Yet hopes and dreams, in daily and political contexts, cannot be separated from the societies that produce them.

This is where belief and faith are essential to rethinking what individual and social aspirations may involve. In the fading dreams of more communal politics, in both secular and cultural terms, what bonds and regeneration of belief may be necessary across political movements – for instance, in gay, feminist and Marxist collectives? In writing and other forms of cultural and critical debates, this involves having access to knowledge, and the tools to create and produce other ways of expressing the despair and alienation in social and economic life. Writer Christos Tsiolkas and I reflect on this and on believing – the hopeful connections between how we live, the space of public dialogue, and bonds of love and responsibility that we can restore between ourselves and others. Tsiolkas' fiction and non-fiction writings explore the conflicts and tensions of living across different cultural, sexual and political realities in Australia. In these writings, sexuality, class relations and intercultural racism are central themes. His writing evokes the need for hopeful alternatives in the midst of cultural and political despair.

Faith, hope and belief

Mary: There is a link between hope, faith and belief. To survive in this world, these are essential things. So to begin, what are your thoughts on this, and the potential for creative hopes and dreams?

Christos: Hope and faith are two words that are interrelated for me. My struggle – and it is an ongoing struggle – is trying to locate hope and faith in new forms and in new ways. In that sense I have always tried to develop a political argument in my work, whether it is in fiction or non-fiction. And what tends to happen is that I keep going back to notions of family, community and even, to some extent, notions of religious faith in order to locate a forward direction for the characters I write about. For a while I was really nervous about doing that and I thought: Am I simply reconstructing a conservative idea of family or religion or community? That's what I struggle against. I am almost nostalgically looking back to those places, and I think that's partly a reflection on the confusions of post-modernism and the cultural moment we're in, and a struggle against some of the more fundamentalist tenets of the politics I came through. I'm thinking there of communism, gay and queer politics, and feminism. That's quite a broad range, isn't it!

Yes, and we'll return to it. But what about faith and the confusions of the culture and era that we live in?

This may be a roundabout way of getting into faith, but I will explain something that happened to me. When I was in my early adolescence I became a member of one of the Protestant churches for a while. It was a terrible experience in the long run because I think it was about feeling shameful and trying to hide my sexuality, and also feeling dislocated from the community around me. In that way it was quite a repressive and ugly church, I think – all about hating the body. But at that time, all I knew really was that somehow God promised salvation. I came out of the experience shunning the idea of God and shunning the idea of faith. And then I came to a point in my life about six years ago where I was very unhappy, I was very distressed, and I was also around a group of people who were in similar states, and two of them who committed suicide. And I found myself praying for the first time since I was a 15-year-old boy, and I wasn't praying to a god in any sense, but the very act of prayer itself assisted me. Now you can call that meditation or a whole variety of secular terms to explain it, but when I talk about faith it is about that sense of being. It is very easy to look out into this world and just see ugliness – because that's what it is. I still get angry about this world because it's an increasingly harsh world. We all know that, and we are all living in that reality, whichever side of the fence we find ourselves on. And without the belief that things will change, I don't know how you go on – how you don't succumb to that distress.

So, for a long time after that religious experience, communism and Marxism and those forms of politics offered another version of faith, but those two collapsed when I was in my early twenties. Just because those politics and that religious experience collapsed doesn't mean I can't draw both from the knowledge of those bodies of thought, and from the actual lived experience. What was interesting was that, after that experience of prayer, I went back to reading Friedrich Nietzsche. I read book after book by him, and he gave me another sense of faith and the *will* to live.

When I talk about faith I mean the actual experience of believing in the future. I mean faith is a really difficult term to talk about because I am secular and I am living in a secular age – and it does stem so much from a religious experience. But how do we find ways of translating that into our lives now? I guess it is a project that a lot of us are engaged in.

Yes, I think so. I would agree with you there about the need to have faith or some future, otherwise you would fall into a sort of void of nothingness…

Well, yes – and I was actually going to talk about the experience of doing a teaching diploma at the moment, and teaching out at high schools. I was really aware over that teaching period of how important it was to actually give dreams to a lot of the young people I was working with. Because I was shocked by the number of 13-, 14- and 15-year-olds who responded to questions about the future in terms of 'I want to die'. I mean that's not being melodramatic. It was a school for a local working-class community, or what they are increasingly calling an underclass – whatever that term means

– in the outer suburbs of Melbourne. And it seemed to me that nothing in the curriculum was encouraging dreams or any notions of faith. So it seemed important that I believed *in* them. I actually just gave them faith in themselves and told them that there are possibilities in their life. But also I gave them knowledge. Now, they already have a knowledge of how hard life is – you know, a lot of them have no parents or have lived on the streets, or come from families of third or fourth generations of unemployment. So they don't actually need to be told that any more; they understand that reality quite well. It's how you give them knowledge about the way this society works and about how to challenge a social role that says, 'You will never amount to anything'. That's what they are being told, and then they are living that reality and that truth inside a popular culture which tells them that they should be a millionaire!

Which is about the importance of imagination – I mean as a writer you can use that as a tool to create characters and provide another sense of justice through writing. Imagination gives us the tools to create other alternatives, and I wonder how important it is to give that imagination to people...

Oh, I think it's crucial. I use the term 'dreams' and that is part of what imagination is – the ability to dream possibilities and to dream a future. And without that ability to imagine you end up locked in a very narrow range of roles and expectations, and that's really destructive. It's really funny, because almost the last decade of my life I've been turning away from some of the great dreams of political struggle, and moving to something really simple like wanting to work in public education. And to make education *public* again in Australia, rather than, as I was saying to you before this conversation, 'poverty education'. To make education real and to teach kids how to read – when I say read I don't only mean the printed word but how to read television, the media, films, and so on. These kids are actually quite savvy in a way, but the range of material they get is really narrow. And that's what you want to challenge. But part of that is also about giving. It's also teaching those skills of how to write, make films and videos, etc. And hopefully in this capacity we can have an effect.

So this giving is showing that there are different ways of working in the world at the moment. But it is a society which is becoming more conservative in terms of the cultural images and the cultural texts that are being circulated. I think it is even more imperative for journalists, for writers, for anyone working in what's called the 'cultural industry' to talk about alternatives and produce alternatives, and to try and disseminate those to the best of our ability. No matter how hard it is – and *it is hard* – we all know that.

Yes, because it has to do with issues of class, and cultural experience – which I would like to develop a bit later... But for the moment, I want to return to political feelings and faith – you do still see Marxist thinking and post-Marxist ideas as relevant?

I do, most definitely.

And its kind of relevance in your own political position and framing of struggles and issues? You call yourself at different times an anarchist or democratic socialist, depending on the activity or the task you are addressing, and I guess that may also reflect the broader issues around the cultural work we are engaged in...

I am very aware that I am not someone who can pretend to be an academic theorist on culture or economics, but from my own reading of Marx and my experience of Marxism what I appreciate is the ethical component of understanding the economic organisation of society. And given that we are still living in capitalism, I have yet to come across a body of work that actually explains and makes sense of some of the economic relationships that I live and we all live under. For me that is the recurring influence of Marx and post-Marxist writing. In terms of being cagey about what I call myself, it is because I am very aware of the legacy of the communist states. And that's where the suspicion of that term comes from, and that may not be anything more than the fact that I am caught within this historical moment. This may change. What is inevitable for me is that communism as an ideal did turn into a fundamentalist system of beliefs, whether it was expressed in totalitarianism in the Soviet Union or the particular way Marxist groups have worked in the West.

I guess if there is anything I am struggling to do it is to argue against fundamentalism at the moment, of any kind – whether it is religious, political, economic – whatever form it takes. And the other big challenge is to no longer believe in the utopian idea that, you know, a social society or an economic system will change overnight through revolution. When I call myself 'democratic socialist' now and look toward the principles within that, it is simply acknowledging that *transformation* is much more difficult than simply taking over the means of production. I don't know if we can use that analogy any more.

Sure.

But whatever term I use to describe political engagements, it depends on the audience I am speaking to. The really important thing for me is that I still firmly consider myself as someone from the Left, and that to me means someone who is concerned about exploitation. I think that is about understanding economic exploitation in society and also believing in the role of the state, and how that must also involve the redistribution of wealth – that is, allowing ordinary people to have a control in the way that wealth is produced.

It is also more than that too, isn't it? When you were raising the ethical dimension or what gives you faith in certain systems of belief, it is precisely the ethics, right? And what I understand your work to be – and this is something you can contest with me – is some notion of human relationships as well. For instance, the impact of living in the society which we do at the moment, and how it is increasingly unequal. But I suppose the task is expressing and exploring the new forms of alienation that are going on. That comes back to the point you made about the kids you've been teaching – how they are experiencing and living out the conditions of poverty and alienation, and they don't have to be continually reminded of it. I think those forms of alienation are important to understand.

Yes, they are. One thing I want to be really clear about is that Marxism has been an incredibly influential body of work, and its history has been incredibly influential to me in understanding something about economics, and trying to express inequality. And it also means that it explains different forms of alienation as well, because I think all these things are interconnected. But it is not simply Marxism itself that explains this. One of the tasks of anyone who finds themselves writing or producing film or ideas in our culture at the moment is to describe exactly, as best as we can, what that alienation is and to give it a voice, and then turn it into the idea of hope and faith – that is, how to go beyond those experiences of alienation. In that sense I am influenced by a wide variety of knowledges and experiences, including feminism and gay politics. But I also think it is important to learn to listen to voices that have emerged from outside the West. So what I try to do in my fiction is to give it that voice, and to give alternative kinds of futures through my characters. But, you know, I often get asked why I write such ugly scenes, and why is my writing so ugly? It is precisely because what I see in these new forms of alienation is acute ugliness and acute pain. As I said before, that is something we all understand and we all experience. But we all turn away from that and I'm guilty of this too.

I mean, I have been closely following the argument about the drug trade and the safe injecting rooms proposed in Australia. I've been going to public meetings, and I am not going there with a 'black and white' answer to any of the issues. Personally, I believe the safe injecting rooms should be given a go as a trial, but I don't actually think they are the answer to the heroin problem. But when I go to public meetings I am still shocked at the level of denial people express about something they see quite clearly in front of their eyes. They know there is a huge problem of alienated, bored, self-destructing young people – and it is not only young people – but it is almost as though they are choosing not to look at what is there. That's what I am trying to describe in my books.

Well, this is about the question of hope. It is the very practice of what we do, and how ideas can express different forms of ugliness and pain that are essential to understanding life in the present. I'm particularly interested in how you try to express that ugliness and people's experience of working-class life now. I guess it is the very practice of doing it – that is the ethics, and how those ideas enter the public sphere...

I want to explain a bit more about fundamentalism because I think it is important in understanding what I am attempting to do, and also cultural work more generally. I think one of the dangerous things about any political or religious expression is that its tenets can fall into quite clear moral abstractions – 'this is right' or 'this is wrong'. For instance, religion does that, but so do so many forms of politics. What I want to do is look at the humanity of even the most abject, or what we consider the most evil, of circumstances or persons. I don't choose to look at something like, say, paedophilia or violence or aggression because I just want to exploit those things. What I want to do is actually present those experiences as human, not without obviously having an ethical stance on what my characters do. But I don't want them to be simply judged *as* evil. I don't want them to be judged as people who should be excommunicated or cut away from the social.

And, you know, what is happening in our society more and more is we are making those moral definitions about people. We are filling up our prisons, not only here but places like the US, because we are falling under the sway of politicians and leaders who talk about a black and white world – of the good person and the bad person. And this is increasingly so with crime, law and order, and the mandatory sentencing issues we see here in Australia around Aboriginal people and asylum-seekers. I think we are complicit in that as long as we fall into those kinds of arguments. And that's why I believe that by showing the *humanity* of someone, even though they are involved in the most despicable of acts, you can actually make a difference. I believe that the power of the human imagination is that we can go down that road, and we can understand what leads someone to do that. But I think a lot of people are fearful of what lies in their imagination. Now I've got to make this clear – it's not about simply exploiting that, saying that I am just writing this to shock you for shock's sake. I believe every time I have depicted an act of extreme violence or sex it has been in a context of wanting to raise a series of ethical and political questions. I'm interested in both extremities *and* politics. Is that clear?

Yes, it does make sense. And when you say humanity it seems to me to be impor-tant as well. I would like to rethink what it is to be human actually, and...

Yes, are we neo-humanists!?

Well, maybe! I think it is important because there is a certain disillusionment with politics now, right? And this is going to be a curly question – you've talked about some of the limitations you see in gay, feminist and queer politics when people get stuck with the idea of 'identity'. Is there a way of moving beyond identity and coming to something like humanism without falling into the traps of what we've all experienced humanism to be in the past?

It is a curly question because part of me feels like saying, 'Can you get back to me when I'm 69 about that?' I am trying to think that one through carefully – because it is about faith, and one of my hopes is that we can do precisely that. I am critical of identity politics but that doesn't mean that I don't understand or I don't believe myself in some of the positive effects of identity. For instance, my criticisms of identity politics come from the concern that in politicising an identity you are actually replicating the exclusion of the 'other' that does happen in a whole range of more conservative and more limited understandings of humanity.

And morality comes into play...

Yes, it comes in very, very strongly. Although I am critical of identity politics, there will be moments when I will align myself with a particular form of politics because I think it is important. The most clear example is homophobic violence. I am quite critical of notions within the gay community and gay expression but I will go out and demonstrate over homophobic violence. I still think it is important to talk to younger people about homophobia. But in terms of the human subject, that's an area I'm still exploring, to be honest, Mary.

Well, I am too. In some respects that's why I am asking people to think about what hope might be and what human hope might involve. Can we think of some kind of humanness without ideas of ownership and property and destructive forms of power? Is there another way to exist that takes us away from this? I don't know, but going through this process is helping me to think more concretely about the potential for human hope...

I'll throw this idea in – In terms of organising a community and, within that, different communities, it is important that there is a respect for difference, and that includes a respect for different moral codes. So it's about trying to understand how you could form those kinds of communities. Could I give you an example about what I mean?

Yes.

In the same way that lesbian and gay activists will ask the Christian or the Jewish or the Islamic churches or whatever to accommodate a modern, secular notion of sexuality, I think it is important that gay men and lesbians understand the imperative of people with religious faith. This is about a kind of mutual acceptance and it is not about tolerance. I think it is really a *mutual acceptance* – that you can actually live side by side in a community, as neighbours and as friends and as work colleagues or whatever, with people who don't necessarily share the same ethical and moral code. For me that seems to be one of the possible ways forward. And that's why I keep coming back to this notion of fundamentalism or exclusivity in terms of ethical or political thought. I mean that's where I see the danger.

Yes, in any kind of political action. But it also seems to be about acceptance and it is about some level of recognition, which is closely connected to issues of responsibility, too, in terms of an individual's responsibility in this world. And I think that there is a responsibility between the individual and their role in the community or their relationship to the community...

We see ourselves as consumers and individuals in this world, and so there is very little or almost limited understanding of what kind of responsibility we have as members of a community. I think that's partly a result of the increasing individualisation of the world we live in, and it is also an effect of the discrediting of certain communal forms of politics, Left politics and things like that. Responsibility is obviously really important to me in terms of trying to rethink communal politics. It seems to me there are aspects of individualism that have been constructive to the identity politics that have emerged, but that will need to be curtailed by a different, a more communal sense of society. I think that is inevitable. So I do think there are productive aspects of 'individuality' and, to go back to sexuality, your sexual life does not need to be bound by the perimeters of community and family, and that has given rise to what we have now, which is the modern gay movement.

So what I am saying is not necessarily that I want to go back to point zero and forget what has occurred. But in itself it has not been enough, and there may be aspects of communal life and communal responsibility, and intergenerational responsibility, that have been forgotten in this striving for individualised sexuality. I mean those are still very complicated areas for me; I am still trying to work them through – but I think they are really important to address and that's why I keep coming back to that notion of family.

Bonds

Which is where I'll take you. Some of the themes in your books The Jesus Man *and* Loaded *are about a certain kind of ugliness within communities and families, but at the same time you express the intimacy as well. And this presents interesting ideas about the potential bonds that we can have in terms of community and family. I want to ask you a little bit more about your idea of family, and how it isn't just about blood relations but is about something else – perhaps it is about new communities?*

What I am saying is to look at the idea of the family and also to look critically at the history of family – trying to understand it, and trying to explore it – and this is from my own experience as well, what has been constructive and what has been positive in that notion of family.

What has been constructive?

Well, I think it has been the idea of responsibility because, in the end, you are involved in a relationship with another person and you need to be responsible to that. You need to maintain and keep some faith about it. So whatever differences may arise between you as individuals, the relationship will be ongoing – and because of the nature of the Greek family I grew up in, the notion of the extended family was important. And that's something I really admire because, whether you are talking about a baby or person approaching the end of their life, you are talking about a shared responsibility to those two beings, and I think that is dropping away now. However, none of this is to deny the incredible brutality that can and does happen in families. We would all be idiots if we didn't understand that.

So I am not talking about going back to some kind of patriarchal norm of the family. I am just saying that there are bonds in the family that I think are important and that we can extend, for example, to our work relationships. What is happening in our work relations more and more is a loss of shared relations. I've been working for over 20 years of my life and there used to be a *camaraderie* – and that is what I would call it – amongst workers. It is increasingly what the 'individual contract' has effaced; this is its purpose. Those shared relations are now looked on suspiciously – for instance, if you go out together and spend some time around the bloody coffee machine, sharing a fag, doing stuff, which used to be the biggest pleasure of the actual work space for me. Increasingly we are told, and come to believe, that if you want the bourgeois life you will work as an atomised being. And in that way you don't have any of kind of real interaction with other human beings. So when I look towards the idea of family it's saying that those bonds – they don't have to be blood bonds, but those kinds of shared responsibilities, shared commitments, shared affections and shared love, to use those terms – are still possible.

One of the nicest things about being back with young people has been seeing the affinity and the affection that they can have for each other, which you don't really see any more in the adult world. For instance, you don't see people walking down the corridor of their workplace hand in hand or with an arm around each other. It has also been instructive to be back at school to see how the 'fag' is still excluded and the racism that still takes place in that environment. I am not approaching either youth or family or any of those ideas idealistically, but saying what is possible within them.

Which comes back, I think, to the point about possible futures and

*alternatives for people. The difficulties with some of the ideological strands
of Marxism was a kind of utopian future ideal, but all of this comes back to
the 'present', which is important to you, and perhaps that is about hope
and faith and love...*

The present is the moment you are in, and by necessity you have to explore
it. I think that is one of the problems with the kind of bourgeois traditional
notion of the writer, because I think that's been about writing *the great
novel in the future*. They are all about bypassing the present and being in
the future moment. And that's another utopian fantasy. That's not to say
that I'm not prey to those dreams – we all are, and I would be a bullshitter
if I told you otherwise. But I remember people saying when I wrote *The
Jesus Man*: 'Are you sure you want to write about Pauline Hanson and the
One Nation Party in Australia, because that will limit you to a particular
moment in time?' And I said 'Yes', I did, because whatever that moment in
time was, it was an important moment to write about. And the present is the
moment I want to explore, because that is the only moment I can talk about
or express with any confidence. And so if I am going to find *hope* I have to
find it within what we are living.

*Yes, and the limitations of writing the great novel is that utopian fantasy,
because writing is about collaborating with others, and finding a way of it
being a lived practice or tool for cultural expression between people, which
is what dialogue is for me...*

Writing is collaboration. And more and more my writing is taking me towards
theatre and other spaces where the collaboration is actually on the ground.
I am frustrated with the idea of the great genius writer. To me that is a
bourgeois lie, and I will call it that because, as I have already said to you, the
analogy for me is, well, if the genius exists, how come it exists only on one
side of the Yarra River, to give a Melbourne example. I think what I do is *work*,
and that is my politics speaking but that is the best way for me to understand
writing. I mean I am involved in a craft. There may be talent, but there is
talent in a cabinetmaker or in a really good artisan of any sort, right?

What I want from the community that I do my work in is to have the support and *camaraderie* that I find essential in a workplace. For me the biggest disillusionment about writing is that it doesn't exist. In general, most writers are not interested in that kind of relationship with each other. They are much more interested in individualised, privatised and secluded relationships.

But what is hopeful is that I have been lucky to come into contact with a range of people who are working in film, theatre, painting, writing or whatever who do share those kinds of aspirations about their work – they do see what they are doing as a trade and a skill that will develop over time. What I think they also share is an understanding that there are other important things in the world that will inform their art, and I think that's crucial.

That seems to me to be about inspiration...

It is inspiration. Look, we are talking in Australia at the beginning of the new millennium, and there is something about the Australian context – and we are talking about responsibility and art and creative work – that's been let go of to a large extent. Perhaps the best way to explain this is with an example. I was the angriest I have been over the last few months when the refugees who were in the Woomera camp in South Australia protested and went on the streets. Those people, who have suffered in ways that I can never imagine, all they wanted was to talk to journalists, to actually get their story printed, put on television to be told, so people would know what conditions they were living under. I read the papers quite closely over that period and I think there was only one journalist who actually talked to individuals involved in the protest. This journalist didn't write an opinion piece about what they thought when they woke up that day and saw on the television. So I am using that as an example of the *irresponsibility* in terms of creative work that I see in this country.

I see journalism and the media as part of that irresponsibility. I felt shamed about that coverage, and lack of it, because I actually think that wouldn't have happened in America. In America I think there would have been enough of a tradition of critical journalism that would have enabled those people to have found a voice – even if it was not within the mainstream – it would have been there. And it is very easy to blame John Howard – I do. It is very easy to blame globalisation and the market – I do. But there is something about the complicity of us as writers, film-makers and journalists that is involved in that as well. Most likely we think it is too hard. We don't even know how to talk about it – we are scared about being too 'politically correct' or about showing any passion or commitment to ideas. I think we are really floundering, and you can see it in our creative expression and political analysis. There are exceptions, but in the main it seems to me quite a grim point for Australian culture at the moment.

*

On reflection we can see, almost two years later, some of those problems that angered you – the public debate around asylum-seekers and refugees is severely limited in this country... And the only way it seems to me to address it is by grass-roots activism and the hope that their 'real' stories will start to hit the Australian consciousness...

The last year has been literally shattering for me in terms of my understanding of being 'Australian'. The racism and fury directed to refugee boat people, their incarceration, the demonisation of their lives and experience, has been a slap in the face. It has reminded me that this is a deeply racist country. I wanted to fuck it all off – I mean Australia – and go elsewhere to live.

Yes.

It felt like I would always be a wog for this country, that no matter what struggles were involved in people coming to this country, no matter what rhetoric was spouted about multiculturalism and integration, the truth was that unless you were an Anglo this country would hate you. I wasn't alone in feeling this, still feeling this. Heaps of people I know felt this and are feeling this. This has been a historically reactionary moment for this country, and it has literally been a return to a colonial xenophobic understanding of what constitutes an 'Australian'.

Yes, and the hope of what it is to be Australian, then, is built on fear and resentment...

I think what was most despairing was the feeling that this racism permeated every level of class and strata in this country. And these feelings haven't left me – I'm still angry, but it has simply reminded me that we live in an economically ferocious time, in a deeply conservative and reactionary world, and the Left has an enormous amount of work to do. If anything positive has come out of this moment – and I hesitate using the term 'positive' given the wretchedness of the experiences undergone by the refugees – it is that it has reminded me that humane and non-racist politics must reside in the Left. In terms of a more hopeful, egalitarian society we have many decades of work ahead of us.

For me the political work that needs to be done is around the conditions of refugees and asylum-seekers in *this country*. The refusal to allow the *Tampa* to land in Australia happened only a few weeks before the bombing of the World Trade Center. What became clear to me over those months was that the *Tampa* was a much more defining and crucial date than September 11. I am speaking to you as an Australian. This may put me in a minority, but I think it is important to keep stressing this distinction – at work, in writing, in politics.

Counter-cultures

Earlier we were beginning to address the relationship between class, sexuality and migrant experience. You talk about wanting to find new ways to talk about class experience, which I think is imperative. So how can we express those relationships?

...I am hesitating because it is such a big question for me, in terms of trying to make sense of what class is and how it is lived in Australia at this present moment. I think my background heavily influences this project – my parents were factory workers and they were migrants who came to this country. So that experience has been paramount in understanding how I emerged in this culture, and so class isn't an abstract notion for me, it's part of my life. At the same time there is no doubt that the experience of going to university and being a writer has made me more 'middle-class'. I have a consciousness that there is a certain privilege in my position, because I can find work and I have had some level of success as a writer. But the feeling of being responsible to notions of class and speaking about them hasn't left me – and that's what I want to continue doing in my work. What I have worked on in the last few years has been all about the collapse of the working-class economy. Whether it is in theatre, with *Who's Afraid of the Working Class?*, or *The Jesus Man*, which is a story about a man's spiral into terror that begins when he loses his job in the new economy.

But I think for a long time I was too obsessed about class, in the sense of 'How do I fit into that relationship of class – was I middle-class or was I working-class?' – and this is where the school experience has been great because it slapped me around a bit. When I was with those young people who were living in conditions of poverty – there are a whole range of things I can say about that – the fundamental social fact that was determining their aspirations, their lives, and their experience was unemployment. And the fact that the traditional skills and crafts and jobs of working-class people have been annihilated in the current economy. So unemployment seems to me the fundamental thing to investigate, not only in terms of Australia but in large parts of the world now. And the fact that this society has no space for people who find themselves on the other side of the wealth, in poverty, outside the IT society, outside entertainment, outside all those things.

What about class and your own family? – because I think that language itself becomes a class issue. What I mean is that speaking different languages and across cultural experiences within families can be fraught, and that class experience and language can become a form of alienation within migrant cultures...

I think one of the hardest struggles within my family has been finding a common language between us, and that's obviously an effect of migration. My parents grew up in a country where the first language was Greek, and I grew up in a country where the first language was English. It has also been made more tense and difficult by the fact that I received an education and they never did. So that's a perpetual question, and when I look at what I write I try and think through the language and think who I might be excluding by writing in a particular way or using particular words. It is a very difficult area, and one of the dangers is that populism in our recent thought and culture says that if you are engaged in any kind of theoretical, cultural, intellectual work, you are by necessity elitist.

I think that belief is misguided, because there is a desperate need for complex and thoughtful public debate...

Yes, and I guess that the return to populism is about mistaking ideas or mistaking complexity, and it is about not acknowledging that there are ways of arguing, speaking and communicating complex thought that are not elitist. And I do get worried that the hunger for black and white terms means that we are not engaged in thinking through issues, so that is an important struggle for me in terms of how I try and write. But given what I said about family, I think one of the delights of my life is that I think that Mum, Dad and I have been able to find, through a lot of work on both sides, a language which is shared – and which is simply about putting our beliefs on the table and understanding that.

I think that's the point. We don't have a language yet to express that and, coming back to some of your stuff about the future and where possibility may lie, there is the need to find ways to express and communicate all the struggles that are going on to provide some new language of belief...

Yes, I think that will emerge, and where I can see signs of hope is in the ways these can be represented, not just in migrant communities but 'across the board'. For instance, there is a film I've heard about related to the idea of hope, where young people were given a camera to record 10-minute segments about their lives. These kids were living on the streets and poverty-stricken, and the film was giving them the opportunity to document their lives. But I keep thinking – and this is optimism and I may be completely wrong on this – that there will be interesting ideas and politics emerging from the former Eastern bloc nations. I think that their experience of communism has been so terrible, and their contemporary experience of capitalism has been so terrible, that new ideas will emerge from that. I also increasingly think that the experience of being a refugee – of having to live a stateless life – will mean that eventually people will put that experience, hopefully, into print and into film and into an oral tradition that in the future will inform the ways in which we think about this present moment.

And what it means to be human…

Exactly. What it means to live these experiences and – to return to class – what class means at the moment is also changing. But the paramount factor is that the difference between the most wealthy and the most poor is widening so fast in Australia that at some point that will emerge in our cultural production. Even if it is not stated explicitly, it will emerge through fear, paranoia and terror. I will be interested and fascinated by that development. But I am much more interested at the moment to actually talk about that with people at an intellectual level. That's what I find missing in a lot of the conversations that I have with artists and I am really hungry for that. And I think it is partly a fear of politics at the moment, or fear of being able to talk politically, because I think there is a suspicion about it.

There is a difference between 'politics' and the idea of 'the political'. 'The political' is a more active way of looking at it – it is about doing and creating things. Whereas if you situate 'politics' as the end-game you almost shut down the possibility of trying to be active or thinking about doing things, you know what I mean?

Yes.

It has something to do with contesting your own systems of belief, but it is also about passion, too…

It definitely has to do with passion, and I think you are right about the difference between a closed system, which is politics, and political activity. And political activity is happening all around us. It is happening in Aboriginal communities around reconciliation and the reclaiming of a history that has been silenced and shunned in Australia. It is happening around ecological issues; around the Gay and Lesbian Mardi Gras in a way – that is political activity. I am speaking only for myself at the moment, but what I think is missing is an engagement around class. But I think that is bound to happen because all those forms of political activity are occurring under the same social and economic conditions. What I am excited about is the links that will begin to be made around class – that is, emerging from different sites and different perspectives. I think anyone with a committed and responsible sense of the social will find it impossible to talk about any political activity without trying to understand the nature of class and the disparity of wealth.

I agree. In a lot of intellectual work this aspect has been lost, because there has been a real concentration around questions of identity. In the last decade or so the question of class has dropped out of the equation, and there is a necessity now to form new understandings of how all of these things are interrelated in real and concrete ways.

Well, it has to do with the fact that the ideas of class emerged from the Left and the socialist/communist tradition, and that's been discredited. The free market, the individual, economic rationalist ideas hold sway at the moment. So we are not going to find the experience of working-class life being expressed in those places where people have a much more conservative idea of economics. I get a real sense with a lot of writers, film-makers and people involved in the cultural industry that they no longer feel a responsibility about talking about the social. I find that distressing, because it is not like the artist hasn't been privileged for a long time. It is not like 20 years ago the world was full of working-class writers and film-makers – and in fact, look at the English tradition: most of them came from two universities. So that reality hasn't changed *but what has changed* is the sense of responsibility that artists feel about their work.

So for me it's a twofold struggle in terms of talking about art and class. One is the new struggle of reinstating the notion of responsibility in artist practice, and the second one, which is an ongoing and perpetual struggle, is getting access to the tools and skills of artistic reproduction to places where they have been denied to people. For instance, who gets the right to speak on radio, who gets the right to make films, or who is able to write and to give expression to their lives and their experiences. And another point that is really important to come back to is basic issues around health and schooling – in the past, no matter what mistakes were made, at least there was an attempt to create a public education and health system. So even in the language of liberal democracy, there was an attempt to give access and opportunity to everyone. But now those basic rights are being dismantled and taken away. So where are people going to get the skills to communicate their lives? I think it is really important that artists keep that in mind and think about the spaces where they reproduce or produce their work.

Well, I guess that's what you did in the play Who's Afraid of the Working Class? *I'd like to ask you about that intersection of a public space and the relations between class, sexuality and power, which is part of how you tried to communicate those ideas...*

Yes, that was a collaborative play. There were five of us involved in the actual writing of it who all had a history in Left politics. We were invited along to write and produce the play with the Melbourne Workers' Theatre, which was celebrating its tenth anniversary. The theatre company began in the 1980s and the idea was that it would actually go out to workplaces and it would involve working people in the theatrical experience. So writers would come in and write plays in collaboration with workers in a variety of sites. And that's a really important part of theatre history in Melbourne. When we came together to write the play we realised that we were all uncertain about what class meant in the 1990s. We had 3 or 4 years by that time of the Kennett Liberal government in Victoria, and had seen a complete dismantling of public space, public utilities and public commitments, if you like. And we also knew it was to be a play that was not going out to work spaces any more – it was to be in a theatre, and so we approached that play knowing full well that the majority of the audience would be a bourgeois theatre audience. So we wanted to confront that audience with their expectations of theatre and their expectations of what class was. And that's why, I think, sexuality, class, race – which we wrote about – all involve ideas and notions of power. We wanted the audience not to feel alienated by the experience but to actually look at themselves when they walked out of the theatre and onto the street, where there were homeless people living. And to actually think about some of the limitations of identity politics that they might espouse.

One of the things that was explored – but only to a limited extent – in that play, and does interest me now, is a rising fear about what that 'underclass' represents. I think that's what is behind so much of the 'law and order' rhetoric, not only of the conservative parties but of the Labor Party as well. It is a politics of fear. And I think that fear rises because people know that people are hungry, desperate and angry. And of course those things are also more highly charged in a society which is dominated by television and the image which keeps promising more and more consumer goods.

As I said before, in your writing you do convey certain kinds of disillusionment, fear and alienation, but it is actually giving that experience some form. And that can proliferate and provide another counter-culture, or maybe not even a counter-culture, but it seems to me that is where the hope is...

It's an interesting word, 'counter-culture', and I would call it that. We do need another counter-culture because this culture is so conservative at the moment. I think cultural production and artistic work has become so enmeshed in corporate culture that we do need some sense of a counter-culture, and what we need is some sense of like-minded artists, writers or whatever finding different ways of working. Which isn't to say, 'No, I will never take the private dollar'. It is about saying that the private dollar isn't enough. There are ways we want to work, and there are things that we want to communicate, that the private sector will never finance.

Well, precisely – because it doesn't want to hear about it!

I think in corporate cultures there is a mass market, and it's niche markets that are aimed for, not work that exists outside of that. And for me that's probably where part of the work has to be done by us – actually trying to form those collaborations and also trying to find ways of funding ourselves.

That's what you are doing with your writing magazine Refo, *because it is about collaboration and it is about finding another kind of way of funding, and producing writers' works that would never be published in a more corporate world...*

George Papaellinas and I talked for a number of years about doing a self-funded publication that is not dependent on the corporate dollar or on the big publishing houses – and, as you said, to give expression to the writing that doesn't find a voice or expression in the Australian culture. But whatever happens with *Refo* there is a satisfaction that George and I did this thing and that we've invited other people to be part of it. So part of what we want to do with *Refo* is actually bring royalties back to the writers. In that sense, whether it is a success or a failure economically, it feels like a success in terms of it being an initiative that was produced.

It's opening up the spaces for that, isn't it?

Yes.

And finding new ways of belonging to different kinds of community, artistic or otherwise?

Well, yes. We have to actually create those spaces for ourselves because they are not being funded and they are not being made for us. I think the ABC [Australian Broadcasting Corporation] is a fine example of that at the moment, you know, with the slashing of its budget and the new corporate culture coming in. So there too you are going to have less space for the articulation of certain ideas, and certain ways of producing radio.

I think there is courage needed in producing alternative culture expression, and how that impacts on understanding ourselves as a community and the responsibilities we have to each other...

Yes. It also means that we have a responsibility to try and find the humanity, as I said earlier, of everyone, and to not exclude anyone from the social body. I think in political activity of any kind that's what we have to strive for.

6
HOPE, PASSION, POLITICS
A conversation with Chantal Mouffe and Ernesto Laclau

Hope is tied to the passions that make up our everyday reflections on the world, and to our political activities. When we strongly feel that there is an injustice to ourselves we may vent anger or hatred onto the world or others. In the political sphere these passions can take on a variety of forms. For instance, passion and politics shape the historical and contemporary contingencies of the Left – and the populist movements of the Right, where hope can be part of more aberrant calls for national and political unity. To investigate these passions and hopes requires a critique of the neo-liberal – or economic rationalist – forms of capitalism that operate today, and how they produce alienation in both personal and social terms. Yet this cannot be done without rethinking the basic questions of human emancipation and freedom, and the sites of struggle and power relations that emerge in different cultural and political environments.

Chantal Mouffe and Ernesto Laclau, political theorists and philosophers, engage in a dialogue with me about these issues, and what might be more global notions of hope and human emancipation – how, in contemporary struggles, hope may lie for the Left in active calls for justice and new forms of freedom and resistance. What 'radicalisation' of democracy, we ask, is necessary in the dimensions of politics? What are some of the resources available in our cultures that can make this the project of democratic societies? What tenets of equality and economic justice could be part of a vision for new social and political imaginaries? Laclau and Mouffe, who are based in London, have over the last 30 years explored these passionate alternatives for the Left. Their writings provide philosophical analyses of hegemonic social relations – the language games and power structures that occur in societies, and the need for radical pluralist democracies. This radicalisation has been central to contemporary debates for social and political change. In their visions for politics – which come from their travels,

experience and work in different countries and critical contexts – hope lies
in the contingency of life and political struggle.

On hope and passion

Mary: By looking at hope in the crossovers of everyday life and political
struggles, we can explore how feelings of hope and despair occur in our
lives. I want to begin by asking both of you about these hopes, and the
idea of the political.

Chantal: I think it is very important for people to believe in some kind of
future and that there are alternatives to the current political situation. I
think even in the ordinary realm of life there is a need to look forward
to something and to feel some kind of meaning in life. In the field of the
political it is very important that people think that their present condition
could be better, and this is something which has been lost today. In the past
there was the idea of a socialist future for some people, but this horizon has
now been smashed for many people. In many respects it's not so bad that
we have a completely new start, but of course there are many dangerous
ways to understand that. But now we have gone too far – people are told
there is no alternative to the neo-liberal hegemony, and that it is here to
stay. I have been arguing that this is very negative, as many people are no
longer interested in politics because most democratic parties don't offer
them any alternatives... But the whole question of the rise of the right-wing
populist Jörg Haider movement in Austria, for example, is linked to this lack
of hope that can be found in the democratic system. In fact all my work
about 'passion' could be seen in a way as about hope, or the horizon of
expectation and the lack of it.

Ernesto: I would like to add something to that – the notion of hope is to
some extent linked to the question of human emancipation. People feel that
they are curtailed in their possible developments in a variety of directions,
and they create an imaginary of transcending these limitations, and that is
where the place of hope could happen. Now I think there is in some sense an
end of hope, if by *hope* we understand something which is transcending all
possible human conditions – in terms of the fulfilment of a perfect state of

liberation, emancipation, etc. But on the other hand there is a proliferation of new hopes, new demands, and these demands can be put together to create some kind of more feasible social imaginary. This is not to say that our expectations are any less than in the past, but that at any moment in time we have to construct partial social imaginaries of transformation that can push emancipatory politics in many directions. But we no longer have these eschatological notions of hope – yet hope is something which is very much populating our dreams, present in our struggles, and so on. So I think the task of the Left is to provide some more global notions of emancipation. But these notions have to be constructed around a particularised item, rather than in terms of an ultimate fulfilment of a post-human society which is presupposed in the classical emancipatory position.

Could you tell me about the idea of passion, then, in terms of another way of conceiving hope and the links between passion and this notion of a social imaginary?

CM: Well, I think that when you speak of the need for a social imaginary you are already implying that what moves people is not exclusively interests or rationality but what I call 'passion'. People who are rationalists do not believe in the role of the social imaginary. They believe that people need to find ways to act rationally according to their interests in a rationalist choice model, or to find moral universal rules in another model. What they don't believe in is the process of symbols or in the construction of personality, because it is a different way to think about the construction of human identities. When you introduce this notion of a social imaginary it implies that you are leaving the rationalist perspective behind. The term 'passion' is some kind of place-holder for all those things that cannot be reduced to interest or rationality – you know: fantasies, desire, all those things that a rationalist approach is unable to understand in the very construction of human subjectivity and identity.

EL: Also, I think that one has to point out that, whenever there is an attempt at transcending a certain social system, there exists in the discursive elements which organise it something which is given through 'empty terms'. For instance, if you say you want something like human liberation in a certain context it is going be an empty term, but the *content* is going to be provided by a plurality of demands which establish an equivalential relationship between them – and this has been a key point in our analysis. So the more the social demands are organised in an equivalent way, the more empty the discourse of liberation will be, but this *emptiness* is the source of its force. I take a position here which is diametrically opposed to that of rational choice theorists, because they believe the ideal of emancipation has a final and definable content. On the contrary, emancipation for me is to put together some kind of dream which becomes more and more empty as new demands become associated with it. When people thought about the socialisation of the means of production in classical socialist discourses, or when people thought about the market in Eastern Europe after '89, these were very concrete forms of the organisation of the social. But, for the people, they evoke a much larger set of elements, and this is what I would call an empty signifier, which can evoke different demands in different situations. For instance, every oppressed group in a situation in which a repressive regime falls, maximises its expectation – because what is falling is not that particular form of oppression, it's oppression in general. So there is a wide development of hopes coming from different groups and, I think, hope is something which is ineradicable and is inherent in any kind of political or social mobilisation.

CM: Yes, hope is ineradicable, but it can be mobilised in many different ways, and that was the point I was making with respect to right-wing movements. The desire for hope is ineradicable, but if democratic political parties and democratic systems do not provide a vehicle for this then we are in the situation in which other forms of hope are articulated. I think this is very important to analyse. In the context of what I call a deficit of democratic politics to address this question of hope, we can understand the different forms of fundamentalism. For instance, in terms of religious fundamentalism, because they offer precisely a discourse of hope which is something that people can't find in politics or the hope that can be found in nationalist movements. And of course right-wing parties in the context of politics are offering a discourse to articulate, to give sense, direction, to this demand for something new. So hope can be something that is played in many dangerous ways...

Yes, that's my interest – this mobilisation of hope. There is often a lack of hope for people in terms of future possibilities. So those people who have been disenfranchised – whether it is economically, culturally or socially – do tend to move towards right-wing parties that offer them some other form of hope. This hope provides a reconfirmation of their identity in some way and I think that is the danger – once you start to essentialise those hopes by identification. That's one point. The other issue is that the idea of hope may not necessarily always be about the future – a utopian dream and ideal we must attain – but in terms of democracy it is about a 'future to come'. That is, as you both have written, the radicalisation of democracy is never complete and never totalised. It is always, in a sense, both possible and impossible. But the first part of the question to you both is that idea of the mobilisation of hope...

CM: That is why I insist on the need for political theory to recognise this dimension of passion and the fact that people need to have those affects of their imagination mobilised towards something. In fact, even people who are not having many problems in terms of security, etc, also require this mobilisation of passion. Theorists tend to believe that if you are satisfied, you know, if you have enough to eat, then you don't need to look towards something new. I think that is wrong – it's not simply the poor who want to get a better situation, but people in general need to have that hope of something different to look forward to. And, in fact, I do think we are in a dangerous situation today. I think it is very important to realise that, in circumstances in which the future seems so bleak for people, this is the moment when right-wing movements are the ones who provide hope. In fact, recent studies about the rise of Hitler in Germany, for instance, have shown that one of the attractions of his movement was that he was the one who was offering German people a new idea about what Germany could be; he was bringing hope to German people. That is really terrible to realise, but this has been a very important element in the rise of this movement. At the beginning many people were attracted by that because it gave them hope. And, you know, I am looking at Russia today and I am really afraid. Because one can see many analogies between the situation of the rise of Hitler in Germany and the situation in Russia today. So right-wing movements can come and capture the imagination of the people because they are the ones who say now, 'We are going to be able to make you proud of being Russian again'. And, of course, the situation in democratic countries is less dramatic but is also very worrying in exactly that same direction.

EL: It is important to see what the structure of hope is as a type of discourse. Hope is always related to something which is lacking. For instance, you hope for order if you are confronted with a situation of radical disorder. You hope for justice if you are confronted with a situation of radical injustice. It is always related to a certain lack which is the reverse of the discourse of hope. The point is, and here I agree very much with what Chantal has said, that the concrete content which is going to incarnate that need for something which is unspecified is not given from the very beginning. To give you an extreme case, Thomas Hobbes' *Leviathan*, where you have a civil society which is confronted with a situation of a radical lack of order – which is the state of nature. So the will of the ruler, whatever the content of the will is, is going to be good insofar as it can establish some order, because when people are confronted with radical disorder any order will do insofar as it is an *order*. Now who contributes to that order can change at any time, and this where you can have right-wing populism or you can have left-wing possibility, and so on. What we have to define in this hegemonic game is the attempt to channel this particular content and this broad social hope which has no precise content of its own. Hegemony, in that sense, means articulating an empty term, such as 'justice', to concrete contents which can give a precise reference in a particular context.

The drama of the Left today is that it has a certain handicap in the hegemonic game, and other discourses like 'moral majority' and so on have had the upper hand in the last few years, simply because the discourse of the Left has been associated to contents which are very difficult to put together in terms of a more widespread social imaginary. So without hope, there is no society, because no society is able to cope with what simply exists. But to say we are going to administer a little bit better what exists is not a strong enough response. And if you have a discourse in which the Left is seen as one more administrative discourse for something that the Right is doing anyway – without contributing to this dimension of a new social imaginary – then what you are going to have is the aberrant emergence of right-wing discourses which Chantal was just speaking about.

New social imaginaries – radical democracies

I want to come back to what Ernesto is saying about the hegemonic game and the question of emancipation. In Contingency, Hegemony, Universality *and* Hegemony and Socialist Strategy *there is a discussion about the relationship of power and hegemony, and that it is intrinsic to society. In some ways that relationship offers a possibility for the radical forms of democracy that you are talking about. Can you talk a little bit more about that relationship of hegemony and the radical kind of democratic project that is necessary today?*

CM: I would like to discuss this question of how to understand this radical project. There has been a formulation given of our work by Slavoj Žižek and, no matter how much I agree with him, the way in which we understand radical democracy is very different. In fact, the same term used by people like Jürgen Habermas also implies a very different understanding of democracy. In our work it means the *radical impossibility* of democracy. This understanding of radical democracy is related to what Jacques Derrida calls the 'democracy to come'; this involves recognising that democracy is something which will never be completely fulfilled. And, of course, this is linked to what Ernesto was saying before about the need to understand emancipation as something which would never be complete in a traditional model. But I think that this creates problems in terms of the kind of projects that the Left can offer, because it implies a secularisation of politics. This is very difficult to carry out, because it is much easier to mobilise passion, and that is why right-wing movements are usually more successful at doing it. Furthermore, the belief that you are going to arrive at some absolute definition of a democratic project is also problematic, and that's why when there was the idea that socialism would *finally arrive*, people would be able to mobilise their passions very strongly around that ideal. But today, and that is part of the project of radical democracy, you've got to abandon this idea, we have to rethink democracy in a different way – recognising the contingency of it. Relations of power cannot disappear, because they are constitutive of the social – and many of the points we make in the *Hegemony* book are precisely indicating that. So we need to secularise left-wing politics.

I think this question of the radicalisation of democracy involves the understanding that democracy is never going to be completely realised, but it is something which will always need to be a *project* which we are going to fight for, but knowing that we will never be able to reach it. I think it needs a transformation of people's understanding of their political action. People really need to be enthusiastic about political struggle and, at the same time, be aware that there is no final goal – *democracy is a process* which we are continually working towards. So we are clearly facing a difficulty in terms of the way passion can be mobilised. It involves accepting the contingent nature of our struggle. But it is also very important to acknowledge the specificity of our project, which is precisely to introduce this dimension of the radical impossibility of the perfect fulfilment of democracy.

EL: It is important to point out that the *impossibility* of this radical fulfilment has some philosophical grounding, simply because it is impossible to fill a complete series. For instance, let's suppose you have in a certain neighbourhood people making demands about water, other people making demands about lack of jobs and others making demands about police harassment, and so on. At some point all these demands will make people feel that they are part of a certain totality, because all these people are having demands against something which is unspecified, whether it be the system and so on. But once you have a relation of equivalence between these demands you have something which approaches what, in Rousseauian terms, we could call a 'collective will' – *volonté générale*.

Now the difficulties of the Rousseauian approach is that he would have to assume a certain contingency within this equivalence which was absolutely universal. What we find today is a *spread* of demands which only partly coalesce around a more general collective will. And this collective will is something which can be created and expanded in many directions. I remember 20 years ago people said in San Francisco that the condition for a really vibrant collective will existed because there were the demands of the Chicanos, of black people and gay people. So all the constituencies for a popular will existed, however nothing of that kind happened, simply because the demands of some groups clashed with the demands of other groups.

So a collective will is again a moment of hope, it is an empty signifier which tends to realise something which is not possible to fulfil in practice. The point is we can expand a collective will which embraces a lot of democratic demands, and you can have democratic expansion, but other demands are not going to be present there. So these demands are the names of ideals which by definition cannot be fulfilled – although they operate as a *force* in bringing together a set of relations that otherwise would be dispersing in their mere particularity. I think the whole dialectic between the universal and particular depends precisely on the force of people's demands and the impossibility of fulfilling demands. And this is the nature and contingency of democratic action.

CM: I would like to insist that this impossibility should not be seen in a negative way. I think the trick or the point of this is important in order to transform the way people think about it, because there is a way of people saying that it is impossible and we will never be able to reach a fully realised democracy, but we still need to maintain this *as* the goal. In fact this is very much the way Habermas understands the realisation of democracy when he says it is a regulative idea. What we argue is different. For us the impossibility is not empirical but conceptual. Indeed the idea of perfect realisation of a pluralist democracy is a self-refuting ideal. Imagine a pluralist democracy that would be perfectly realised and everyone would agree. That would no longer be pluralist democracy because there wouldn't be any differences – it would be a completely static situation and, in fact, that is the dream of a totalitarian society. What we are arguing is that to conceive of a pluralist democracy as something that can be absolutely fulfilled indicates the end of pluralism. So we really need to take pluralism seriously, and this links obviously to an argument we were previously doing against the traditional Left, who saw pluralism as something negative. I think one of the most important issues is that we need to introduce into the Left this recognition of pluralism. To value pluralism. If you value pluralism then you will be alive to the idea that the impossibility of democracy or some final goal is not an impediment, or something negative. You can see it as something positive. And, on that basis, one can mobilise enthusiasm and say, 'Well yes, we will never reach it, but thank God we will never reach it, because that would be the end of the democracy'. So I think that is also an important distinction.

EL: I would like to add something to that. I think our position has to be differentiated from other types of approaches which have dealt with this issue. For instance, Slavoj Žižek's argument is that in order to have a politics there is a need for a certain element of naturalisation in the validity of democratic demands, or in another version, what has been called 'strategic essentialism'. Now I think both approaches try to deal with this problem in an inadequate way. If I assert some demands and I see that these demands at some point incarnate demands for justice and so on, which as I said are empty signifiers, I don't need to say that there is an essential link between the two. All I need to say is that at this moment, historically, it is worth fighting for these objectives. And to keep open the possibility of other incarnations is something which we cannot deny, because that possibility is always present in democratic struggle. So the argument about essentialising or naturalising, even in strategic terms, I don't think is needed in order to assert what is behind the will or plurality of democratic demands.

You have spoken about the idea of 'articulation' in your work, and what you are saying seems to me to be about articulating in a historical moment what your demands are – what you would wish to claim or fight for in democratic struggles. In terms of re-articulating, as you've been doing now with your idea about democracy and so on, can I ask you specifically about the importance of re-articulating certain kinds of socialist strategies? What is the relationship between re-articulating socialist principles and a radical democratic project?

EL: Well, socialism I could say is a link to some particular type of demand. For us socialism is simply a component of a radical democratic project – it is not something which is beyond it. For instance, at the end of the eighteenth century there was the beginning of the democratic revolution, the French revolution and so on, where there was the attempt at asserting the principles of equality at the level of the public space of citizenship. In socialism there is the extension of that principle of equality to economic relations. In contemporary society there are many other relations that claim to be treated in an unequal way, and the expansion of the democratic revolution has moved in a variety of directions. So for us, socialism is definitely a component of these wider processes. Now the question is that the more diversified the demands of equality, the *less* the principle of equality is attached to particular contents, and the principle of equality can also be applied to contents that in a democratic way we would definitely reject, because it is a general and formal principle. That is why the struggle is a hegemonic struggle.

The hegemonic struggle means these two sides. On the one hand, the universalisation of a principle beyond the particular contents that are argued for. But on the other hand, giving those particularities the role of representing a universality transcending it. For instance, the concrete workers demands of *solidarnosc* came to represent the wider emancipatory aspirations of the Polish people. Now the two sides of it are ultimately incompatible with each other. But this incompatibility is not a problem. The problem is how one can play different language games within these possibilities which ultimately exclude each other, but as we are not living in an ultimate environment these can be played out in a variety of ways.

CM: I think, with respect to this question of socialism, it is interesting to note that the situation today is in a certain sense the reverse of the one when we wrote *Hegemony and Socialist Struggle*. When the book was published in 1985 (we wrote it the preceding year) we were arguing that the problem with the Left was that it was exclusively concerned with class struggles and the socialist aspect of the transformation of the relations of production. We suggested that the Left was not sensitive enough to other issues that were called the 'new social movements' or other forms of oppression. We were arguing that it was important to articulate the struggles of the working class with the struggles of the new movements, those struggling – like feminism and environmentalism – against other forms of subordination. In a certain sense, today what has become dominant is those struggles in the new forms of oppression, and it is true that some people like Richard Rorty have been recently arguing 'back to the class struggle', because that component of class has been lost. There are many reasons for this and one certainly is linked to the collapse of communism – that socialism has become some kind of bad thing. You can't even refer to it without automatically appearing to be someone who wants to bring back those dreadful regimes. I think that it is alright to fight against racism and sexism and all those issues, but one should not lose sight of the aspect of class. I think 'class' is a problematic term, but we can't lose sight of the traditional socialist struggles for economic equalities and so on, which have recently been played down.

That's one of the major questions I want to address. What interests me at the moment is precisely that kind of evacuation of class, and I know the term does have a legacy and difficulty in understanding its new formations – class and power are far more complex now. It's complicated not just in an economic sense but also in a cultural sense – for example, not being educated enough leads to less access to work, and there are the social ramifications of more and more inequality. So what's the real importance of thinking the complexity of class and reconsidering issues of justice, emancipation and the democratic project you are talking about? I am also thinking of the huge amounts of unemployment at the moment – the new forms of unemployment where no job is secure or even getting a job is more and more difficult, and the sense of despair and disillusionment that comes with that. I see this as related to new forms of social stratification and class organisation.

EL: The notion of class as elaborated by Karl Marx consisted in asserting that there is a certain position in the relation of production which was the point around which a class identity was constituted. Now by 'class' it was not meant just economic inequality, because economic inequality exists in the world we live in, and is even more pronounced as a result of globalisation than in the nineteenth century. The problem is not about class inequality or social inequality, but rather whether social inequality can be conceptualised in terms of classes – that is, the position of the human agent in that relation of production. You have mentioned unemployment. There is no doubt that unemployment is a source of wide social inequalities, but the unemployed cannot be conceptualised in terms of class. This was a problem that Marx was already thinking about in the nineteenth century. What did he say about the unemployed? He said the unemployed are simply the industrial reserve army. That is, there is a tendency in capitalism to put wages down, and the way of putting wages down after a boom of accumulation is by expelling the workers who become unemployed. But those workers who became unemployed were still functional for capitalism in that the level of wages was put down to the subsistence level. What happens if unemployment develops beyond the point in which it is functional for capital accumulation – that is, unemployment becomes of such a magnitude that the workers no longer play a functional role in terms of the working class in the classical sense? This was something perceived by Trotsky in the 1930s. He said that if unemployment continues in the way that exists in the world today we will have to entirely reconsider the Marxist theory of classes.

Today unemployment has become a structural phenomenon, largely – as a result of processes associated with globalisation – beyond anything which can be dealt with in terms of economic mechanisms. So when you have unemployment of this nature you have huge social inequality and so on. But the possibility of conceptualising this social unevenness in terms of classes would presuppose a stable bond within the relations of production which no longer applies – because these people are no longer a part of this process. So one thing to insist is that the Left has advanced too much in the cultural field, and has not conceived the structural problems linked with capitalism today. Another thing to say is that this consideration should proceed along a class analysis in the classical sense, which I think has become less and less obvious.

CM: Yes, I also agree that the problem today is not so much around the question of class but around a critique of the capitalist system. And I think that is where the analysis has to be done. One of the reasons why I think there is no hope today for future possibility is precisely because people feel there is no alternative to the capitalist system, and even more to the neoliberal form of capitalism which is dominant today. And the Left is in great part responsible for that, because they seem to have capitulated to this dominance of capitalism and they are not thinking of another alternative. What I think is really missing is an analysis of the problem caused by capitalism and the neo-liberal form of globalisation. For instance, there is the belief that because of globalisation nothing is possible, and this has become the dominant discourse, the discourse of Tony Blair. Socialist parties in Europe today say, 'Well, because of globalisation we cannot really do anything fundamental in terms of changing capitalism and the neo-liberal hegemony'. Of course they don't call it that but for them it is basically the acceptance of this situation because of globalisation. What we need in this new socialist imaginary we were thinking about is the mobilisation of passion in a different way, different from right-wing populism. And that is the very condition of possibility – that an alternative is going to be imagined to the present neo-liberal system. If there is no possibility that things could be different, then one is not going to be able to oppose globalisation. There are different strategies within globalisation and I think this is what the Left should be able to offer. They should be able to say, 'Well, we are going to accept globalisation because there are many important and positive things in globalisation, but we are going to propose another strategy to organise it'. Of course, this includes certainly a critique of some of the modes of regulation in the capitalist system.

When we speak of a critique of capitalism, we must be aware that we cannot go back to the language of before: 'Smash the capitalist system and establish a completely new socialist system'. This is not a discourse which can be acceptable, because capitalism is such a simple word to refer to many different modes of regulation. I mean, it questions that we should accept the market economy but we shouldn't see that everything is going to be organised around the law of the market. For instance, in France they have a slogan, 'The market economy, yes. But market society, no'. What neo-liberalism wants is to have not only the market economy but also to transform the whole of the society into a market. And this is where I think the Left can really come up with some new strategies and proposals. We have to accept that we are not going to dream of a completely different system, but that there are certainly many different forms of regulation of capitalisation which are possible, and certain forms which are more compatible with the struggle for equality, and so on. And this should constitute the nucleus of a left-wing project. So I think that redefining those socialist lines is really what is needed today.

EL: Yes, certainly the regulation school in France, regulation theory and so on, had advanced a different kind of discourse which has not had too many repercussions in terms of the political Left. The work of Aletta Norval especially has emphasised the political mechanisms through which capitalist accumulation becomes possible. But I think it has potential in terms of understanding the way in which the market itself is politically constructed and mediated, which is not simply an economic mechanism as understood in the nineteenth-century image. And once we introduce the dimension of regulation many alternatives immediately become possible.

*

Reflections on life and politics

How does your critical work emerge out of your personal hopes and the experience of living across different countries and social relations? I am thinking about the idea of 'nomadic identity' and life (something you have written about, Chantal) and your backgrounds – Ernesto, you're originally from Argentina, and Chantal, you're from Belgium.

CM: Well I'm not sure how to answer that, it's a bit difficult. I must say that I was born in Belgium but I left a very long time ago and I don't have any real identification with Belgium. I am a French-speaking Belgian. I have always said that Belgium is not a country, because there are two separated communities that don't have anything in common (the Flemish and the Walloons). So you can't have a strong identification with Belgium. But I do certainly feel very European. That is something I became very aware of when I went to spend some time in the US. When I was there I realised: even as much as I like New York, I am European. I have worked very much on Antonio Gramsci and there have also been very strong links with Italy. I have also lived in Latin America (as I speak Spanish) and I also have a lot of contacts with Ernesto there. At the moment I am working in Austria and I have been working in France for a long time. But my identity is not so nomadic in the sense that I don't feel any identification, because I really do feel European. For me this is something which is part of my identity. But I just want to say something about this issue you raise about nomadic identity, because I think there is a danger in generalising experiences. Intellectuals like us might live a nomadic life because we teach in London but we live in Paris and the US and so on. But I think that we must recognise that for many people 'belonging' is important. There is a certain problem today that many intellectuals are theorising on the basis of their own experience, and they believe that everyone is living that experience. That is the problem with a lot of recent political theory which is generalising from the experience of a certain class of intellectual. I feel that is really wrong. It impedes them in understanding or considering the rationale of a movement of people who belong to a specific territory, or even those not necessarily in a nation or state. For instance, take the case of France, the identity of being a Briton is becoming very important. So I think that one must be aware that belonging is not something archaic or outmoded, or to dismiss it because of the idea that with globalisation we are all going to become 'cosmopolitan citizens'.

EL: Well, my experience is obviously a bit different from that. I am Argentinian and that Latin American component of my identity has always been very strong. When I made the transition to Europe at the end of the 1960s I arrived into a Europe that was putting into question the same kinds of left-wing certainties which we were addressing in Argentina. For example, in Argentina what was important in the late 1960s was the emergence of Peronism as a powerful force. Peronism, as a political phenomenon, was beyond any 'class' or differently specific base in terms of the social structure.

For me, the constitution of a mass identity was very important in order to break with the classist perspective that had been there – the traditional perspective of the Left – which actually, given the force of things, was never really mine at that moment in Argentina. I remember with the impact of Louis Althusser there was the idea that the contradiction in social life was over-determined, as far as it included a plurality irreducible to the Hegelian notion of determined contradiction. This perspective was some way of mediating class identity in terms of something else. So when I arrived in Europe it was a Europe post-1968, and exactly at that moment it was when new discourses of the Left were putting into question those certainties. There was a natural, let's say, feeding backward and forward from one experience to the other. I never had the feeling of having moved to a completely different type of reality. And I was always against this sharp distinction between metropolitan countries and Third World countries. In some senses, Third World countries presented in a most radical way an experience that the central countries were starting to develop.

That makes sense to me. We still call other countries 'Third World', and the radicalisation within those countries is never fully realised – whether it is subsumed under a European identity or global perspective or whatever. So there is a real lack of understanding of what the possibilities might be or what other countries can offer...

EL: Yes, absolutely. At the same time, Argentina is a country with a whole superstructure of a highly developed country, but with an infrastructural weakness of a developing country. So in some senses, you participate in both worlds. The kind of culture that I received as a student in Argentina was a totally European culture. We were moving from the French bookshop to the Italian bookshop (where we read *Rinascita*, the weekly paper of the Italian communist party) and then to the English bookshop. But at the same time there was a populist movement around Peronism which was of a completely different kind. So there was a refraction between the kind of theory we were receiving from Europe and the concrete social reality in which we were living there. For instance, the critiques of dialectical reason were very influential in Argentina in the early 1960s – the analysis of Latin American reality in terms of 'constitutive excess' – and then the impact of Althusser was also very important. So we were always attempting to think of some other kind of theorisation that escaped the patterns of classical Marxism. In some ways, in terms of a country, I think Argentina is similar to Australia. It was a country which was populated by indigenous people and it was colonised by European immigration. For instance, in Buenos Aires in 1914, for every 10 inhabitants 7 were foreigners of European origin. And, like Australia, even the staple production of the country was the same – wheat, wool and so on. In that respect it is 'atypical' from the point of view of Latin American standards, where you have a basic population, basic economy, and immigration was less important, but that is part of the complicated business that history has given to us.

In some respects there is always a kind of disjuncture between the importation of theoretical models from other places and the concrete reality of living in one place. I am thinking whether that's always the case, and how it is related to your own thinking about the notions of contingency and historical struggle. To be a human subject, or to conceive of emancipation, you are always shaped by different ideas and experiences – in an abstract and critical way, but also by the very lived experience that propels those hopes.

EL: Let's see if I grasp exactly what you mean. When I went to Europe in 1969 I was thinking very much in terms of Argentina, even though I had established contact with the people of the *New Left Review* and I started publishing there and so on. But my main point of reference was Argentina. At that moment – it was perhaps one of the earlier effects of globalisation – there was a movement towards a more international kind of discourse of the Left than what I had moved in before. So if there is some kind of break in my experience it is by the fact that I made a transition from being an Argentinian militant and Leftist to somebody who belonged to this more general movement of ideas. But it was a passage without ideological breaks, and also there was in the 1970s a long period of military dictatorship which meant I could not go back to Argentina, and that helped the process of transition. But my roots are there and I cannot joke about it. In one interview in *New Reflections on the Revolution of Our Time* I said James Joyce returned all of his life to his original experiences in Dublin, and all his writing was around those experiences. My experience in Argentina in the 1960s was a constant – and is still the constant reference point for understanding a variety of intellectual and political issues. In that interview I said that when I read Derrida, Lacan, Barthes and so on immediately I relate it to events of my political experience in Argentina in that era. It's not that I am only thinking in terms of psychoanalytical or philosophical texts, so it is a process of translation which actually shaped my perspective.

That's what I was getting at, and the last point you made is very interesting. It's that idea of translation and the experiences that continue to shape your life and writing – there is a relationship between the past and the present there. It occurs to me that there is always this translation or continuum between life and critical work...

CM: Yes, probably. For me, what I find intellectually creative and productive is the fact of having lived in so many different places. And I always find it extremely interesting to live in different kinds of cultures because it does pose questions which you would not think of if you were living constantly in one place. For example, I can see the difference between my friends and myself in Paris because the French tend to be very 'hexagonal' – 'Franco-French' as they call it. They tend to see things exclusively from the French point of view. I realise when I pose something they say, 'Oh yes, you've been caught up in the Anglo-Saxon mode', or 'You spend too much time in America'. I mean the question of multiculturalism, feminism or anything like that I couldn't have seen in the same way if I remained in France. And, for instance, simply seeing things from the point of view of London or Paris is so interesting, because sometimes you have the feeling that things are completely different. I remember the time of the Gulf War. I was teaching in Paris and going back to London, watching TV there and reading the newspaper. I was wondering if it was the same event that was taking place because the way it was seen from France and from Britain was so completely different. I think that is important because you are bombarded with different images and you are forced to pose questions. But, as I was saying before, this is a particular kind of experience of the intellectual and one cannot expect that this is going to be the normal way of life for everyone.

I'd like to come back to that issue. You were saying there are certain dangers with the idea of 'nomadic identity' that's used in a lot of critical theory, and the idea of the 'cosmopolitan intellectual'. At the level of intellectual life, we are talking about quite specific experiences, because we can travel to different countries and so on. But I wonder at some level, when people do want to belong and feel some sense of familiarity with a place, how it might be possible to have a positive sense of identity – a sense of belonging that extends the relations between ourselves and others. It is also a question of defining the very essence of human identity and belonging – I don't mean 'essence' in a negative way, but as a vital source of living.

CM: I think it is important to understand that the very condition for having an identity is the presence of what one could call the 'constitutive outside'. The *other* is in fact the condition of my identity. But there is a danger that identity is going to be constructed in opposition to the other. I think if we realise that the 'other' is also the condition for my identity then we can establish a different kind of relation to otherness. I mean there are many different questions that can be developed around that. For instance, I have been particularly interested in the relation of Muslim or Arab cultures in France, because there are right-wing movements that are emphasising that European identity has been constructed in opposition to the Muslim world – Christian against Muslim and so on. So I think if we are going to be able to envisage or fight against that, we can follow a line which has also been introduced by the historian Alain de Libera, who wrote a very interesting book called *To Think the Middle Ages*. He was a historian but his aim was very political. He shows how Muslim and Arab cultures have been very important in the very constitution of French culture.

Importantly, he was trying to change the perception of French people to the Arab population and immigrants, to show how these cultures can enrich our culture instead of seeing them as people who come and endanger our culture, since these cultures have been moulded or fashioned by them. And this is something I have been arguing about with people in Austria. For instance, in Austria there is resistance to the enlargement of the European community. It is very important to realise that the opening of the Eastern countries, etc, should not be seen as a threat to them but, on the contrary, something that is going to be an enrichment for them. So I don't think one should be against identity, but it comes back to the whole question of negotiating with other identities. And I think that is important and that's why we should not say to people, 'Oh, you should stop being Austrian, you should all become European', but try to redefine what it means to be Austrian or French in order to bring many different strands of culture and history into that definition. In the case of Austria, of course, the relation with the Austro-Hungarian empire is there – you don't have to invent it – it is there to be brought back to the fore, for people to recover an identity which has been suppressed in the last 50 years.

Yes, it comes back to the point about the rise of the Right and issues we raised at the beginning of the conversation. In countries like Australia and Austria the rise of the Right seems to be linked to a hope for some kind of future ideal where the migrant or the foreigner has to be 'expelled' from social and political discourse. The 'other' is seen as competing with the so-called natives' resources and lifestyles. We haven't yet been successful in trying to re-articulate or invent other ways to be hopeful in the Left, because in terms of the political there's still a very strong nationalist fervour and everyday racism...

EL: Yes, but I would only add that to some extent the frontiers are less even than in the past, and they require more of a political construction. For instance, if you find a skinhead in Germany today, obviously this frontier is a *frontier* which is not simply seen as the materiality of the presence of the other; it is some kind of a need for an other which has to be constructed out of the most obvious one. This need involves the creation of some sort of identity in a historical climate in which no strong identity is provided. One can see the history of the Left – in the period of the Second International and even after the First World War – as an attempt to create a frontier in terms of class which went beyond all national boundaries. Now that attempt failed. It failed in 1914 and it failed later on with communism. In the end the national fact always predominated over the class division. But one could say that the leftist movement which was successful was the Liberation Movement in Italy at the end of the Second World War. They were successful because they combined the element of class identity with a plurality of other elements. In some sense they created new political frontiers in a much more a complex way.

The problem today is, I think, largely the result of antagonisms that are no longer located around one simple issue or point. So now there are sources of antagonisms which are spread over the social spectrum and which can be constructed in completely different fashions. And the way of universalising this plurality of antagonisms around a single frontier is an open question. That's what Chantal was saying before about the construction of identities in the new Right in Europe today, which goes exactly in that same direction. The ability of the Left to construct or to mobilise all these potential antagonisms around the construction of a new frontier is something which has been diminishing over the last 20 years. So in the end what we have are very traditional types of discourses which are not able to create anything. For instance, the last progressive social imaginary in America was Roosevelt's New Deal, which had a set of phenomena associated with it. The global mobilisations and social imaginaries that are created these days have been around the 'moral majority' – issues in which the Right has a clear priority. It is at that level that I see the future of democratic politics being fought – whether it is possible to create a more global social imaginary or whether this macro politics is going to be entirely in the hands of the Left.

CM: I think that your question shows precisely what I have been trying to say in different ways. It is the shortcomings of the Left which are linked to the rationalist approach and the lack of understanding around passion in the neo-liberal imaginary. Clearly this is what is at stake today in the fight against racism, xenophobia and right-wing populism in general. To take the case of Austria again (but it could also be France), the way the Left is addressing the rise of racism and xenophobia in its mobilisation through right-wing discourses is by a more moralist discourse. They are saying, 'You should not be racist', and they make reference to the universal abstract principle about human rights – all people are equal. Some people even use scientific discourse. For instance, I've heard people in France say, 'Well it is a question of teaching these people that there is no race, so they shouldn't be racist', and believing it is a question of scientific knowledge that proves race doesn't exist. So they believe this logic is going to stop people being racist. I think that is ridiculous. In this rationalist view it is a question of speaking rationally to these people in order to make them act rationally or to make them accept moral principles. But what is at stake is the creation of other forms of identities in which the foreigner is not going to be seen or depicted by the racist or xenophobic discourses. The fear of the enlargement of the East which is mobilised by the Jörg Haider movement is not going to be fought by reference to those abstract principles. It must involve constructing other forms of identity which are going to make people change their perceptions towards the East – for instance, as I was saying, to see this as some question of an enrichment of culture and not as a threat.

Here I think we come back to this question of hope that you are raising, because hope is something that can be very easily articulated into *fear*. Hope becoming fear. And in that case you don't see the situation as something that is positive, is hopeful, that may be an enrichment to life, but as a fear that you must defend yourself against. But the same 'affect' can be mobilised towards something *positive* and, for instance, the enlargement of the European community offers great possibilities for Austria – in the sense that it won't simply be the border of Europe but it will become more of a centre with new definitions of its identity. So it is all a question of mobilising the affect towards hope instead of fear. I think that is what the Left has not been able to understand, and that's why they are so bad at fighting against right-wing populism. I mean, it is really a hegemonic struggle that is at stake here. But a hegemonic struggle is not a matter of rational and moral argument, and too much of the fight against racism is done on the basis of a moral argument because they see racism as some kind of moral disease. And they believe it should be fought at that level, not realising that it is always a question of specific economic and social conditions which are the origin of those racist identities. So you can only fight against racism by constructing other forms of identities.

EL: If I can add something to that point, I think that the Right and the Left are not fighting at the same level. On the one hand, there is an attempt by the Right to articulate various problems that people have into some kind of political imaginary, and on the other hand, there is a retreat by the Left into a purely moral discourse which doesn't enter into the hegemonic game. I was previously mentioning the case of the New Deal in America. The New Deal was a discourse which mobilised people, with elements coming from the so-called progressive era in America. It provided a vast set of demands which were equivalentially linked to the development of a progressive imaginary. So once this progressive imaginary was acting there *as a* political alternative you could have many possibilities within it. For instance, the Communist Party largely developed in America at the moment that this kind of possibility presented itself and many other possibilities were aroused. So 'progressive communist', etc, was part of a broad political imaginary. In this movement there were also moralist causes there, but causes of different kinds were given within this more global political phenomenon which is the social imaginary. The main difficulty of the Left is that the fight today does not take place at that level of the political imaginary. And it relies on a rationalist discourse about rights, conceived in a purely abstract way without entering that hegemonic field, and without that engagement there is no possibility of a progressive political alternative. The future of the Left as a political alternative depends on its ability to present its own aims as those embodying the global emancipatory aims of society as a whole.

New frontiers

Returning to the idea of passion and affect, it is precisely those mobilisations of fear and associated feelings in response to the other – those people who are almost categorised as subhuman – or the extremities of economic realities or whatever, in a country that drives certain racist or nationalist attitudes. In conceiving of something like a 'revolution to come' or ideas about a hopeful community or communities – which has to do with passion not just in the intellectual work we do but in terms of understanding it in everyday life – what might be a way of thinking about affect and the idea of revolution?

CM: I am not very keen on the term 'revolution' because I am not sure what that would mean in a pluralist democracy. I am not saying that revolution should be forever excluded, because in some conditions you need to have a revolution in order to establish the basis for a democratic system. So I am not against violence and I don't think it should be forever precluded. But in democratic societies, you know, even really existing democratic societies with all their failings, I don't see the need for a revolution. When we are speaking of radical pluralist democracy we are really insisting on the radicalisation of the institutions of existing democracies. It is an immanent critique, because we are not going to build completely different societies. In fact we believe that the symbolic resources exist in our societies for this *radicalisation*. The political principles which are sustained by those societies (even if they are not particularly put into practice) are, after all, liberty and equality for everyone. I don't think one can find more radical principles than those. So the problem with our societies is not that the ideal is not there, but that they are not put into practice. So we should strive towards putting those ideals into practice. That's why I don't think we need a revolution. But in order to have this project of the radicalisation of democracy one needs to mobilise affects and, of course, when I speak of passion, affects are very much part of it – our desires, fantasies and so on.

And again I want to insist on the shortcomings of the model of democracy today, which tends to present democracy as some kind of set of procedures. I think we need to create democratic subjects who are *passionate* about democracy, who don't see democracy as a procedure that involves simply mediating among interest groups, but see it as a *project*, as something that is worth defending and fighting for. But that means we've got to have a different kind of democratic politics than the one we've got today. And when I speak of the need for an 'agonistic' public sphere – where dissent could be expressed – in this sphere real alternatives could be offered and people could feel that their voice would be heard, and the fact they are *active* is going to make a difference. This requires that there is an alternative offered to the current modes of democratic organisation. But if you say, 'Well, there is no alternative; we can only humanly manage the capitalist system a bit better', this is not conducive to a vibrant political and public sphere. But I think without that vibrant public sphere, without alternatives, we are not going to be able to create democratic political subjects whose passions are going to be organised for the development of this radicalisation of the democratic project.

EL: I would like to add the following: in order to have this radical imaginary what you need to do is create a political frontier. Now how do you create a political frontier? By presenting some objectives which are a horizon unifying all partial struggles. To give you a banal example: when we were students at university the distinction between left-wing students and right-wing students was about the concrete aims that we were proposing – for instance, reducing the price of the ticket in the student restaurant, or increasing the number of hours in which the library was going to be open, and so on. In those situations, right-wing politics meant that the concrete character of the demand was all that the struggle was about, and if the demand was satisfied, then the identity of the people intervening in the struggle disappeared. Now for left-wing students like us the possibility was different. It was to create a horizon embracing demands covering a whole field. In some sense our worst enemies were the administrators who came up with a solution to the problem – not in the sense that we would have rejected the solution, but that we saw these struggles as one episode in a wider political struggle. So radical democracy means the ability to construct a frontier that draws on symbolic resources that our society has, as Chantal pointed out, but presents this link to a set of demands which transcend what the society can fulfil at a certain moment, and gives some kind of global direction to the struggles.

From this point of view the difficulty today is that this broader spectrum of politics, which once included the classical forms of communism, has disintegrated. So the concreteness of the struggle is not linked to any kind of long-term prospect of transformation and, I think, that is what is important to create. We have today the beginning of a new type of struggle – as shown in the anti-globalisation movements, which started pointing in the direction of a new social imaginary. This is a line of political action that we have to pursue. Mobilisations are still too incipient and unstructured but are, anyway, creating the terrain in which a new politics can be conceived. To make it explicit is our task in the years to come.

7
'ON THE SIDE OF LIFE' –
JOY AND THE CAPACITY OF BEING
A conversation with Ghassan Hage

We live in cultures where security and comfort are seen as the motifs for the betterment of life and happiness. You have a home, a car, a job, and you earn more and more to make that house your comfort zone. No-one or no thing can come between you and the security you seek in this form of cultural belonging. Yet, in the era of late capitalism, these hopes are increasingly less able to be fulfilled. Instability at work, instability in social relations, and cultural mobility make the dream home an imagined resting place. In this view of the world the reality of our being and living becomes part of limited definitions of social and cultural exchange. We want more money, more success to protect ourselves from the threat *of insecurity. If we extend the home to our national visions of unity and economic security, those who enter it may be unwanted guests and threats to our homely comforts. In this view of hope our lives are subsumed by a deferral of gratification – the hope for things to come in cultural, aesthetic or monetary terms – visions of life that make all hospitality a cultural risk. What, then, might be an ethics of hope, a hope not based on threat and deferral? How might it relate to joy as another kind of contentment – the affirmation of life as it emerges and in the transitions and movements of our everyday life and relationships?*

Sydney-based anthropologist Ghassan Hage and I reflect on these relations of hope, and how, within capitalism itself, hope is not evenly distributed amongst the population. The effect of this unevenness is a complex mix of envy, guilt and resentment that becomes established in communities – in the formation of identities and across ethnic, social and class lines – both real and imagined. In this dialogue we explore what it means to belong to a community and to feel at home, where migrants and 'natives' experience belonging, ideas of security, comfort and hospitality in immediate and daily ways. The political consequences of these experiences are apparent across the globe, and what we need is to find ways to hope differently. It is the ethical responsibility of intellectuals to understand how hope aligns with politics, and what directions can be possible for affirming hope in anti-capitalist and joyful ways.

Ghassan Hage's writings on 'whiteness' and ideas of being and belonging have been influential in contemporary political debates on how we might understand national identities and political economies – the tensions, hopes and concerns for building new philosophies that are on the side of life.

The distribution of hope

Mary: We often think about hope in positive ways – as the 'good' or some future ideal to work toward, but hope may mean many different things in our everyday understanding of happiness or in the field of politics. I'd like to start by asking you about these hopes.

Ghassan: Hope is a word that usually has such positive significations, and when I use it I worry that people might think that I am necessarily talking about a positive condition. But hope can be positive or negative. In philosophy there is a tradition from Spinoza to Nietzsche that sees hope negatively. In this tradition hope is equated too often with 'religious hope' in the sense of Karl Marx's 'opium of the people'. Here hope becomes a negation or a deferral of life. In Spinoza you also get a sense of hope as the absence of the pursuit of joy. Instead of living an ethic of joy, we live an ethic of hope, and that becomes an ethic of deferring joy which fits in very much with the idea of saving and deferring gratification. This is similar to the thesis developed later by Henri Marcuse about enjoyment being subjected to the logic of capitalism – you suffer now in the hope you might enjoy later without this enjoyment really every arriving. This is the kind of hope which, as Nietzsche saw it, was against life.

But there is also a hope which is on the side of life, so to speak. There is the hope associated with Spinoza's endeavours which is like a bodily principle of hope, which drives us to continue to want to live, no matter what. And there is also the hope associated with what Pierre Bourdieu calls *illusio* – the existence of something to live for, what gives life a meaning, which again, to continue the intellectual connections, is not dissimilar to Jacques Lacan's understanding of the 'constituting fantasy'.

So in approaching existence from a perspective of hope we get a very ambivalent ethics of happiness. That's why we need to look at what kind of hope a society encourages rather than simply whether it gives people hope or not. In relation to capitalism this allows for a triple critique. First, we can argue that capitalism reduces the ethic of joy to an ethic of hope and deferral, and we can criticise this in the name of a long-term political aim, reinstating an ethic of joy. Second, we can also adopt a critical attitude to the ideologies of hope that capitalism encourages, and which reduce hope to dreams of upward social mobility. But, thirdly, we can also adopt a short-term critical perspective. We begin by accepting whatever hope capitalism has to offer, but as a next step we argue that capitalism does not even manage to distribute this kind of truncated hope evenly amongst the population. So not only does it withhold joy, but it actually doesn't even give hope to people in an equal manner. So this distribution of hope becomes the politics of the immediate but, at the same time, if you just concentrate on the question of the distribution of hope you lose sight of the fact that there is a greater ethic in life, the ethic of joy, which is the basis of a far more radical critique of capitalism.

What, then, would this ethic of joy involve?

Well, for Spinoza, joy comes from a simple change to the *better* in the state of the body. That is, it is an experience of reaching a higher stage in the capacities to act, associate and deploy oneself in or with one's environment which constitutes us as a specific 'thing' in Spinoza's language. So joy is not the experience of a static state of being, no matter how 'high' that state is. Joy is the experience of a growth from one state of being to a more efficient one *as it is happening*. It is the experience of that quantum leap of the body, of the self as it is moving into a higher capacity to act. Importantly, for Spinoza, we are capable of reaching even greater joyful leaps when we combine communally with others. Sadness is the opposite. So from a prescriptive perspective (that sounds awful!) we can say that we are aiming for a society which allows us to communally maximise the experience of this quantum leap. I think this idea of an 'increase' in being, but only at an individual level, is also found in Bourdieu's notion of the *accumulation* of capital.

So joy involves the capacity to experience life as a transition and movement in one's own state of being, because it is not premised on the deferral of gratification or a future-oriented project or plan. It is an affirmative state of existence. Can you explain how this links with the idea of the accumulation of capital – what are you precisely getting at here?

Bourdieu notes somewhere that he sees human beings as motivated by the need to accumulate 'being'. In this understanding of the human there is a core criticism of most philosophies of being encapsulated by Shakespeare's 'To be or not to be, that is the question'. Bourdieu is saying precisely that to be or not to be is *not* the question, because for him being is not an either/or question. People don't either have being or not have it, people are constantly striving to accumulate being. Some people are scraping the bottom of the barrel to get a bit of being in life. So being is not equally distributed, if you like, amongst the population. Now, for Bourdieu, symbolic capital is that socially specific thing that people accumulate and from which they derive being. In *Pascalian Meditations* he talks of the accumulation of symbolic capital as the accumulation of *raisons d'être* – the accumulation of reasons to live. Each person accumulates whatever gives them a buzz in life, but what they choose is determined by their circumstances – that's ultimately what capital is for Bourdieu. Furthermore, capitals are specific to the fields in which they are valued – the more you accumulate the more you become capable of operating efficiently in that field. It's in this sense that I've established a connection between Bourdieu's notion of accumulation and Spinoza's notion of joy.

As you say, hope and 'being' are not evenly distributed amongst the population, and this directly links to the loss of hope that is experienced by people in a nation. You have written about 'whiteness' and how the category itself needs to be investigated to understand the crisis of identity that has happened in Australia, and elsewhere, which has led to new types of nationalism and racism. I think in your book White Nation *you were starting to develop the relationship between this loss and the loss of hope. So when we talk about hope not being evenly distributed, what does that crisis of loss entail for a country like Australia?*

Well, let's go into whiteness a bit first, would that be the best way to move into it?

Yes.

I must say now when I reflect on *White Nation* I think that whiteness is not as satisfactorily dealt with in the book as I would have liked to have dealt with it, given its importance for the whole work. Many of the issues people have publicly or privately raised with me in relation to whiteness showed a misunderstanding of what I was aiming for, and I feel that it is I who has created that space for misunderstanding, I think. I should have insisted a lot more on the specificity of colonial whiteness. That is, what does it mean to talk about a whiteness that is a specific historical product of colonialism? Some of the historical writings on whiteness today have shown how, in the precolonial era, forms of white identification existed on many continents – in the Arab world and China, for example. European colonialism monopolised whiteness; that is, it shrunk the geography of whiteness and made it an entirely European attribute. But the other important point that needs to be emphasised here is the association of whiteness with colonial/ European civilisation. Being white did not make everyone civilised, but it made every white European think that they had the *capacity* to be civilised. So whiteness works like a kind of imaginary bank account that you have but you can't access, but *you* are happy to have this bank account because ultimately you think that *you* can access it.

More capital?

Exactly. More capital. More being. More hope. We can say in a Bourdieuian fashion that the accumulation of whiteness allowed for the accumulation of more colonial being. So what happens is that the colonial project has led to a move away from class as the principle for the distribution of the 'hope to be civilised' and replaced it with 'race'. For instance, if you look at England and France, the recipients of what we call today 'racist thinking' were always the working classes. They were the people conceived of as innately unable to access civilisation 'by their very nature'. So, being working-class or being part of the masses meant that you were conceived of as a bad breed and there was nothing that could be done about it – no hope of ever becoming civilised. Now notice the change that happens with colonialism and the shifting from class to race – suddenly those French and English working class, who according to their previously conceived class identity had no hope of accessing civilisation, became primarily French or British 'whites' and gained with it the 'hope of access'. Here we have the hope principle at its best – being white did not make you immediately 'highly civilised', it just gave you access to the possibility, it interpellated you as someone who could try and be highly civilised. The economic state of deprivation you're now in as a white national mightn't have changed much from when you were considered as inherently uncivilised, but at least your whiteness gave you hope of a better life. The no-hopers, those who by definition could not access colonial civilisation, the ones who couldn't and shouldn't even bother to try, were now the blacks!

But what is interesting today is that, I think, we are witnessing a return to class as the principle for the distribution of this *capacity* to be civilised. One of the most important phenomena that we are witnessing is the cultural pluralism among the middle classes and the upper classes which has meant that race as a principle for the distribution of the 'hope to be civilised' is no longer as functional to capitalism as it used to be. As many have argued, global capitalism promotes and is promoted by a kind of 'multicultural civilisation'. Many white working class are seeing themselves as unable to access this civilisation. On the other hand, there are too many black people, Asian people and other Third-World-looking people – as I call them – who are starting to have access to the goodies we associate with civilisation. These include aesthetic goods, such as being spunky, appearing nicely on the camera etc, and economic goods, being an investor and what have you.

If you look at Asian people in Australia today there is a division between three categories. There is first the category of the 'spunky Asians', the ones who feature in corporate advertisings. There is the category of the 'Asian investors', who are welcomed as migrants. And finally there is the category of the 'Asian piece-worker'. This is one category of Asians that is starting to be completely marginalised, even if not especially within multicultural discourse! – even though this remains a very fundamental reality in Australia. So we are seeing class being the determining criterion for your inclusion in global multiculturalism. Now a similar process is happening amongst white people; that is, it is the working class who are being increasingly denied access to the *capacity* to multicultural civilisation. So maybe we can say that multicultural capitalism is leading to processes of deracialisation of whiteness, and the reintroduction of class as the mechanism for the distribution of the hope to be civilised in the era of globalisation.

In the Asian example your use of the three kinds of categories – the spunky Asian, the investor-type Asian and then the worker in a sweat-shop or factory situation – opens out another form of class analysis. What you are pointing to seems to be class not within a dominant/minority model, or the ruling class/working split, but within ethnic cultures themselves, and the ways they are presented. The struggles of class mobility within an ethnic culture become also, to use a word of yours, 'worrying' and that's what is interesting me now: class in all of its transmutations. So how do we begin to untangle some of these issues within communities? For instance, in a family you can have different entry and exit points in the distribution of hope, and that is class related. Often children of migrants experience hope and class quite differently from their parents...

Well, I think your question is very interesting itself because 15 years ago someone might have said, 'Okay, you are talking about all this class stuff, we know all that; let's talk about identity'. I think it captures something which is very much part of what I consciously see as I move into reintroducing political economy – and, more importantly, *critical* political economy – back into the analysis of identity, because a very large chunk of work on identity in the last 20 years or so has often been done without a solid empirical grounding. So in a sense your question talks to my most dominant fantasy at the moment, which is to create an anthropology which combines critical political economy, psychoanalysis and philosophical issues, and fuse them together in looking at the questions of identification and hope. And I think that the need to introduce class is partly the product of the 'historical conjuncture', as we used to say.

At one level there is always a need to introduce class. I mean it is not that class happened 20 years ago and disappeared for 10 years and it has come back again. I think what has gone and come back is more the culture and the consciousness of class and the academic awareness of the importance of class that went with them. So here, I think, I am straightforwardly being the product of my time. When people were more conscious of their own class identity I was a class analyst. And when people stopped valorising it I stopped being a class analyst, and now that they have become conscious of class again I've returned to it. So maybe the real heroes were people who were struggling all along with trying to maintain the importance of class as an analytical category...

It is precisely those questions that I skimmed over when I was looking at identity, and when I came to the end of my book Foreign Dialogues *I realised this was a primary question that was underlying the issues. I realised I had to address it in my own life because I live between classes in a sense – between my parents' working-class life and my 'educated class' – and then within a more cultural sphere, of being a 'public' intellectual and not being part of a university structure. So where do you place yourself? There are so many different class relations there and I think that's why I want to keep working at, I suppose, becoming conscious of class again – the historical and social conditions that have changed how we understand it. Are you suggesting another kind of class consciousness here?*

I am not sure. I know that as far as I am concerned, my own class consciousness involves consciousness of my own specificity as an academic and the position of academics within the capitalist class structures, and the ethical responsibilities such an ambivalently privileged position entails. So one of the things that is becoming obvious to me today is that, if you are a social scientist and remain blind to the processes of class exploitation that are happening around you, there is something unethical about it. To keep talking about repressed and marginalised identities, difference, and what have you, can lock you in a middle-class struggle of identity affirmation at the very time when, because of the way capitalism is developing, the difficulties and miseries that people are encountering in life because of their class position have become so much more important than the miseries of identity and misrepresentation – or, even in a more complex way, they emerge within the miseries of identity and misrepresentation. Now, to be clear, this does not mean that the move of critical theory into the analysis of identity is something that should be regretted. It has given us an immensely useful body of concepts and insights. But I fear that many of us have somehow retreated from a confrontation with a critique of capitalism, and facilitated the dominance of the rampant neo-liberal ideology we are witnessing today.

So there is a need to reintroduce an intellectual counter-hegemonic resistance to *capitalism* (not to 'modernity' or 'post-modernity' or 'post-colonialism')... or rather, we need to join with those who have been doing this work of resistance in the 'Western underground' and in the Third World. I don't like to grade intellectual work too much and say 'This analysis is more important than that one', but I ultimately would say class analysis is more urgent today. Most people are beyond worrying about being classified as silly dogmatic Marxists. But I would probably go further: I'd say that I'd rather be classified as a dogmatic Marxist than as someone who is only interested in 'identity politics'. As always, the best is to try and combine the two tendencies.

Yes. It is important to understand the workings of identity as part of analysing the accumulation of being in capitalism and new class formations...

Yes. Approaching class from the perspective of 'being' can have important ramifications on notions of class struggle, for instance. It invites us to understand what 'being' a member of a class is. Whether being a member of the upper class or the working class, it is still about a human mode of being – a being with its hopes, envies, weaknesses and all sorts of things like that. So it invites us not to fall into associating being in an economically exploited position with being virtuous. It would help us to refuse to idealise victims and deposit in them 'the good', whether they are the working class or subjugated racial subjects – just because life is tough for them doesn't mean they are 'good'. I mean, you can be under the thumb and be a very nasty human being. So the perspective from the angle of identity and being can help us de-moralise a bit the analysis of class exploitation.

Sure, sure. And, I guess, there is a real need to analyse the relations of envy and resentment in relation to that subjugation. This involves understanding the conditions that make people want to cling to identities (which you point to in the discussion of whiteness) and the hope that is invested in them within a capitalist system...

Yes... exactly.

How long can we stay for dinner?
I think in your work, and certainly over the last 10 years that I've come across it, you've been very much concerned with addressing, as we have already discussed, the question of being. That is, what it is to live *and* be, *almost in an existential sense. And, connected to this, what it is to be at 'home' or not at home in a place and how this idea of 'homeliness' is related to a notion of community. In a way I now find 'identity' a very annoying and narrowing term for understanding those experiences. In fact, I think the concept of being, and what you were saying earlier about Spinoza, is a much richer way of talking about the human capacity for living and existence.*

Richer than what?

Richer than an idea of just identity. I think being evokes a broader sense of life – not just a metaphysical one, but how through the constitution of language and thought we come to understand what it means to be human, and that, to me, is hope.

I'm not sure I would oppose the two terms. I don't think you are either. I think that identity is a kind of relation to or consciousness of being. I think it is the most manifest part of being when it comes to listening to people speaking in an interview, for example. Unlike academics in the humanities, social scientists, in the sense of people whose work involves empirical investigations of social phenomena, have often shied away from fuzzy concepts such as being – what on earth *do* you research when you are doing empirical research about being? So the question was left in the hands of philosophers. But I totally agree with Bourdieu that philosophers are much better at asking the difficult questions than at actually working them through – because they work them at the level of ideas, rather than through empirical research. So I think that there must be 'a sociology and an anthropology of being' or 'a sociology and an anthropology of hope', because such a mode of investigation would raise questions that can only be answered – insofar as they can be answered – empirically. Part of my own research project on migration at the moment is to try and operationalise (sorry about such an awful word) notions such as being. The notion of homeliness comes in handy here, because I think it provides a key, and an attempt to find categories with which you can empirically start studying something like the pursuit of being.

What being at home might mean?

What it *does* mean. Immediately when you speak about the pursuit of homeliness, even though we are still into fuzzy, vague terms, we've come down a bit more tangibly from the pursuit of being – and suddenly the imagination starts working on something more concrete depending on the image...

Of the home...

And what it is, and in itself that's an interesting empirical project – for instance, the different images of home that come to people's minds as soon they are speaking about or unconsciously thinking about homeliness. So, yes, I think part of my project here is to refine the breaking down of homeliness into various aspects like familiarity, community, security and hope.

Yes, it means learning to feel uncomfortable with 'comfort' or contentment – intellectual or otherwise – and the hopes that we can so actively take for granted within capitalism. You know, what is familiar, secure, hopeful, really needs to be explored through a variety of experiences...

Yes. I am trying to give homely imaginaries a more socio-historically specific content – for instance, in relation to our discussion on hope. It is clear that homeliness and hope are related, but not in the same way for everyone. For Lebanese economic migrants, for example, whose conceptions of homeliness are highly affected by the economic imperative which has defined their lives as migrants, homeliness and hope are clearly structured around the capitalist logic of upward social mobility. But I was very intrigued when interviewing an old Lebanese peasant last year. I noted that he had a disposition towards contentment (without any of the romanticisations that the concept invites) around which his whole 'homeliness' was structured. I felt that such a disposition was so thoroughly anti-migrant and anti-capitalist. It made me think that one of the most important radical tasks of creative intellectuals today is to try and think of modes of hoping differently. We talk a lot about cultural difference these days, but really I feel that capitalism has integrated all cultural differences so thoroughly that I haven't met many people who *hoped differently* in the middle of all this cultural difference.

So in the pursuit of homeliness and your work on community there is an important relationship between how you feel at home or not at home, and how you perceive yourself in a community. Can you give me an example of that concrete work and the relationship to a community or fantasy of a community... Is that too big?

An example?

Yes, I guess there are too many examples...

Well, the sense of community is clearly a sense of articulation to others, concretely speaking – the feeling of connection, of sharing, or recognition. Homeliness comes from all this. But, as we mentioned earlier in relation to Spinoza, homeliness is also achieved when individual bodies can actually find a more useful and better pursuit for joy in combination with other bodies. So this combination of bodies itself, even in its physical sense, has a basis for thinking the importance of the homeliness of communities. Benedict Anderson's idea of 'imagined communities' has rightly been considered an important innovation in thinking about communities in general. But paradoxically, it seems to have limited our imagination as far as how we think of communities. After all, communities are not just imagined; they are also so many bodies relating to each other. They are a practical ensemble of relations between people that one uses as a support in the pursuit of being. So being part of a community provides a very important objective and subjective gratification for people. That's what *feeling* part of a community, as opposed to just imagining, can convey. It is objective in the sense that you want to be part of a community only if you feel you are capable of achieving more by being part of it than you can on your own – and subjective in that you kind of 'take on' the greatness of so many more people when you are living in a community. Like I, as an individual, am hopeless at cricket, but that doesn't stop me from feeling that 'we', Australians, are brilliant at it. Because 'community' can do so much for you, you develop a sense of owing it when it actually does. You want to give it something in return.

There is no doubt that this can be seen in doing research on migration – where there is a constant question around the need for communality – which is part and parcel of the process of immigration, emigration, and of leaving and of settling. I can't help but think here that in my experience (and this is something which people haven't worked on much, I think) there is an incredible element of guilt that accompanies the process of migration, when people leave their societies while feeling that they owe them something. In migration, especially under the era of capitalism and colonialism, there is a transformation of the self into a *homo economicus* at the expense of a *homo moralis*. For instance, the classical 'economic migrants' – regardless of what they experience – are people who say, 'I'm gonna kiss my communal life good-bye in the aim of pursuing economic success'. And here we come to this issue of hope, because there is always an element of deferred gratification when the migrants say, 'I'll just give my communal life a miss for a while so I can make some money, and then I'll come back home and enjoy life in my community'.

In my ethnographic work I'm always very sensitive to the desire for community expressed by migrants. Often it is a desire that oozes guilt for having left a communal life for the pursuit of an economic life. For instance, in many interviews people say to me, 'You can't make friends here like you can in the old country; it's different'. I have noted that this concern for friendship is, at another level, a kind of transference of the guilt for having given up friendship for economic pursuit. And, as a matter of fact, most people never experience good friendship. The image of a good friendship will remain as part of those 'back home fantasies' where deep human relations are imagined to still happen. I think the principle of communality which is working here is through the presence of an ideal, and its practical absence is heightened by the process of migration.

I mean guilt, yes. In the sense I am understanding what you are saying in relation to economic pursuit – transferring yourself into a better life, economically, and that's certainly the history of my family, although it never worked. They are not any kind of economic success story. So I suppose it is about the question of the loss of hope or loss of the capacity to feel connected – but it is not just guilt, though. It is also about a certain dream that went wrong or something.

Oh no, it's not just guilt at all, I agree. I think it is also very important to say that guilt will vary from one person to the next, and the extent to which it is experienced, if it is experienced at all. And that's something which is interesting me a lot at the moment – the ambivalent feelings that the migrant has towards their home country. I feel sometimes that I'm trying to develop a notion of 'centripetal envy'. This is the fantasy of belonging to a society which pulls you in, a society that keeps you. Now what I mean here is the migrant leaves home and wants to idealise the home but, at the same time, it's the home that has failed to keep them – and so, here, the home is thought of as the 'mother with the bad breast'. On one hand I want to love my mother but on the other hand, my mother is not feeding me, *damn it*, she's pushed me out! I'm under a centrifugal force and I land somewhere among people who are *in* and so I envy my hosts. My host is someone whose mother has kept them – I hate them for it. One wonders to what extent the racism of the host can be sometimes the most wonderful thing that could happen to the migrant, psychologically speaking. It provides them with a good reason to hate people they already hate for a 'bad' reason. There is something very relieving about finding a good excuse to hate someone you already hate. Which doesn't mean that the person who is racist is less racist or does not deserve to be hated but, at the same time... just as well he's there!

Well, I just think how many times I've heard that in my family and I suppose you would have heard it too. In my experience it was all about the Australians not being up to scratch. So, growing up, it was all about Australians as the other, the people who were really being hostile, not inviting, that kind of thing...

Poor migrants! We're really getting stuck into them, aren't we? I'm a bit uncomfortable – we'll have to start bashing white Australians soon or I'll feel bad...! But no, you're right. I have seen this happening in my recent work on the migrant discourses about the Aboriginal question. The discourse is that the Anglos have stolen the land from the Aboriginal people, right? Now that's also a wonderful event from a migrant perspective, because it enables them to say, 'I don't owe you white people anything. You didn't give me anything in the first place; you stole that land – Why are you telling me that you have accepted me on your land? You're bastards, thieves, killers, etc'. And I think even among the politically correct migrant – who joined in with the 'we must apologise to indigenous Australians' – there is an extra element of *jouissance* that oozes in. It's good to see the history of the whities catching up with them!

That raises the important question about the relationship between migrant discourses and indigenous issues. It does become problematic if they are basing the discourse on an apology from somebody that, as you say, has already done them wrong. So, in a way, they are not addressing their own questions to indigenous and other communities, using your idea of spatial logic. They are not going across or moving in horizontal fashion to the communities where they are living – they are looking at the host as the problem... But let's go to the question about the host – to the country that takes in guests. Clearly a notion of invitation involves a certain fantasy of unconditionality – but we all know that this is not the case for migrants and refugees. So how does a community work in relationship to the host country?

The very idea of 'host' is already ideologically loaded – most people who call themselves hosts have never issued any invitation, as far as I know. So I think the discourse of host often allows some people to have *fantasies of control*. The very idea of hosting, welcoming, etc, assumes a certain control. Now there are some people who have power to welcome and decide how many migrants come in, but the thing is, they are not the people who get the most mileage out of discourse of 'we are the hosts' and 'one should be able to decide who comes into one's home'. I don't think those who use the host language most have much control over anything really; they just fantasise about it. And the discourse of the host is linked also with the discourse of the guest, and there might be something therapeutic about the notion of host/guest in the sense that it allows for an imaginary transitional moment after which everyone goes 'home'.

Like at a dinner party?

Well yes, I think that's precisely it. The dinner ends – that's what so nice about it! The guests eat and leave. They just don't stay on and on and on! How much can one eat and party in one evening – there's a limit!

That's the problem – the guest keeps on staying. Well, they've been invited to stay but they have really outstayed their welcome in this scenario...

Yes, 'guest' is a very time-dependent concept, and I think that is why it becomes so problematic when used in relation to migration, because it often exceeds its time. When it exceeds its time it becomes a category that brings out the very contradictions it is trying to hide. For what is true about hosts is true about guests – if you're living somewhere that you consider somebody else's home, how long are you going to keep on wanting to relate to the owner as the host? If your stay extends long enough you start feeling at home despite yourself; you might also become a rapacious human being despite yourself, claiming the house as simply your own. There is something about our humanity which cannot allow us to live in a guest-/host-dependent relationship beyond a certain time. In the process of migration I think that is what happens. On the one hand migrants themselves, by the very nature of their length of stay, can no longer find it in them to act as guests, and the host easily becomes an irrelevant category. And at the same time the host will start seeing the migrant as trespassing rather than as a guest – and this is often where the tension emanates from.

But this is an ideological tension because, as I said, most of the people who see themselves as hosts are not in a position to host much in the first place. To host, to offer refuge, is part of an economy of 'giving hope'. But not many people really have that much hope to give. That's why you have such a strong support for the government's anti-refugee stance. People are so short on hope – neo-liberalism excludes them from the networks where hope is circulating; they become refugees in their own country... the refugees of the interior.

This relates to the distribution of hope, class and the loss of whiteness that we discussed earlier. Those who have fantasies of control are often in a precarious social and political position, and this forms resentment and projects it onto the outsider, whether it is the migrant or the state of refugees in Australia. So there is a vital link between these fantasies and the attitudes that dominate how the national debates are staged in this country. Which is also, I guess, a broader question around 'hospitality'...

Exactly.

The materiality of being

All the issues discussed raise ethical questions. As you've said yourself, the ethical role of the intellectual involves understanding how humans struggle to maintain a certain viability in the world. How does this ethic, and trying to understand cultural and political experiences, impact on what you see as the responsibility of intellectuals?

It is always very difficult to talk about this because I often find myself being put in a kind of priestly position... or putting myself in it, really. And this is not by pure chance, because I think there is a priestly element in the intellectual disposition. And even though I am a secular intellectual there is something attractive about it which I do like. Let me give as an example something that always stuck in my mind following the massacre that Martin Bryant committed in Tasmania. Of course when he did that he was evil incarnate. But there was this fantastic moment when a priest went to see him and listened to him. This priest did not define him as 'evil' as everyone was doing at the time, and he did not use any concept of what Martin Bryant was or wasn't; he simply listened to him. Now for me this is something very similar to the role of the intellectuals. In society there are already people categorising things as good or evil. To be clear, it's not a question of arguing that the people who do this shouldn't be doing it – I am not saying that at all. They ought to be and this is how society works – if someone commits something which is asocial we condemn them. But I think that there are some people who have a role to *not* enter that game, and it is the role of the intellectuals. So it is not a substitute role for the people who try to fight struggles, and it is not the role which aims to be critical of the people who fight struggles in the name of justice, etc, etc. But it is simply that function which can add an important ethical dimension to these *struggles as they are fought*. It won't stop them and it's ridiculous to assume that it would, because it is unrealistic to think that intellectuals have such a power – but it is simply what they can do.

It is a question of evaluating what difference does intellectual work make to life in general, given the limited capacity it has to influence social life. My position comes from – I like to think – a very materialist evaluation of the capacity of intellectual products to have an impact on the social world, which is again inherited from Bourdieu. (Now I am going to have a hard time convincing people that I am capable of original thoughts!)

That materialism is also about the kind of work you do, isn't it? Which is very much empirically based with conversations, and uses your own life experience and that sort of thing. Is that how you are defining materialism, in a sense: the critical tools that can be brought to intellectual work and the 'everyday'?

That's definitely part of it, but it is also simply a question of an almost anatomical look at intellectual work. For instance, I want to follow my book physically as it is moving – to find out where is it landing, in whose hands, how many hands, how many minds, how does it circulate? It is a total physical approach to see what the sphere of influence is, once it has landed somewhere. And I think it's minimal. One of the greatest illusions we intellectuals have – and we don't like to believe it – is how minimal the impact of our work is. And it is because of the minimality of this impact, or rather it is because we don't want to face it, that we fall back into the total fantasy of omnipotence of thought.

It is this illusion that is necessary to face, and that's why the relationship between intellectual work and life experience often breaks open that sense of omnipotence. I want to ask you in more detail about how much of living in Lebanon and through a civil war, and then coming to Australia and being an intellectual here and so on, have framed your own sense of self and informed your critical work?

Yes, of course those experiences have informed my critical work. You may have noticed in *White Nation* that the instinctive part of my writing was attacking Hansonites' usage of metaphors of civil war in Australia. You know, when Pauline Hanson asked rhetorically, 'Do you want civil war?', that really shitted me! I think that people who talk about war and civil war, etc, in such a vacuous manner are often insulting to the ear of someone who has walked on a ground where blood was still dripping.

Because no-one who has seen war can imagine it as a useful fantasy in any possible way and play little stupid language games with it – it is your worst possible nightmare. And I think the idea of playing with the concept of war can only emanate from people who haven't got a single idea of what violence means. And this is also my problem with spunky revolutionaries who attack me for dismissing violence as such, and they say, 'What about revolutionary violence or something like this?' To me they are all part of the same breed. And perhaps the belief that violence is a means to something else frees them from the fact that they have not experienced violence, and that frees them to think of it, and good luck to them. So whether it is for a revolutionary liberational mode or whatever, I am not going to join in. I can't join. This is one important way that the civil war has shaped my life and ethical position.

Another important aspect, specifically in regard to Lebanon, is my understanding of cultural pluralism. Often in Australia, despite the fact that we have so many Lebanese here, the cultural and social commentary remains limited. For instance, the former Commissioner of Police comments about the 'Lebanese' and 'Middle Eastern-looking people'. In this commentary there is a slotting into the public mind of Lebanon as some kind of backward-looking Third World country, and there is nothing there, etc. But what people forget is that Lebanon was a culturally pluralist nation. I grew up with Muslims and Christians, and it was difficult but there were people struggling to keep Lebanon pluralist all the time. So my experience of Lebanon has given me a sensitivity, and a keen eye to spot people who proclaim realities which become self-realising prophecies – such as people who say, 'Whenever you have cultural difference you will end up having a war'. To me, people like this are actively plotting for war. Statements like this are what set up part of this process, because cultural pluralism does not lead to anything. Cultural pluralism is something you struggle to maintain like anything else in life. It is not a given: it does not sit there for you, it does not produce magical realities, but it does not produce hell either. You work on it. So because I saw Lebanon turn from such a pluralist country into a war situation, I am a very good spotter of people who aim to create social tension under the guise of wanting to preserve national unity, and all those sorts of things. Of course when you talk about the influence of migration there are many areas that one discovers, but these are the two that immediately come to mind now. I don't think that my experience of migration itself helped me understand migration in general.

Really?

No, I think it positioned me in a good place to be able to look at migration, but I came to Australia from Lebanon in the mid-70s as a student, not as someone looking for work, and I very quickly moved into Anglo-Celtic student circles, through friendship... and marriage!

But there would have been fractures in your life, though? You would have experienced a different mode of being in terms of your relationship to Lebanon and Australia. You would have had to invent a new kind of relationship?

No, no, that is always an interesting question – this question of crossing borders and experiencing migration. Now I never experienced myself as migrating to Australia. I experienced myself as a university student who in Lebanon was interested mainly in jazz rock and spunky women (Frank Zappa rules!) and all I felt was, 'Here I am now living in Sydney; let's hope I can still continue engaging in these same deeply intellectual pursuits'. I never uttered the word: I have 'migrated' to Australia. I always thought 'I am living in Australia'. Later in my research I became very aware that this was a common experience for middle-class people rich in economic and educational capital. The richer you are in those capitals, the more cosmopolitan you are, and the more you experience the world as your turf. You meet other people like you and you never ask where have you 'migrated to'. You only ask, where are you living now? 'I'm living in New York, I'm living in Sydney'. And that's what I used to think: 'I'm living in Sydney'.

Well, that's interesting. It comes back to the question of class and how it is experienced. If you have access to cultural capital, and are in a certain position when you do migrate, then your access to power is quite different from somebody who doesn't have those entry points. I mean, from my experience, the fractures and pain of living across cultures has been very strong – we never had access to power and we didn't have a privileged class position.

Yes, there's no doubt this is something important. It is also worth remembering that Sydney is essentially a working-class city as far as migration is concerned. I actually lost consciousness of this until recently when I went back to Beirut and someone I knew from my teenage years asked me where I was living, and I answered Australia, and he looked astonished and said: 'What! You are in *Estrohliyo*?' By saying *Estrohliyo* this person was affecting a northern Lebanese peasant accent, and what was meant by the comment was 'How the hell did you end up in Australia? – only Lebanese peasants end up in Australia'. By the way, it was because of my personal history that I ended up in Sydney – my mother spent most of her life here before she went to Lebanon to marry my father and stay. But her family (my maternal grandparents and my uncles and aunts) all stayed here in Australia.

Anyway, so I didn't have a common trajectory for people like me. Most of my friends were in the Paris, London, New York triangle. And I think that this experience put me in an uneasy location *vis-à-vis* Australia and *vis-à-vis* the Lebanese community in Australia. But I also think that it allowed me a certain intellectual lucidity around issues of class, privilege and cultural difference.

An ethics of joy

Well, one last thing. Is it joyous communities or hopeful communities that we aim for? I mean, what might be a hopeful and maybe a joyous community?

Joyful community, ultimately, I think. But as we are talking it seems to me that maybe we shouldn't oppose joy and hope, but think of joy as that particularly positive variant of hope that is 'on the side of life'. Otherwise, hope as the deferral of joy becomes a variant of *ressentiment* – a surrender to the logic of deferral, masquerading as a higher ethics used to justify the non-pursuit of joy. Maybe, until the revolution, we should aim for the possibility of affirming a joyful hope, a hope that emerges from a refusal of the capitalist logic of deferral, and derives joy from that very refusal.

8
THE REST OF THE WORLD
A conversation with Gayatri Spivak

The image of our world is that all aspects of global communication are possible. People in the remotest of villages and places can have access to the networks of global exchange – the free markets of trade and opportunity. But what false hopes and promises does this involve when differing access to technologies, knowledge and cultural agencies occurs in 'the rest of the world' – those countries seen as Third World and 'other' – where the space to imagine is often colonised, and life is seen as an 'instrumental blip' in the circuits of global capital. This is where the promise of free and willing subjects participating in the global exchange of labour, commodities and communication continues to uphold inequality and exploitation, where hope is vital, yet difficult to sustain against the new abstract nature of corporate markets and the global dominance of financial control.

So what hope might this involve? It is about a kind of faith in crisis – crisis as a turning point, in individual and political terms. Feminist writer and literary theorist Gayatri Spivak and I reflect on the relationship of hope and crisis in the language of political struggles and cultural resistance, where imagination and the dissolving of identities are part of this crisis and hope. In this conversation we explore the ways that Marxist and Leftist thinking could possibly intervene in the new eras of global capital and cultural exchange. This is a challenge to the Left and its attitudes towards cultural difference, and what may be the ethical and active ways of resisting global exploitation in the rest of the world.

Gayatri Spivak teaches in the US but works extensively in Third World countries as an activist looking for new ways to create democratic structures and global resistance. Her feminist and post-colonial work is at the forefront of current philosophical and political understandings of language, ethics and cultural translation, where it is necessary to evoke hope in the very languages and experiences that frame our critical and political perspectives.

Crisis – a site of hope

Mary: To start, I'd like to look at the link between hope and crisis in critical thinking and political struggles. I'm interested in your reflections on this 'crisis' and how it can provide a vehicle for hope...

Gayatri: For me, the relation between hope and crisis is about *bringing to crisis* – that is, an energy in excess of crisis – dependent on the uncertainties of who and what brings a situation to crisis. I learnt the idea of bringing to crisis from the Subaltern Studies Collective, who saw in the work of groups that were cut off from lines of colonial mobility a kind of resistance and insurgency that metropolitan theorists defined as 'prepolitical'.[1] They saw that what was termed 'culture' or 'religion' was brought to crisis and became continuous with something that needed to be resisted. This resistance became a form of militancy. So, for me, bringing to crisis is an enabling moment. On the other hand, *who* brings something to crisis is never clear, because any moment of decision, singular or collective, is that moment which you cannot plan for. So crisis is an un-anticipatable moment which makes something inherited perhaps jump into something other, and fix onto something that is opposed. For me, crisis is not the leap of faith because it brings faith into crisis, but rather it is the leap of hope. And that's how I would connect the potential of crisis and hope in resistances of all kinds. But if it's not understood that bringing to crisis is a mark or a *site of hope*, then one turns that situation into a polarity and loses precisely the critical power of bringing to crisis, of *krinein*. After all, the terms 'critical' and 'crisis' are related. I think this also points to something that my mother once said with reference to English, that it is 'someone's mother tongue' and that you respect the fact that words are in language.

It is precisely that – words are in language. And is it your own crisis or maybe your movement or transition in languages – you have Bengali and English —that is part of the crisis and hope in the writing, thinking and living between cultures?

I am bilingual, of course, in Bengali and English. But, for me, all languages are an 'invitation'. My mother gave me this idea in 1985, standing at an airport, where a kind of accent in English, upstate New York (and I apologise in advance), jarred me. (I was a student long ago at Cornell University located in that area.) Mother and I had been in Paris at the College International where there had been this wonderful academic French. My mother had taken some trouble to learn French – nobody expected her to do that. The assumption was it's Gayatri's mother, an old Bengali lady, and she has just come because Gayatri is showing her Paris. After a week of wonderful academic French, and Mother making her effort, suddenly there was this kind of English at the airport. I turn to her and say (I translate this now from the Bengali idiom), 'Gosh, you know, you can't lift it into your ear'. And she turns to me and she says, also in Bengali, 'Dear, someone's mother tongue'. And now *that* is the invitation to the imagination of all languages – that it is someone's mother tongue. So in fact learning to be a revolutionary, and Karl Marx says this also, is like that moment in a foreign language when you no longer refer to your mother tongue. So the so-called foreign language – I *love* English and Bengali is *certainly* my mother tongue – is when that foreign language becomes also someone's and the someone is bracketed. It is as if you imagine it as your mother. You *don't* lose your mother by taking on a foreign language; in fact you expand her! So that she begins to be identical with the world and, yes, that's the moment of hopeful crisis too. It's like riding a bicycle – you have that moment of crisis where suddenly you are riding and before that you were falling. It's that moment of crisis that is the moment of hope, that you are going to be able to negotiate with the other in her mother tongue, *as if it were yours*. You don't have to know it perfectly – it is an attitude thing, you know what I am saying?

I do. I am thinking very much about the imagination and the notion of invitation. In some ways you're talking about Marx and learning to be a revolutionary – to enter into a foreign language you don't leave behind your mother tongue. Rather, you are recreating it in the new language, and that is the hopeful crisis. So you do need the capacity *for imagination, then?*

Well, you have it. Imagination is something that you don't need to be educated into. There are two ways of looking at this language stuff. One of them is where you don't lose your mother tongue, and on the other hand it is also true that when you migrate, for example, the child has a different mother tongue. That is what's so wonderful about it – the fact that the mother tongue can be transplanted and it changes. The mother is a graft. As Ferdinand de Saussure very correctly pointed out, every generation inherits a language. The language does not belong to the so-called native speaker; it has a history before the birth of that person and will continue after the death of that person. Therefore we insert ourselves into the stream of language, on loan almost, so the idea of language as the bulwark of identity allows us to see that identity itself is interesting insofar as it can dissolve.

Yes, this dissolving is necessary so we don't attach ourselves to an identity... which makes me think in some ways that is hopeful – the transplanting of language – and that we have this in-built capacity for imagination. But your work is very much about when that space is colonised, both within a national political sense, but also when the individual is colonised. How does imagination or invitation work in that sense?

Well, it depends if it is thrust upon you – so that you are not encouraged to imagine it. You see, one of the things about imagination is that it is fed by knowledge work, so that you can imagine something only if you have been living a life where a lot of 'knowledge work' is being done. I don't necessarily mean institutional knowledge work. I will give you an example. I've been teaching a wonderful novel, by my colleague Maryse Condé, called *Heremakhonon*. On the surface it is a simple story of an upper-class girl from Martinique going to a West African country to find her identity – as she says, and I use these words as a quote obviously, 'niggers with ancestors'. There a woman clearly without much institutional education says to her, '*Really* you are from a place where people don't have Fulani and Ebo and Wolof and Hausa?' She gives this huge train of names of many, many African languages. Now the young woman, who has her mind already made up about her search for identity, doesn't even hear that, and the only thing that she hears is that the woman also says, 'Someone so pretty as you...' And one of my graduate students, a very politically correct young man from Iran who certainly knows how to criticise the US for not listening, says, 'Well, this is a weak moment in the novel because you wouldn't really expect someone who is uneducated to know the names of so many languages'. I looked around the class, and of course that response is totally focused in an academic atmosphere where you know names of discrete languages. Whereas if you live in a situation where there is completely pre-colonial open hybridity – people moving, walking – you know these names without thinking that it is a particularly intellectual exercise. It is in that sense that I talk about how the invitation is extended. If the invitation is 'You'd better learn this for institutional validation or *else*', then you are not a guest and that's not an invitation. There is an American idiom which was in use a lot when I came to the US in 1961 which is, 'You want to do this or that'. In Texas they would say, 'You need to do blah blah...' But actually what it meant was, 'I would like you to do this'. Now that's not an invitation. I don't want to do it *nor* do I need to do it. It is the other person who is requiring you to do it and the idiom picks up on the fact that this coercive situation is being disguised as an invitation. So there are invitations and invitations – you have to see what the nature of the hospitality is.

I'm thinking in Australia there is the notion of migrants as 'guests', and the idea of hospitality which is often conditional... Are you saying it's how the invitation is offered or something?

You know, institutionally, if you think about an invitation as basically unconditional (I mean, otherwise it is not really an invitation), if or when you open your premises to a guest, by definition this guest is supposedly the master rather than the host. That's the whole deal about 'guestship' rather than being a guest at a hotel or an immigrant. So that model is a fuzzy model, as defined by Lotfi Zadeh, whereas citizenship, immigration *or* hotels are an abstract structure. 'Nation' is fuzzy and 'state' is abstract, 'citizenship' is abstract and 'identity' is fuzzy – one goes by the name of the other. My mother is an American citizen; I am not. So there is a difference in our travelling. Those things are abstract but the idea of guest/host invitation is fuzzy. In the fuzzy area you have this image of unconditionality, which then begins to operate in the abstract area like a little mole, subversively. That's what I was trying to say, whereas the invitation in language is *completely* unconditional – because you are not obliged to learn a language well because language moves by its users' so-called 'mistakes'. You are only obliged to learn it well when you are entering abstract structures.

It becomes formalised in that sense.

Well, your linguistic ability becomes formalised. Language itself is never formalised. Language in its mode of existence is always breaking the form that it had a second ago – that's how language moves. But the requirements can be formalised.

In a slightly detoured way, this comes back to the issue of 'knowledge work' you spoke of earlier. Recently you spoke about a relationship of 'knowing and doing' in the workings of late capitalism and telecommunications, and that is one of the biggest issues today. If we don't see the crisis or fractured relationship between them as a possible site of hope, then we lose the critical power to analyse and assess the impact of these in a changing global economy. Is it 'knowing' in the sense of knowledge production, and 'doing' in the sense of how the knowledge is practised in different cultures?

Knowing and doing. No, knowing for me is a much, much bigger word than knowledge production. Of course it is related. I talk about those two things in relation to this idea of selling knowledge – 'knowledge work' – which telecommunication is using in order to bring untapped markets into finance capital. In finance capital, money does not in fact beget money, but, because the competitive markets in negotiable instruments do not touch base with the production of tangible commodities constantly and directly, their volume of circulation can be exponentially larger. When, through the immediate possibility of accessing databases, we acquired 'command over information', to call that 'knowledge' was already undermining the hard internalising process which knowing something requires. Now, thanks to the Internet, we have an ephemeral access to lots of information, and this completely insubstantial and poor-quality phenomenon is also called 'knowledge'! That is indeed a wonderful subterfuge.

I don't have a moral position on this, but when it is sold to disadvantaged groups *as knowledge*, then knowing and doing (I say reading and writing also) – those two parts of being human – are shoved under the carpet. It can then be a drama organised by the movement of capital as the *abstract* as such. In the past it required more coding – it doesn't require that much coding any more because it can actually be sold as knowledge. This is not the old argument about the sociology of knowledge. This is an argument about needing to bring back the fractured relationship between knowing and doing. You cannot necessarily play a game well if you know how to describe its rules. This gap is getting flattened out by the exigencies of telecommunication, indistinguishable from the circuits of finance capital. It has to represent knowledge as immediately active in the world if accessed electronically. And indeed when 'knowledge' is data, it is so.

The rest of the world – new organisations of capital

The example that comes to mind is one that you were talking about at a recent conference. It was an advertisement of a Bangladeshi woman with a mobile phone, and that image seemed to me to be about the way she becomes another commodity that you are selling to. Is that what you mean about the circuits of finance capital?

Not really. I am not against commodification in the way romantic anti-capitalism is. It was actually the picture of an African woman and we mustn't confuse the two. Bangladesh is rather a different kind of case – it is not an 'emerging market'. This image is a US advertising logo – a very lovely tall, slim African woman wearing cloth holding her cellphone. I think that logo is a false promise. The idea that to have a cellphone means to be able to communicate is a false idea. You must have an infrastructural effort which will then welcome this woman into the mould of communication which a cellphone calls for, and also into a critical mode. Otherwise what is being fabricated is a 'general will' for exploitation in the exploited, and this is *profoundly* unfair to exploited people. It's as if she is being treated as a subject. She becomes an instrument in the movement of capital. Marx said that the capitalist carried the subject of capital. That's the burden that is being put on the shoulder of this African woman, not even as free labour but simply as an instrumental *blip* in the circuit of finance capital. Now the free labour argument is where Marx had his hope in the commodification of labour power – that once it is commodified then it can be turned around. Marx's hope about commodification was also to be able to abstract – that abstraction is not all negative... Because commodification of labour power whose *use* produces value cannot be understood if one thinks of commodification as a bad thing in a romantic anti-capitalist way, or commodification through its fetish character.

So the 'fetish' of the commodity is not necessarily how we can understand labour and power?

There is no such thing in Marx as the fetishisation of commodity or commodity fetishism. All of that is made up later. For Marx the fetish character of the commodity is simply that the commodity is not a relationship between things; it is a relationship between people. That doesn't mean that one person commodifies the other so much as the worker or the agent of production can use the commodification of labour power by turning it into socialist uses – whether one agrees with that or not... After all, the dream of international socialism is now pretty much gone. But what I would like to come back to is that that logo, or the credit-baiting of the poor rural woman in Africa, is not commodification. It is the bypassing of infrastructural labour, and the creation of a general will for a post-industrial finance capitalism, which is used as evidence that the very poor really do want this. It's a very different tactic than industrial capitalism. That's what we have to realise, and commodification arguments are not going to apply to this, and therefore the *other side* is going to win the argument very easily if you say it is commodification. They say, 'What do you mean?' We are acknowledging that these are communicating subjects.

I want to ask you about this aspect of Marx. It seems to me that you are offering a criticism, or perhaps a different way of understanding exchange relations between people and objects in the world, through a notion of 'use value'. And I'm interested in how we can revisit Marx in contemporary contexts to understand the new forms of capital, labour and social exploitation. Or, to put the question another way, how is your reading or taking up of Marx offering this?

I think that this business about finance capital is something you really have to develop further than industrial capitalism. I am not an economist. There are wonderful Marxist studies – for example Amiya Bagchi, who used to be my teacher, his work on banking, and, closer to home, Saskia Sassen's work, although her politics are becoming somewhat dubious now. I would also mention David Laibman's work in this context. You move along the same trajectory but it's not industrial capitalism, although industrial capitalism, world trade, etc, certainly manages the crisis of finance capital and you need to know that too. And even post-Fordism in the lower reaches is like the industrial capitalism that Marx described. But the idea of finding the possibility of value, rather than only use, in 'use value' is something most people don't even think as an interesting part in Marx any more, because it was never really understood. It is obscure because it is counter-intuitive. What Marx is saying there is simply that it is in exchange that value appears, and that's for everyone, and the worker must understand that the made object *itself* contains the possibility of its use value.

I sometimes say to my students, when you look at all those nutritional constituents of food there it is – the made object *made* for consumption but you see its use *value* right there. That possibility of being commensurable is in the made object, *not* in the non-made object. That's why Marx says a thing can be used and not really be of value in that way. He talks about air, earth and things like that. With that particular intuition I am not really doing anything very special there, I am just, as a teacher of literature, keeping my nose on the page and trying to read as it is written on the page. Because I see that in the stock response and clichéd minds of British empiricism and rationalism – and Friedrich Engels also, who isn't Marx – there is the constant correction of these counter-intuitive issues. For example, the idea of abstraction I discussed – the guys who translated Marx, who are all men (not that it matters), don't understand what on earth Marx is talking about when he discusses abstraction, because their minds are made up in advance that use is concrete, exchange is abstract. But where Marx says, 'abstract from this object of use', they say, 'subtract'. But the German word '*abstrahieren*' is certainly not subtract, you can hear the cognate but they can't say it. When Marx says value is contentless, they say value is slight in content. In '*inhaltslos*', '*los*' is less and '*Inhalt*' is content. How does that translate to 'slight in content' in version after version?

The other thing that I was saying about this is that the power of abstraction contained in the made object must be understood rather than just simply seen as appearing in exchange, which is what the untrained mind thinks. In this sense, then, a socialist society, although making vigorous use of the abstract production of capital, can be a true community – *gemeinschaftlich-gesellschaftlich* – because abstraction is implicit in the made object of use. But this too was never understood and always mistranslated as 'this is common to all social forms'. The last time I talked about this was before I left the US with two students who are doing an independent study on Marx. They came to my place and one of them said, 'My goodness, I see you are not saying anything; you are just looking at the page as it is written, but I am having to undo years and decades of indoctrination'. In America he is what is called a *red diaper baby* – his parents are communists and this is something that is in-bred – this idea that use is concrete, exchange is abstract, and Marx is all for concrete use. But Marx is not like that at all. So, as I said, I don't think I'm doing anything very new, I'm doing something very old-fashioned – reading the page carefully.

'Human All-too-Human?'

To take up Marx, in reading your work and in particular your book A Critique of Postcolonial Reason, *you make a point about Marx and the relationship of humans to capital. From my understanding, Marx is saying that there is a relationship of humans to capital. That is, human nature is not defined by capital* per se *but rather in relation to it. How do we describe*

*the human being if we are thinking of Marx, and we are thinking of new
ways of understanding class relations, and so on? Is there another way of
understanding what it means to be human, or is it always in relation to
some kind of object outside the self?*

Well, Marx is writing, after all, at a certain time, and Marx comes from a
certain educational background. It seems to me that in the early Marx,
when he is talking about 'species life' and 'species being', the species life
understanding of the human being is that... nature is the great body without
organs of the human being and human life is simply nature, breathing in
and out. This is what Marx will much later call the 'realm of freedom'. It's
not possible to plan anything there – people live and die as natural beings.
Species being, on the other hand, is where each human being should be
an example of the universal human being and universal human rights. And
this is Marx's inheritance – he was born in 1818, right? What is different is
that Marx's version of the public use of reason, to quote Immanuel Kant, is
from below rather than from above. That's his distinction. If one is looking
at Marx in the middle years, what he really comes to is that the human
being is a site of difference – he or she can make more than they need. And
in that difference, in that fault line, is the emergence of capital. That's the
relationship between being human and the self-determination of capital:
the human being as the agent of work. On the other side there are all
those other issues around species life, etc. For me that's enough. But the
class subject, of course, is a self-conscious subject – that is, informed by
class consciousness. Now, in *Capital – Volume 3*, the last three chapters
as Engels arranged them, 'On the analysis of the production process', 'The
illusion created by competition', 'Relations of distribution and relations of
production', and the chapter on 'Classes' which is unfinished, Marx argues
that one must not take the lineament of industrial capitalism – especially in
Britain, which was well advanced in the nineteenth century – as the eternal
lineament of the class struggle. Marx jokingly says that would be like
taking wage labour and profits as the 'trinity formula' — it's like you make a
religion out of Marxism, if you think this is the model with which you must
always work. So Marx was looking forward to a way of thinking which would

not be circumscribed by his historical circumstances.

When you get to the chapter on 'Classes', Marx says that class by itself is not a sufficient tool of analysis. When it is tied to that historically emergent trinity formula of profit, ground-rent, and wages, then it's useful. On the other hand, given that we are not out of the clutches of industrial capitalism – there *is* world trade – although we should not think of class as the determining instance of resistance, for then we forget what is outside of capital logic, nonetheless the problem of forgetting class because of the emphasis on identity is a huge class-specific problem in the metropole, and it works well for exploitation. So class cannot be the determining instance, because there is a lot happening outside of the US and other metropolitan countries which is not accessible to class logic. Yet liberal multiculturalism in the US and other metropolitan countries ignores the question of class and becomes an instrument of upward class mobility, and thus diffuses the question of race as well. Generally, globalisation and its relationship to disenfranchised people in the global South, in whom a general will for exploitation is being produced, cannot be accessible to a class logic alone. So class cannot be a determining instance. The international union movement is riven by racism. But at the same time to ignore class as an instrument of analysis is to give in to the other side. Class has now become a conflictual but crucial instrument of analysis.

You were saying that the international union movement is racist, and what I am understanding by that movement more generally is that it is premised on class. Now if that class logic does not work, say, in a country that doesn't function in the same ways as liberal multiculturalism does in the US, there are people from the US advocating class logic in those different countries. So how do you begin to understand class, then?

It's not the US that advocates class. Generally, in other countries, it's Marxism that advocates class. I didn't say really that the international union movement was racist, I was saying it was riven by racism, split. It does seem to me that their commitment really is not so much to class as it is to organisation, because management and labour are no longer really seen as class differentiated, since management involves the working class just enough so that the boss' loss can be managed by passing the loss on to the worker. The worker wants the boss to succeed. Labour is moved into pension plans (401K in the US), partial ownership of the means of production, stock options, etc. This works to undo the pre-Fordist and Fordist binary opposition between labour and management which is still intact in parts of the bottom layer of the global South and the South-in-the-North – although the unorganised sector, 'permanent casuals', the shadow economy, etc, make the binary less workable in other ways there. In the academy you hear people talking about having been working class as if that is some kind of origin. The actual issue is organisation – organised labour, unorganised labour, feminised unorganised labour, home working, the disappearance of the factory floor through post-Fordism, etc. The place where class should be an issue is outside the labour movement in metropolitan multiculturalism.

Yes, I think so.

You can't turn back the clock in world trade and relate it to the class struggle on the model of the capitalist and worker wrestling each other to the ground. On the other hand, in liberal multiculturalism the question of class is incredibly important – especially when you look at the migrants' moment of exodus and the moments of re-entry. These are issues that really have to be thought through, how the so-called national frontiers have now become demographic as they used to be in the old days – pre-capitalist frontiers, not territorial ones. You have Indian-Americans fuelling the Indian elections for Hindu nationalism. These demographic frontiers have now become virtualised. (At the time of revising this conversation, one thinks of NATO against 'Islam'.) This analysis of the uses of virtualisation is a critique of the selling of telecommunication as value-free access to knowledge. When you begin to look at the re-entry of the second generation, the third generation, marked by geopolitical difference denegated (to use Freud's term) by nostalgia, you're into very complex issues. And that's where a sort of tear-jerking politics of the migrant destabilising the basically white-dominant state is pathetic in many ways. It's narcissistic and self-deluded. Everything is then reduced to that thing that nobody knows what it is: *culture* – that's where class becomes very important, it seems to me.

Working the political: ethics and activism

You are a writer and an activist. How does activism in relation to your work and to your life provide a kind of ethical practice which may be about the different sites of hope?

It has at least two elements that are different but also interrelated. One is an attachment to international counter-globalising alliances, and the other is a focused commitment to the training of teachers who teach children at the very bottom layer of large democracies like India. The latter calls on my skill as a thinker on my feet, because I have to learn from the children of these groups with whom I do not share a historical past. Of course they are Indian citizens as I am, but nonetheless that kind of crude theory of national identity belongs with the metropolis. I share more with you than I do with these groups, and in fact caste Hindu groups like mine have oppressed them. I have to learn painstakingly from the children the ways I can train the teachers, who are also very deprived and ill-educated persons, in order to devise habits of democratic culture. There is no narrative of this analytically developed in my writing because I don't know enough to generalise. As far as I have been able to discover in the last 10 years, these issues are so specific to locations that if I really devoted my attention to generalising I would lose the ability to learn anything. So my focus is to be completely useful in devising habits of democratic culture in small groups of the largest sector of the future electorate – the children of the rural poorest – and frankly, to find recruits. I don't find recruits that easily. Recently I have had a disappointment, because the requirements for this kind of work are very different from the NGO (non-government organisation) level and social agency level of requirements.

On the other front, hanging out with international grass-roots resistance lines – ecological, agricultural, against pharmaceutical dumping, against geo-engineering, against bio-piracy, and the like – what I learn there I do write about. For example, the idea that globalisation can be strategy-driven rather than crisis-driven if there is some recognition that this resistance has existed for a rather long time, certainly 25 years or more – and that the structure of that resistance is not like 'little Britain' Marxism, as historians would say. It is the little Britain Left orthodoxy that really despises me. The resentment that bubbles up is just amazing. They can continue to build Jerusalem in England's green and pleasant land but that's not where the world is anymore. There is a complete failure of communication there, and I don't think they can bring themselves to read me because if they did try to understand they would see that I was not someone who just wrote confusingly. I am not someone who paralyses people or who advocates inaction but I certainly do think that, since I am also an activist, to deny one's own folded-togetherness with the other side will lead to practice that is doomed to fail in the short or the long run.

And, as I have said a number of times now, the kinds of resistances I just described are not new social movements – they are only new social movements if you define them from Europe. And this established pattern of constant running interference against these international agencies – Leslie Sklar calls them 'disruptions' – has come to represent the real front against globalisation. It's not Left party politics. Given that the role of the state in terms of economic restructuring has seen barriers removed one by one between national and the international economies, the idea of constitutional redress in the states of the global South is less and less viable. It is the finance capital market which now has authority, legitimation, etc. In that situation the idea of who wins elections is important – it is always better if a Left party wins elections. I am certainly an old Leftie in that sense and I will work for that kind of direction – but that is not the main story. And to say we must have universals, of course we must have universals – whoever said no? – but on the other hand they are not the universals that you get if you work according to what Marx already was smart enough to call the 'trinity formula'. But this little Britain-Left-conservatism still think that they can adjudicate the fate of the entire Left movement in the world, and it's a very, very scary phenomenon. Today, at the time of revising this conversation, it should be mentioned that constant contact with these groups also shows the US' destructive face, which well-meaning Americans may not be aware of.

You are saying that you had to learn from the children. For me, this links to your work on translation – and this is a different point but it seems to me connected in some ways – that in translation, and in the translating of other cultures, you have to learn the language of others. You have to learn to speak in that language, and is that the kind of ethical issue in doing the work there?

The questions are very simple. I don't organise them analytically because I think I would lose the impetus and the ability to learn. What kind of habits can you inculcate in smart children being taught by very wonderful human beings, generally ill-educated themselves, who have not been able to break into the upward mobility? How am I going to fight the idea of the sale of votes? How are you going to devise something that is going to be acceptable to these teachers who have in their hands children who are as smart as any children anywhere? I have to think about that kind of practical stuff. Although these places are really far away from the cellphone circuits or micro-credit circuits of technology, if the cellphone and computers come – this is the part you are calling translation – what kind of intellectual habits can be devised in these little mud floor classrooms, so that these children will be able to use artificial intelligence without being magically beholden to the disingenuous false promises of unmediated cyber-literacy?

In the aboriginal areas I am dealing with groups that are so deprived that, certainly among the women, the great genealogical memories are still active. I didn't realise this, because one is so used to having orality described as enforced illiteracy. It was only about two or three years into my work I began to realise this, because I've only been interested in training the teachers. In the evenings, on the other hand, you don't have anything to do and so the women entertain themselves together. I'm also a woman and so I am in the women's entertainment quota. At first they didn't take my efforts at joining in their music seriously, and then when they began to take it seriously I couldn't keep up with all of it. Suddenly I realised that I,

Gayatri Spivak, with a fairly strong literate memory, could not keep up with this damn thing! I have heard the great Hindu epics done in big cultural centres in New Delhi – for example, women doing the Pandavnis, as they are called, and I have been told, 'Look here's the oral formulaic'. But in these remote areas how would I recognise that this was the oral formulaic where they are putting in all this material about police, issues affecting them, etc. I remember being right in the middle of so many women in this one mud room and singing loudly, blowing noses with their fingers and the children pissing, etc – it is not a wonderful scene like the New Delhi scene – and I suddenly realised, my god here's Homer! So the children have already kind of lost this form of memory because there is a national system of education there that is criminally inadequate at this level. And because there is the question of education – the human child is the only animal that is educated into becoming human – you try to see how memory and memorising will not reward certain kinds of things and how you will be excited by certain other kinds of things. So that's what I try to devise by paying great attention to the children and the limited qualifications of the teachers.

When you were just talking about memory, though, it did activate for me that there are other ways of remembering and knowing. If memory is simply understood as remembering in certain ways, then all those other ways of knowing fall out of the picture, and that's what your story suggests to me...

Yes, the only thing is it has to be more abstract, because you and I are talking here in this room in Adelaide. But this is more abstract than what happens right there in those rooms. I mean, I want them to not take too much pride in remembering a lot of stuff, because if they do they will be defeated by the computers so easily. It's going to win immediately. So it is very simple, isn't it? On the other hand, I don't want them not to use the computers – I don't want to deprive them of this wonderful tele-technology. The only thing that I don't want to see is the *unmediated* access to cyber-literacy, which will make them small cogs in the wheel of exploitation. How am I going to give them any help at all in treating the computer or telecommunication computer telephony critically, except on that level – to an extent taking away what is culturally theirs, which is those incredible genealogical memories, which Jacques Derrida, to his credit, recognised as mnemonic writing. That is, you don't just write on material, you write on memory traces, mnemonic material. So I have to deal with the fact that if you acknowledge that artificiality – which I do – then you cannot value it to the extent that it's going to then be simply defeated in the children's minds by what even a bad computer can do.

I'm not thinking directly of that example, but of the artifice of the mind – there is a writing and there is a memory that is written on the mind, not just on paper... I mean it is work that you have done and so on, but it reminded me of the importance of thinking about the relationship between speech and writing...

It doesn't work with these children, because that's what I am undermining – that other writing. Perhaps one of them will read a little post-structuralism at the end of this hard road. They may be examples of it, they may even make its moves, but to have access to its recognised vocabulary? There was only one woman, from the Lodha tribe, who went to university, and she killed herself there. She wanted so much to study anthropology, but there was such incredible discrimination – one woman out of a whole ethnic group. So the situation is really quite miserable. Of course in my work I am very derivative of Derrida, and I'm interested in that relationship between speech and writing, speech as writing, etc. I remain convinced by that work, and it has its repercussions on my understanding – questions of identity, questions of translation, how I teach, and so on.

Something to come...

I'll direct us towards an end, and towards the notion of collectivities and political action. How do you think about hopeful collective actions?

Well, first of all, in order to make political decisions you need to have collectivities, artificial collectivities, and it must be made quite clear that's what they are, even as they are working. So that's why I never, ever, *ever* speak of identity. We know that in order to do things we must all join together, we must work together – that's fine, and as a group this is how we will benefit or we will not benefit. Those are very limited projects. But in the sense of real collectivities, and again I am very derivative from Derrida here, you don't draw knowledge from the doers in an unmediated way or draw doing from knowledge in an unmediated way. In those global movements, if they talked about what they were doing, it would probably be identity talk. But it is silly to imagine that the *doers* know or the *knowers* do – one must keep that crisis going. And what has happened to Marx in that model of identity talk? It has become completely fragmented and the Marxist analysis has been digested. That analysis applies in different ways in the different situations, to credit-baiting differently from the sale of knowledge-power as knowledge. It is almost as if it is one person's textuality internalised by many people flung out into history in a model of *something to come*. That's a collectivity that can keep working, whereas, as I keep saying, any sort of Left conservative model – of, you know, miners striking together, etc – of course those are good, but that's not where it's at in terms of the world we are beginning to live in.

Notes

[1] The Subaltern Studies Collective was founded in 1983. Its founding members were Ranajit Guha and students from the University of Sussex. The Collective has been fundamental to the study of colonial power and the sites of resistance that emerge in countries outside of metropolitan cities and centres.

Part III

Revolutionary Hope

9
THE ART OF LIVING
A conversation with Michel Serres

When we jump for joy our body moves with a kind of exuberance and pleasure, like the sound of a wave when you pick up a sea shell, or the feel of a gentle wind sweeping across your face. But in our relations to the earth and natural environments, little time is given in intellectual or scientific debates to consider these connections of knowing and feeling, those unquantifiable moments that move life forward against a background of despair. In these times, our bodies, our movements, our feelings are changing with new technologies such as the Internet, discoveries in science, biological inventions and artificial intelligence. These transformations have altered our relations to space, time and perception. In these transformations, what are our new social relations to labour and technology? What might be our responsibilities towards the world and nature itself when new communications and inventions have transformed humanity itself? What creativity, risks and joys are possible?

In this dialogue, the French historian and philosopher of science Michel Serres and I explore these connections, and ancient and modern approaches to these questions that may see us look towards 'angels' and different kinds of interlocutions and communications – to take us to new heights, hopes and joys. Serres' writings have been essential to creating a philosophical dialogue that connects different scientific, cultural and literary perspectives and insights into fundamental questions of human existence. His revolutionary perceptions of time and culture embrace the joys, visions and inventions that can build new philosophies for the future – and reflect on the art of living itself.

Renaissance of hope

Mary: I'm interested in where hope may lie as we are transformed by new technologies, and how that relates to our perceptions of the world – how scientific and philosophical questions have changed, and what might be new hopes for our times. I'd like to start by asking you about these 'hopes' and how what you call 'walking wounded' through the violence of our times has influenced your life and work, the philosophical directions and scientific questions...

Michel: In many ways my life has influenced my work. Why? Because I turned 70 about a week ago. So I was born during a very specific period in the last century. My first memories date from the Spanish Civil War, and right after that there was the Second World War, after which there was the whole series of colonial wars in which Europeans set themselves against their former colonies. As a result I knew nothing but war between the ages of 6 and 30, and was deeply affected by this period, which stands out in the last century for having produced, in Spain, a bloody civil war and a totalitarian regime, but also Fascism in Italy, Nazism in Germany, Stalin in the Soviet Union and Mao Tse Tung in China, not to mention regimes such as the Khmer Rouge in what used to be called French Cambodia. And so this whole period, which in many respects can be said to have culminated in the concentration camps and also in the atomic bomb at Hiroshima, was very important for me, and for two reasons. The first of these goes to the – dare I say – political orientation of my work, since very few of my generation were politically active. As a general rule, French intellectuals – the people we *call* French intellectuals – are politically outspoken and given to political analysis. Not so for my generation, which was too deeply affected by all these dramatic and bloody events. The second goes to the specific nature of my work as a historian and philosopher of science. Before the atomic bomb was dropped on Hiroshima, the reigning ideology among scientists was scientism – in other words the idea that science could do no wrong. Hiroshima brought about the first realisation that science could pose an ethical dilemma. Hiroshima marked the introduction of ethics to science. After that came other problems related to the environment, biology or biotechnology, but Hiroshima was unquestionably the first world event that made a whole generation of scientists stop and think. I was a scientist myself, and I became a philosopher the moment the bomb was dropped.

So, in relation to hope, generally speaking, most intellectuals and philosophers today, at least those around me, writing in French, are rather pessimistic. In other words, they write books which are at once critical of the present and pessimistic about the future. Unlike them, I am fundamentally and very actively optimistic. Why? Because the series of events I mentioned earlier are only half the story. As a matter of fact, in the last half century we have lived through even more noteworthy events which have transformed our bodies, our relationship with the world, our relationships with others and so on, and these events are so significant that I can only compare the present day to the Renaissance. In other words we are living through an era where our relationships to our bodies, to the world and to others have been so transformed that it can only be compared to the Renaissance. It seems to me that these transformations are largely positive, and that the role, the duty, of philosophy is to use them to build the house in which future generations will reside. And when one is building the home of future generations, it is one's responsibility to be optimistic and hopeful.

I want to pick up this idea of the home in what might be the ethical place of philosophy and the relationship to something hopeful...

Well, let's examine these transformations more closely. First of all we tend not to notice, here in the West at least, that we have been at peace for half a century. In other words there have been no wars between Western countries for 50 years. To give you an idea of what I mean, consider that the longest period of time before this in which there were no wars was a period of 7 years in the seventeenth century. Therefore this 50-year period counts as exceptional. I don't mean to suggest that there is no more war in the world. On the contrary, there are wars everywhere, but I'm talking about the West, countries like yours and mine. And during this time of peace, the human body has been transformed in the most unexpected way by progress in medicine, pharmacology and biology. To see just how much the human body has been transformed, we'd have to do a chronological account of the history of physical suffering, infectious diseases and epidemics. For instance, at the *Académie Française* we have a collection of items of clothing which date from the beginning of the nineteenth century – today, the human body is so different that an 11-year-old girl would not be able to get into them. But in addition to these changes in the human body there have been other, technological changes, thanks to which the consequences of our actions, of our work, are no longer merely local but global. In other words, the work of my parents or my ancestors had an effect on their family, their farm, and their village, whereas our actions today can have global repercussions.

To give you an example, at the beginning of the twentieth century, depending on the country, anywhere between 70 and 80 per cent of the population were farmers. At the end of the century, depending on the country (and I'm talking about the West again) between 2 and 3 per cent of the population are farmers. Now, consider that agriculture was invented during the Neolithic period, in the Middle East, and involved almost everybody. At the beginning of the twentieth century there was not a single politician, lawyer, writer, worker, engineer, and so on, who had not had, in their youth, a direct experience of agriculture. We've all got a grandfather or great-grandfather who was a farmer. Today, however, there isn't a single politician, entrepreneur, workman, teacher, lawyer, and so on, with an immediate experience of agriculture. This is a *revolution* that has transformed the way humankind has lived since the Neolithic period, and is a particularly striking example of what has happened to us during the last half century.

Firstly, then, we have new bodies, secondly a new universe, a new world for which we must take responsibility even as we transform it. And furthermore, thanks to the new information technologies such as the Internet, our relationships with others have been completely transformed in terms of time and space, as have our cognitive functions, such as memory, calculation, imagination, etc. These transformations, which affect the different domains of work, health and knowledge, make up a 'background' unlike that of 20 or 30 years ago. These changes date from the 70s and 80s, and with them all the questions of philosophy were changed too – questions of cognitive science, questions of biology, sexuality and reproduction. Thus the family has also changed, raising new questions about social structures and how we relate to the world. Given all that, it follows that the foundations of philosophy itself had to be rebuilt.

With all the changes we have at the moment – a different sense of our bodies, different relationships to technology and so on – how do those new connections to the land offer a possibility of renaissance, of hope... in the sense of the responsibility to the land and earth itself, and in what you have called a 'natural contract'.

Our relationship to the world at – let's say – the beginning of the last century, was a local relation, because the farmer worked on his farm and had a local effect on it, with no need to worry about the global effects of his actions. It was very rare to observe any global effects of one's actions or work. Today, however, our actions have a global reach, and we find ourselves asking global questions. What then does it mean to *reconstruct philosophy*? It means that this new relationship we have *to* the world brings with it new responsibilities *towards* the world. Philosophy must explore new ways of thinking about this relationship. It was for this reason that I wrote *The Natural Contract* (*Le Contrat naturel*), a book on the philosophy of law. I was trying to see if this relationship to the world – and by extension to other people, but for the time being let's just leave it at the world – could be determined by another law. There's a good example for you – it was necessary to invent a new law to cover a new relationship to the world.

What does this 'new law' involve?

Well, the law in general, and the specific laws it comprises, are founded on a pre-existing contract which unites those who live under this law and these laws, and subscribe to them, to all intents and purposes anyway. This is how Thomas Hobbes or Jean-Jacques Rousseau understands the social contract. In the same way, laws concerning the environment must be based on a natural contract between humans and nature.

For a long time slaves, foreigners or even women for that matter could not avail themselves of the court system because they weren't legal subjects. Over time they have acquired that right. We have yet to promote the same cause for the different elements of the natural world: *Le Contrat naturel* proposes that they become legal subjects.

Angels

This invention you talk of is important in the creativity and joy needed in promoting new relationships to the world, as opposed to the violence we experience. You reflect on the responsibility of the philosopher, the writer, or what you call the 'augementer' – a person that has to express the harrowing experiences that we live through and the violence. What is this responsibility, and the inspiration we need in writing about the more hopeful, joyous and inventive elements of life?

I've written about violence at length in my books, and this has been a concern of mine for my entire life. We've returned to the question you asked me earlier, about my experiences. I really did see nothing but violence around me between the ages of 6 and 30. Corpses, air raids, the sick and the dead. So violence is a real problem for me. I believe human culture is based almost entirely on the need, albeit often an unconscious need, to limit our violence. Culture was probably invented for that reason, language certainly must have been, almost all religions are cultural constructions which aim to limit our violence. If we didn't, it would be just like Agatha Christie's *Ten Little Niggers*; we'd all be dead by now. And so the problem is how to limit violence. Even sport is a cultural technique for limiting violence. Moreover, everything I've written about religion in general has been determined by the question of violence.

Yet violence is always beginning anew, and continually it contains no information, in the strictest sense of the theory of information, which defines it as proportional to rarity. Therefore when the media announce nothing but violence, they're providing no information whatsoever. Out of this monotony of violence comes sadness. Rare and unexpected, peace or inventiveness interrupt this sad, grey monotony and cause an eruption of joy.

But – this is your point – I've written two books about joy (neither of which, unfortunately, has been translated into English).[1] In the first I did an extremely concrete and realistic analysis of the actions of touching, tasting, hearing and seeing. Unlike classical philosophers, my point was to demonstrate that knowledge does not come from the five senses, but that culture, taste and the good life do. In other words, someone with refined senses is particularly good company, someone with whom you could live a joyful and rich life, but not necessarily a great mind.

So what is the difference between your understanding of the senses and the cultivation of knowledge?

Empiricist philosophy believes that knowledge comes from the senses. In fact it comes from the whole body, its attitudes, gestures and movements. Why get rid of that function of the body which would otherwise just be there to carry meaning around? But culture and good living come from the senses too. As far as I know, no 'formal knowledge' comes from the taste of a great wine, the scent of a perfume, or the sound of the wind and waves. But there is great happiness to be found in the enjoyment of their qualities. *Homo sapiens* originally meant the man who tastes, the man of taste. In fact the Latin verb *sapere*, of which *sapiens* is the present participle, means to have taste. English too has *sapidity* and *sapidness*. He who has none will remain a brute.

*

The bodily senses provide some kind of revolt or the possibility of joy?

Yes. There is a very, very old philosophical tradition on the question of the five senses. And it has to be said that the first to study it seriously were Anglophone philosophers. The first of the great empiricists, such as John Locke or David Hume, stressed the idea that knowledge came from the five senses. At the time, continental philosophy, such as that of René Descartes or Gottfried Leibniz, thought that knowledge was innate, that we carry it in our souls from birth. On the other hand, the English philosophers, the empiricists, stressed most emphatically the idea that we enter into the world without knowledge, which comes to us through the five senses alone. At the time, Anglo-Saxon empiricist philosophy seemed a complete revolution against the idea of innate knowledge. It was a massive transformation, affecting the whole Enlightenment and bringing about a conversion to empiricism. Denis Diderot, for instance, was converted to empiricism – almost all the Encyclopaedists were – and it even went as far as Immanuel Kant, who produced a sort of synthesis between empiricism and German idealism.

Today we're seeing a resurgence of research on the five senses, and it's happening for the most part in laboratories. There is an enormous amount of experimentation being carried out by biologists, neurobiologists and researchers in the cognitive sciences, which has led to significant discoveries, not just about the five senses but about the *seven* senses. We have seven senses because, in addition to the five senses, there is also an internal sense (if I close my eyes, I have a sense of my own body) and another sense, discovered by neurobiologists, which is the sense of movement – in other words how we feel our body when we walk, jump, turn. The first of these is called coenaesthesia, the sense of one's own body, and the second, the sense of movement, kinaesthesia.

So, in my first book on joy, I analysed the senses neither from the point of view of the scientific laboratory nor from that of, for instance, the analytic school, which focuses on questions of language. On the contrary, I approached the five senses from a naïve and experimental perspective. This was a form of revolt for me, a revolt against a narrowly scientific or logical study of the five senses. I was attempting a humanist analysis of the senses in the most concrete and realistic manner possible. I am very, very straightforward, for instance, in the chapter where I spend 30 pages analysing the taste that a sauterne can have, and the sensations it can produce. Work like this is generally looked down on by philosophers. That's why I'm so fond of this book – it gave me, and continues to give me, a great deal of joy. It's rather like a book on the art of living.

The second book I wrote on this subject, I argued that knowledge comes from the entire body. And it was in writing this book, which is illustrated, that I made a discovery about joy. I was trying to find an image of a naked body jumping for joy, but even with the help of a lot of friends, researchers and librarians we could not find a single one. Nowhere in the different iconographies of the world could we find an image of a man or a woman, naked and jumping for joy... In Buddhism, in Asian art, in Judeo-Christianity, in paintings, in photography, there are no representations of nude bodies jumping with joy. It's a discovery – that there is none in history... and that's very interesting. And since I wanted to express the joy of discovery – the joy of invention, in fact, since that's the question you put to me – I had to ask a photographer to photograph someone doing just that – a woman, as it happens, but it could just as well have been a man. We found nothing, so I had to invent one. Joy simply isn't something that registers for intellectuals, writers, even photographers and other image specialists. I created this image of a naked body jumping for joy. I can show you right now... I'll get it.

It's fantastic... because it seems to me that the human body is most often portrayed in the Christian tradition as a body lamenting, grieving or in ecstasy...

No, I don't agree with you. In the Christian tradition, the body is always... described in every possible state. There is, in other words, the body of the pregnant woman, the body giving birth, the joyous body (which is the transfiguration), and also the suffering body, but not *only* the suffering body, quite the contrary. Christianity is a religion of the body, and of the body in every possible state. It is only nineteenth-century Puritanism which clung to the image of the suffering body. But in the Middle Ages, the Renaissance, the eighteenth century, the joyous body figured just as prominently. Today, joy is rarely represented, but not just in Judeo-Christianity.

...And when it comes to suffering, we're terribly unfair to those who came before us. We mustn't forget that when we're sick, when we have a headache, we simply take an aspirin. The modern pharmacy is sufficiently well stocked for us to overcome all kinds of pain. We hardly suffer any more, whereas for our parents, and before our parents, pain was ever-present. The most powerful king of France, Louis XIV, screamed in agony every day surrounded by the best doctors. As a result of this, pain figured prominently in the moral philosophy of our ancestors, because they needed a remedy against inevitable daily suffering. It was meant to help them, and we no longer understand this kind of morality precisely because we don't suffer any more.

You are pointing out there was period when we lived with pain and now, to a certain extent, we can mask that pain, so we have a new kind of relationship to pain and the body...

Yes, given that our relationship to pain has changed so much, it follows that our psychology has been transformed by this absence, or lessening, of pain (of course, I'm not suggesting that no-one suffers any more, suffering is still with us), and our relations with others have changed as well. Furthermore, we should remember that the number of blue-collar workers has decreased as the number of white-collar workers has increased. As a result, the body's relation to a painful work environment has also been transformed, and so in that respect too our relation to the world has changed.

This relates to something that I read in your book, Angels. *There is a whole range of images and voyages in that book. At one point, though, you talk about the bourgeois and the proletariat, and the ways we have come to understand their separation – as oppositional and so on. On that issue, we no longer have as much suffering in the sense of labour as in the past – in terms of blue-collar work, and the new transformations in white-collar work. But it's even more complicated now – because there is a decrease in physical work, but there are even more divisions and suffering – it's another kind of pain, and alienation...*

In the 1960s most philosophers still thought of work in terms of production. Their hero was the hero of Karl Marx, or of John Locke – it was Prometheus, the hero who stole fire from the Olympian gods and gave it to humankind. He was the hero of the industrial revolution. Hermes, on the other hand, was the Greek god of messengers, translators, merchants, or anyone who acts as an intermediary; and in the 60s I wrote five books bearing his name to show that we were entering a *new* social system dominated by messengers, messages and their distribution. I declared this the age of Hermes, and no longer that of Prometheus, because our world is now dominated by the god of communication. This again is about the changeover from a blue-collar workforce to a white-collar workforce, because white-collar workers are almost all messengers – their job is to write to people, telephone people, send faxes, emails and so on. Then a few years after that I decided that Hermes seemed very isolated amongst the gods, and that it would be more interesting, when talking about the world we live in today, to use the image of the billions of angels in heaven. So I wrote a book on angels as an attempt to read the most rigorous and scientific thinking on communication technology – and the kind of society that it implies – through the prism of an ancient and often forgotten philosophical tradition. The results demonstrate that angelology is a very interesting way of reading today's world. Moreover, since my book appeared, all sorts of books about the Internet and computers and so on have come out, and they all have a chapter about angels, because they've realised that *angelus*, in Greek, means messenger.

Let me tell you a little story to explain what I mean. For the last 22 years I've lived in Silicon Valley, in California, because I teach at Stanford University. One of my friends there had bought a factory which made those machines that link computers together. This was the beginnings of the Internet. And when I said to him, 'You're making cherubim', he didn't understand what I meant. At that point I explained that 'cherub' was not in fact a Hebrew word, but that the captive Hebrews in Babylon had adopted this Assyro-Babylonian word which referred to a four-legged creature – a bull with horns, the wings of an eagle, and the face of an old man with a white beard. There was a statue of this cherub in front of the Assyro-Babylonian temple, and it simply meant, 'Outside of this temple you remain an earthly, four-footed beast, like this bull. Enter, and you will have wings to fly through the air, like the eagle; finally, you will receive the wisdom of the old man'. This was a statue with three bodies: an animal body, a flying body, and the body of wisdom. It therefore connected three kingdoms. And if you connect three computers, you get a cherub. This allowed me to understand today's leading-edge technology. You can see how profound social and technological change can be understood through very ancient philosophy, and traditions we sometimes scoff at. In other words I had to wait for computers to come along to understand angels. And, conversely, it was through angels that I came to understand the web. You see?

The art of living

It's the art of living and invention that you mentioned earlier that provides an insight into the philosophical and technological revolutions that are possible. How is this art of living connected to the cherubs and the relationship between science, technology and ancient traditions? That is, the networks and connections between different organisms, and how that might provide a different sense of being – or a different ontological sense of understanding what it means to be human...

If I had to characterise my work, one word, one title, one subject would suffice. My work has only one title, one subject: connection. This is not just because I've taken an interest in questions of communication, or because I've written more than 15 books on the subject, but also because of a book I wrote during that time called *The Parasite* (which has been translated into English). Unfortunately the word 'parasite' doesn't have the same meanings in English that it does in French, where it also means the noise or static in a channel of communication. That sense of the word is absent from English, although it had it for 10 or 15 years during the nineteenth century, and then lost it. And so I've studied accidents of communication quite a lot – not just the networks, not just the messages, but also the accidents that befall the messages.

That noise in the channel of communication, or the 'background', is what inhibits or allows the connections between things? I mean, it is those 'accidents' and the joys that could carry the act of inventiveness, or the passage between different thoughts and objects?

Yes. And I have also written extensively on the connections between disciplines which, in the context of the university, have no links between them. I have tried to formulate a pedagogy that would account for the connections between scientific and literary cultures.[2] I did this because I'm so very preoccupied by the fact that people who study the social sciences know nothing of the physical sciences and *vice versa*, such that those who understand the world we live in understand little about humankind, and those who understand humankind know nothing of the world. At the moment I'm working on questions of biology which are equally bound up with problems of communication – communication between biochemical matter and life itself. What is life? What is thought? These are old questions of connectivity which were completely transformed by advances in biochemistry in the 50s.

I don't think it's an ontology we need, but a *desmology* – in Greek *desmos* means connection, or link. The word is used in medicine, but that doesn't concern us here. What interests me is not so much the state of things but the relations between them. I've concerned myself with nothing but relations for my whole life. Relations come before being. Just as Jean-Paul Sartre said that 'essence precedes existence', I say that 'relationships come before being'.

This idea of relations preceding being, and the point that you refer to earlier, of 'background noise', and the parasite – the noise that forms the background to our lives, and the channels of communication that are possible – makes me think about the connection or the relationship between things. You know, between living organisms and environments, the local and the global, and, from a social point of view, what obstacles can inhibit those relationships...

The question of noise is extremely interesting. For instance, if a car were to start up right now, while we were talking, we wouldn't be able to hear each other any more. So we can consider a dialogue between two or three people to be a fight against the noise which prevents that dialogue from taking place. It is therefore not enough that two interlocutors be engaged with one another; they must also be united against the noise, because noise is the principal enemy of dialogue. There are three of us here, right now: you speak English and I speak French, so there's a lot of noise between us, and the person fighting against the noise is the translator, because she is translating. So she is a part of the dialogue between the two of us. But this person might be either a good translator or a bad translator. If she's a good one she will clear up the noise, and become to a certain extent completely transparent, and she will lose her identity. She will be no more than a channel. But suppose she doesn't want to translate, or that she translates poorly, or that she has some stake in intercepting your message or mine, and all of a sudden you'll notice that the balance of power has tipped in her favour. It follows that the origins of power are bound up with the issue of obstacles to communication. One thing you'll always notice is that it's the intermediary in any given relation who has the most power. For instance, it is always the person who is between the consumer and the producer who makes the most money. The question of connection, noise, translation, intermediaries or obstacles is extremely important, not just in material terms of how the channel functions, but from the social point of view, for the question of how we communicate with each other.

Let me tell you a story. You're familiar with the infamous question of whether angels have gender? We tend to make fun of those philosophers from the Middle Ages who would debate the matter. Now take two lovers, a man and a woman, who aren't getting along for some reason or another. They ask someone to help them, to intervene. But the person who is there to help might seduce the woman, or the man. This third person will intercept the message between the two others. Therefore, to help them properly, this third person must be sexless – a very serious problem indeed. In other words, the question of whether angels have gender is the most fundamental problem of contemporary societies: who will act as intermediary, and how will this person act? This is the problem of noise.

*

The importance of communication and connection is also a question of 'peace' for you – I'm thinking of this on two levels, the importance of peace and solitude, *but also that one has to live in solitude to a certain extent. As a writer you spend a lot of time in solitude. What is the importance of this solitude, the necessity of solitude?*

I'd like to answer your question for a technical reason. Most philosophers today think that philosophy comes only from debate, discussion, dialogue and the monitored exchange of ideas. In such a scenario, philosophy is limited to the discourse exchanged within a group. As far as I'm concerned, dialogue is a perfectly noble occupation. I'd even go so far as to say that the more unlike me another person is, the happier I'll be, because I will learn new things. It's essential to relate to other people. As I said before, relations come before being, so I'm all for relationships. But in my opinion philosophy is not science, nor is it a discipline like others, and in order for the philosopher to achieve certain objectives, solitude is equally essential. In other words you need solitude to have the best intuitions about the real, the true – all the questions of philosophy. In many respects a philosopher who was constantly caught up in discussions and meetings would miss out on almost all of the most profound philosophical intuitions. In my opinion a philosopher must be alone at least half the time. It is solitude alone that enables dialogue with everyone else.

Turbulence of life – time, hope and chaos

I am grappling with the question of time in relation to the idea of noise… For me, the idea of communication, channels and noise relates to all that is the 'background', and the force of living which has to do with time, which you describe as being chaotic and turbulent. So what is the relationship with this time, invention, and hopeful connections to the world?

What we call 'chaos' today and what we called 'chaos' 30 years ago are different things. Why? Because 'chaos' is a Greek word which means 'to pour water', and is therefore related to a kind of disorder, like turbulence, which comes from running water. Today, however, the word 'chaos' points more to chaos theory, which was named – unfortunately, but it's too late to change it now – by people with little understanding of what chaos means. What these people call chaos theory is rather like what we call an initial value problem (*sensibilité aux conditions initiales* – awareness of initial conditions), where we cannot know precisely the initial conditions of any given phenomenon, and as a result cannot predict how that phenomenon will develop. The theory originated with Jules Henri Poincaré and has been further developed today. It pertains to almost all the physical sciences, and touches on the question of time.

Given the above theory, just how do we go about dealing with the question of time? You spoke of the living being a little while ago. You have a watch, and you live with that watch – in other words you get up and have breakfast, meals, go to work at more or less the same times, and so, as a living being, you live in time which is based on planetary orbits. This is the time of timepieces. This is the first kind of time. It is the time of society, it is physical time, it is what physics calls time with a small 't'. This time is practically circular. The fact that it is now 6 pm, a Wednesday, the 20th of September – these are things which have happened thousands of times before and will happen thousands of times again. This time is called reversible time. Secondly, you are young and I am very old, so you are beautiful and I am very ugly. Time, therefore, flows in such a way as to produce deterioration. This is the time of thermodynamics, which moves towards disorder. We live in that time also: I am going to die, and so will you – but much later of course! Then there is a third time, in which my daughter is better looking than me, and my granddaughter better looking than my daughter. This is the time of Darwin, where the evolution of living beings moves towards greater complexity and organisation, were the human brain is more highly developed than that of reptiles.

If life is the unity of the three times I spoke of – reversible time of the planets, or of timepieces; the time defined by the second principle of thermodynamics, that of decay and death; and finally evolutionary time – then joy can only come from the third, which corresponds to the evolution of life, its unexpected bifurcations, one generation's refusal to obey the preceding one, creative outbursts, intuitions of the new. If revolt takes the form of violence, then most of the time it merely imitates that which it opposes, and thereby falls back into the same repetitive time. Invention doesn't necessarily mean opposition, but freely taking another path.

Now, what is life? Life is the relation between these three kinds of time. I don't know how, but the fact that I am alive allows me to connect these three times, which have nothing to do with one another: the time of the planets, the time of heat and fire, and the time of increasing complexity. It is the connection between these three times which gives me an inkling of what life might be.

Postscript – on hope and a time for change

As we return to this conversation, one year later, how does the 'renaissance of hope' you spoke of and our perceptions of it provide the possibility for change? What do we need to do to address new hopes so we can move beyond despair and the violence of these times?

In the First World countries, the last half of the twentieth century gave rise to an evolutionary turn of events which my last book calls *hominescence* (a neologism based on 'adolescence' or 'arborescence'). With the atomic bomb our relation to death is no longer individual but collective, all of humanity now being threatened with annihilation. Our relation to the body has been radically transformed by medicine and pharmacology, our life expectancy prolonged, our very existence changed. Our relation to the world is still being transformed by the disappearance of agriculture as the predominant human activity; and finally, information technology is redefining our relations with others in space and time – and heralding a different manner of knowing, through artificial memory and intelligence. To sum up, when our relations to death, the body, the world, other people and knowledge change, humanity itself is transformed.

The real question today is the distance between those who benefited from this movement of hominescence, and those in Third World countries who haven't. In this disparity we find the greatest problem of the contemporary world. *Our hope is to close this gap.* If we do not, we will pay for this inequality dearly. But, however high the cost, it will always be less than that of a global conflict between the rich and the poor.

Translation during conversation by Louise Burchell; translation of written transcript by Peter Cowley.

Notes
1   The first book is called *Les cinq sens*, and the second book, *Variations sur le corps*.
2   For instance, in Michel Serres' book *The Troubadour of Knowledge (Le Tiers-instruit)*.

10
NAVIGATING MOVEMENTS
A conversation with Brian Massumi

When you walk, each step is the body's movement against falling – each movement is felt in our potential for freedom as we move with the earth's gravitational pull. When we navigate our way through the world, there are different pulls, constraints and freedoms that move us forward and propel us into life. But in the changing face of capitalism, media information and technologies – which circulate the globe in more virtual and less obvious ways – how do the constraints on freedom involve our affective and embodied dimensions of experience? That is, how do we come to feel and respond to life and reality itself when new virtualised forms of power mark our every step, when the media and political activity continually feed on our insecurities – for instance, when a political leader can deploy overseas troops to make a country feel safe and secure in the face of 'terror'? Our beliefs and hopes can be galvanised for this 'good', and as a tool for orchestrating attacks on 'evil' and threats to national security. Against this framework of despair that enacts our relations to the world – violence, terror and the virtual lines of capital flow – what are the hopes for political intervention?

Philosopher Brian Massumi and I explore the hopes that lie across these fields of movement; the potentials for freedom, and the power relations that operate in the new 'societies of control'. These are all ethical issues – about the reality of living, the faith and belief in the world that makes us care for our belonging to it. Massumi's diverse writings and philosophical perspectives radicalise ideas of affect – the experiences and dimensions of living – that are the force of individual and political reality. His writings are concerned with the practice of everyday life, and the relations of experience that engage us in the world, and our ethical practices. He is based in Montreal.

Movements – hope, feeling, affect

Mary: I'd like to think about hope and the affective dimensions of our experience – what freedoms are possible in the new and 'virtualised' global and political economies that frame our lives. To begin, though, what are your thoughts on the potential of hope for these times?

Brian: From my own point of view, the way that a concept like hope can be made useful is when it is *not* connected to an expected success – when it starts to be something different from optimism – because when you start trying to think ahead into the future from the present point, rationally there really isn't much room for hope. Globally it's a very pessimistic affair, with economic inequalities increasing year by year, with health and sanitation levels steadily decreasing in many regions, with the global effects of environmental deterioration already being felt, with conflicts among nations and peoples apparently only getting more intractable, leading to mass displacements of workers and refugees... It seems such a mess that I think it can be paralysing. If hope is the opposite of pessimism, then there's precious little to be had. On the other hand, if hope is separated from concepts of optimism and pessimism, from a wishful projection of success or even some kind of a rational calculation of outcomes, then I think it starts to be interesting – because it places it in the *present*.

Yes – the idea of hope in the present is vital. Otherwise we endlessly look to the future or toward some utopian dream of a better society or life, which can only leave us disappointed, and if we see pessimism as the natural flow from this, we can only be paralysed as you suggest.

Yes, because in every situation there are any number of levels of organisation and tendencies in play, in cooperation with each other or at cross-purposes. The way all the elements interrelate is so complex that it isn't necessarily comprehensible in one go. There's always a sort of vagueness surrounding the situation, an uncertainty about where you might be able to go, and what you might be able to do once you exit that particular context. This uncertainty can actually be empowering – once you realise that it gives you a margin of manoeuvrability and you focus on that, rather than on projecting success or failure. It gives you the feeling that there is always an opening to experiment, to try and see. This brings a sense of potential to the situation. The present's 'boundary condition', to borrow a phrase from science, is never a closed door. It is an open threshold – a threshold of potential. You are only ever in the present in passing. If you look at it that way you don't have to feel boxed in by it, no matter what its horrors, and no matter what, rationally, you expect will come. You may not reach the end of the trail but at least there's a next step. The question of which next step to take is a lot less intimidating than how to reach a far-off goal in a distant future where all our problems will finally be solved. It's utopian thinking, for me, that's 'hopeless'.

So how do your ideas on 'affect' and hope come together here?

In my own work I use the concept of 'affect' as a way of talking about that margin of manoeuvrability, the 'where we might be able to go and what we might be able to do' in every present situation. I guess 'affect' is the word I use for 'hope'. One of the reasons it's such an important concept for me is because it explains why focusing on the next experimental step rather than the big utopian picture isn't really settling for less. It's not exactly going for more, either. It's more like being right where you are – more *intensely*.

To get from affect to intensity you have to understand affect as something other than simply a personal feeling. By 'affect' I don't mean 'emotion' in the everyday sense. The way I use it comes primarily from Spinoza. He talks of the body in terms of its capacity for *affecting* or being *affected*. These are not two different capacities – they always go together. When you affect something, you are at the same time opening yourself up to being affected in turn, and in a slightly different way than you might have been the moment before. You have made a transition, however slight. You have stepped over a threshold. Affect *is* this passing of a threshold, seen from the point of view of the change in capacity. It's crucial to remember that Spinoza uses this to talk about the *body*. What a body is, he says, is what it can *do* as it *goes* along. This is a totally pragmatic definition. A body is defined by what capacities it carries from step to step. What these are exactly is changing constantly. A body's ability to affect or be affected – its charge of affect – isn't something fixed.

So depending on the circumstances, it goes up and down gently like a tide, or maybe storms and crests like a wave, or at times simply bottoms out. It's because this is all attached to the movements of the body that it can't be reduced to emotion. It's not just subjective, which is not to say that there is nothing subjective in it. Spinoza says that every transition is accompanied by a *feeling* of the change in capacity. The affect and the feeling of the transition are not two different things. They're two sides of the same coin, just like affecting and being affected. That's the first sense in which affect is about intensity – every affect is a *doubling*. The experience of a change, an affecting-being affected, is redoubled by an experience of the experience. This gives the body's movements a kind of depth that stays with it across all its transitions – accumulating in memory, in habit, in reflex, in desire, in *tendency*. Emotion is the way the depth of that ongoing experience registers personally at a given moment.

Emotion, then, is only a limited expression of the 'depth' of our experience?

Well, an emotion is a very partial expression of affect. It only draws on a limited selection of memories and only activates certain reflexes or tendencies, for example. No one emotional state can encompass all the depth and breadth of our experiencing of experiencing – all the ways our experience redoubles itself. The same thing could be said for conscious thought. So when we feel a particular emotion or think a particular thought, where have all the other memories, habits, tendencies gone that might have come at the point? And where have the bodily capacities for affecting and being affected that they're inseparable from gone? There's no way they can all be actually expressed at any given point. But they're not totally absent either, because a different selection of them is sure to come up at the next step. They're still there, but virtually – in potential. Affect as a whole, then, is the *virtual co-presence* of potentials.

This is the second way that affect has to do with intensity. There's like a population or swarm of potential ways of affecting or being affected that follows along as we move through life. We always have a vague sense that they're there. That vague sense of potential, we call it our 'freedom', and defend it fiercely. But no matter how certainly we know that the potential is there, it always seems just out of reach, or maybe around the next bend. Because it isn't *actually* there – only virtually. But maybe if we can take little, practical, experimental, strategic measures to expand our emotional register, or limber up our thinking, we can access more of our potential at each step, have more of it actually available. Having more potentials available intensifies our life. We're not enslaved by our situations. Even if we never *have* our freedom, we're always experiencing a *degree* of freedom, or 'wriggle room'. Our degree of freedom at any one time corresponds to how much of our experiential 'depth' we can access towards a next step – how intensely we are living and moving.

Once again it's all about the openness of situations and how we can live that openness. And you have to remember that the way we live it is always entirely *embodied*, and that is never entirely personal – it's never all contained in our emotions and conscious thoughts. That's a way of saying it's not just about us, in isolation. In affect, we are never alone. That's because affects in Spinoza's definition are basically ways of *connecting*, to others and to other situations. They are our angle of participation in processes larger than ourselves. With intensified affect comes a stronger sense of embeddedness in a larger field of life – a heightened sense of belonging, with other people and to other places. Spinoza takes us quite far, but for me his thought needs to be supplemented with the work of thinkers like Henri Bergson, who focuses on the intensities of experience, and William James, who focuses on their connectedness.

When you were just talking about Spinoza and the way you understand affect, I don't want to put a false determination on it, but is it a more primal sense of the capacity to be human and how we feel connections to the world and others? That's almost natural, to a certain extent...

I wouldn't tend to say it's primal, if that means more 'natural'. I don't think affective intensity is any more natural than the ability to stand back and reflect on something, or the ability to pin something down in language. But I guess that it might be considered primal in the sense that it is direct. You don't need a concept of 'mediation' to talk about it. In cultural theory, people often talk as if the body on the one hand, and our emotions, thoughts, and the language we use for them on the other, are totally different realities – as if there has to be something to come between them and put them into touch with each other. This mediation is the way a lot of theorists try to overcome the old Cartesian duality between mind and body, but it actually leaves it in place and just tries to build a bridge between them. But if you define affect the way we just did, then obviously it includes very elaborated functions like language. There's an affect associated with every functioning of the body, from moving your foot to take a step to moving your lips to make words. Affect is simply a body movement looked at from the point of view of its potential – its capacity to come to be, or better, *to come to do*.

Like I said, the directness I'm talking about isn't necessarily a self-presence or self-possession, which is how we normally tend to think of our freedom. If it's direct, it's in the sense that it's directly in *transition* – in the body passing out of the present moment and the situation it's in, towards the next one. But it's also the doubling of the body in the situation – its doubling over into what it might have been or done if it had contrived to live that transition more intensely. A body doesn't coincide with itself. It's not present to itself. It is already on the move to a *next*, at the same time as it is doubling over on itself, bringing its past up to date in the present, through memory, habit, reflex, and so on. Which means you can't even say that a body ever coincides with its affective dimension. It is selecting from it, extracting and *actualising* certain potentials from it. You can think of affect in the broadest sense as what remains of the potential after each or every thing a body says or does – as a perpetual bodily remainder. Looked at from a different angle, this perpetual remainder is an *excess*. It's like a reserve of potential or newness or creativity that is experienced alongside every actual production of meaning in language, or in any performance of a useful function – vaguely but directly experienced, as *something more*, a more to come, a life overspilling as it gathers itself up to move on.

What immediately comes to mind is something like anger. It's a very strong bodily experience, a 'heat of the moment intensity' – it doesn't seem to have a positive charge in some ways, you know, because it is often a reaction against something...

I think affective expressions like anger and laughter are perhaps the most powerful because they interrupt a situation. They are negative in that sense. They interrupt the flow of meaning that's taking place: the normalised interrelations and interactions that are happening and the functions that are being fulfilled. Because of that, they are irruptions of something that doesn't fit. Anger, for example, forces the situation to attention, it forces a pause filled with an intensity that is often too extreme to be expressed in words. Anger often degenerates into noise and inarticulate gestures. This forces the situation to rearray itself around that irruption, and to deal with the intensity in one way or another. In that sense it's brought something positive out – a reconfiguration.

There's always an instantaneous calculation or judgment that takes place as to how you respond to an outburst of anger. But it's not a judgment in the sense that you've gone through all the possibilities and thought it through explicitly – you don't have time for that kind of thing. Instead you use a kind of judgment that takes place instantly and brings your entire body into the situation. The response to anger is usually as gestural as the outburst of anger itself. The overload of the situation is such that, even if you refrain from a gesture, that itself is a gesture. An outburst of anger brings a number of outcomes into direct presence to one another – there could be a peace-making or a move towards violence, there could be a breaking of relations; all the possibilities are present, packed into the present moment. It all happens, again, before there is time for much reflection, if any. So there's a kind of thought that is taking place *in the body*, through a kind of instantaneous assessment of affect, an assessment of potential directions and situational outcomes that isn't separate from our immediate, physical acting-out of our implication in the situation. The philosopher C.S. Peirce had a word for thought that is still couched in bodily feeling, that is still fully bound up with unfolding sensation as it goes into action but before it has been able to articulate itself in conscious reflection and guarded language. He called it 'abduction'.

Right, right. Oh, that's like a kind of capture...

Yes, I think you could say that sensation is the registering of affect that I referred to before – the passing awareness of being at a threshold – and that affect is thinking, bodily – consciously but vaguely, in the sense that is not yet a thought. It's a movement of thought, or a thinking movement. There are certain logical categories, like abduction, that could be used to describe this.

I think of abduction as a kind of stealing of the moment. It has a wide range of meanings too – it could be stealing or it could be an alien force or possession...

Or it could be *you* drawn in by the situation, captured by it, by its eventfulness, rather than you capturing it. But this capture by the situation is not necessarily an oppression. It could be...

It could be the kind of freedom we were just talking about...

Exactly – it could be accompanied by a sense of vitality or vivacity, a sense of being more alive. That's a lot more compelling than coming to 'correct' conclusions or assessing outcomes, although it can also bring results. It might force you to find a margin, a manoeuvre you didn't know you had, and couldn't have just thought your way into. It can change you, expand you. That's what being alive is all about.

So it's hard for me to put positive or negative connotations on affect. That would be to judge it from the outside. It would be going in a moralising direction. Spinoza makes a distinction between a morality and an ethics. To move in an ethical direction, from a Spinozan point of view, is not to attach positive or negative values to actions based on a characterisation or classification of them according to a pre-set system of judgment. It means assessing what kind of potential they tap into and express. Whether a person is going to joke or get angry when they are in a tight spot, that uncertainty produces an affective change in the situation. That affective loading and how it plays out is an ethical act, because it affects where people might go or what they might do as a result. It has consequences.

Ethics, then, is always situational?

Ethics in this sense is completely situational. It's completely pragmatic. And it happens *between* people, in the social gaps. There is no intrinsic good or evil. The ethical value of an action is what it brings out *in* the situation, *for* its transformation, how it breaks sociality open. Ethics is about how we inhabit uncertainty, together. It's not about judging each other right or wrong. For Nietzsche, like Spinoza, there is still a distinction between good and bad, even if there's not one between good and evil. Basically the 'good' is affectively defined as what brings maximum potential and connection to the situation. It is defined in terms of becoming.

Navigations

This makes me think of your idea of 'walking as controlled falling'. In some ways, every step that we take works with gravity so we don't fall, but it's not something we consciously think about, because our body is already moving and is full of both constraint and freedom. I found it interesting because, in some other ways, I've been trying to think about another relationship – between perception and language – and it seems to me that 'affect' and this notion of body movement can provide a more integrated and hopeful way of talking about experience and language.

I like the notion of 'walking as controlled falling'. It's something of a proverb, and Laurie Anderson, among others, has used it. It conveys the sense that freedom, or the ability to move forward and to transit through life, isn't necessarily about escaping from constraints. There are always constraints. When we walk, we're dealing with the constraint of gravity. There's also the constraint of balance, and a need for equilibrium. But, at the same time, to walk you need to throw off the equilibrium, you have to let yourself go into a fall, then you cut it off and regain the balance. You move forward by playing with the constraints, not avoiding them. There's an openness of movement, even though there's no escaping constraint.

It's similar with language. I see it as a play between constraint and room to manoeuvre. If you think of language in the traditional way, as a correspondence between a word with its established meaning on the one hand and a matching perception on the other, then it starts coagulating. It's just being used as a totally conventional system for pointing out things you want other people to recognise. It's all about pointing out what everyone can agree is already there. When you think about it, though, there's a unique feeling to every experience that comes along, and the exact details of it can never be exhausted by linguistic expression. That's partly because no two people in the same situation will have had exactly the same experience of it – they would be able to argue and discuss the nuances endlessly. And it's partly because there was just *too much there* between them to be completely articulated – especially if you think about what was only there potentially, or virtually. But there are uses of language that can bring that inadequation between language and experience to the fore in a way that can convey the 'too much' of the situation – its charge – in a way that actually fosters *new* experiences.

Humour is a prime example. So is poetic expression, taken in its broadest sense. So language is two-pronged: it is a capture of experience, it codifies and normalises it and makes it communicable by providing a neutral frame of reference. But at the same time it can convey what I would call 'singularities of experience', the kinds of affective movements we were talking about before that are totally situation-specific, but in an open kind of way. Experiencing this potential for change, experiencing the eventfulness and uniqueness of every situation, even the most conventional ones, that's not necessarily about commanding movement – it's about navigating movement. It's about being immersed in an experience that is already under way. It's about being bodily attuned to opportunities in the movement, going with the flow. It's more like surfing the situation, or tweaking it, than commanding or programming it. The command paradigm approaches experience as if we were somehow outside it, looking in, like disembodied subjects handling an object. But our experiences aren't objects. They're us, they're what we're made of. We *are* our situations, we *are* our moving through them. We are our *participation* – not some abstract entity that is somehow outside looking in at it all.

The movement in language is important and it opens another door or window to perception. But I suppose, as intellectuals, there is the problem of the codification of language within critical discourse and theoretical writing – where that language can stop movement, and it can express everything in particular terms or methods that cut off the potential of understanding freedom or experience...

'Critical' practices aimed at increasing potentials for freedom and for movement are inadequate, because in order to critique something in any kind of definitive way you have to pin it down. In a way it is an almost sadistic enterprise that separates something out, attributes set characteristics to it, then applies a final judgment to it – objectifies it, in a moralising kind of way. I understand that using a 'critical method' is not the same as 'being critical'. But still I think there is always that moralising undertone to critique. Because of that, I think, it loses contact with other more moving dimensions of experience. It doesn't allow for other kinds of practices that might not have so much to do with mastery and judgment as with affective connection and abductive participation.

The non-judgmental is interesting, you know, because you are always somehow implicated in trying to make judgments... To not make judgments in critical thought is a very hard thing to do. It takes a lot courage to move in that direction, because otherwise...

Well, it requires a willingness to take risks, to make mistakes and even to come across as silly. A critical perspective that tries to come to a definitive judgment on something is always in some way a failure, because it is happening at a remove from the process it's judging. Something could have happened in the intervening time, or something barely perceptible might have been happening away from the centre of critical focus. These developments may become important later. The process of pinning down and separating out is also a weakness in judgment, because it doesn't allow for these seeds of change, connections in the making that might not be activated or obvious at the moment. In a sense, judgmental reason is an extremely weak form of thought, precisely because it is so sure of itself. This is not to say that it shouldn't be used. But I think it should be complemented by other practices of thought; it shouldn't be relied on exclusively. It's limiting if it's the only, or even the primary, stance of the intellectual.

A case in point is the anti-globalisation movement. It's easy to find weaknesses in it, in its tactics or in its analysis of capitalism. If you wait around for a movement to come along that corresponds to your particular image of the correct approach, you'll be waiting your life away. Nothing is ever that neat. But luckily people didn't wait around. They jumped right in and started experimenting and networking, step by step. As a result, new connections have been made between people and movements operating in different regions of the world, on different political levels, from the most local grass-roots levels up to the most established NGOs, using different organisational structures. In a very short period of time the entire discourse surrounding globalisation has shifted. Actually, not only surrounding it but inside its institutions also – it's now impossible for an international meeting to take place without issues of poverty and health being on the agenda. It's far from a solution, but it's a start. It's ongoing. That's the point: to keep on going.

The constraints of freedom

The idea of 'controlled walking' is a good example of what you were just talking about, in terms of the limitations on the self and the freedoms that are possible. But I am also thinking about it as relating to the idea of 'societies of control' – which you have written about. We now live in societies of control, so how do control and power in this new age also offer the possibility of freedom?

In physics there is a very famous problem that heavily influenced the development of chaos theory. It's called the 'three-body problem', where you have completely deterministic projectories of bodies constrained by Newtonian laws. For example, if you have two bodies interacting, through gravity for example, everything is calculable and foreseeable. If you know where they are in relation to each at one moment, you can project a path and figure out where they were at any given moment in the past, or at a time in the future. But if you have three of them together what happens is that a margin of unpredictability creeps in. The paths can't be accurately determined after a point. They can turn erratic, ending up at totally different places than you'd expect. What has happened? How can chance creep into a totally deterministic system? It's not that the bodies have somehow broken the laws of physics. What happens is interference, or resonation. It's not really discrete bodies and paths interacting. It's *fields*. Gravity is a field – a field of potential attraction, collision, orbit, of potential centripetal and centrifugal movements. All these potentials form such complex interference patterns when three fields overlap that a measure of indeterminacy creeps in. It's not that we just don't have a detailed enough knowledge to predict. Accurate prediction is impossible because the indeterminacy is *objective*. So there's an objective degree of freedom even in the most deterministic system. Something in the coming together of movements, even according to the strictest of laws, flips the constraints over into conditions of freedom. It's a relational effect, a complexity effect. Affect is like our human gravitational field, and what we call our freedom are its relational flips. Freedom is not about breaking or escaping constraints. It's about flipping them over into degrees of freedom. You can't really escape the constraints.

No body can escape gravity. Laws are part of what we are, they're intrinsic to our identities. No human can simply escape gender, for example. The cultural 'laws' of gender are part of what makes us who we are, they're part of the process that produced us as individuals. You can't just step out of gender identity. But just maybe you can take steps to encourage gender to flip. That can't be an individual undertaking. It involves tweaking the interference and resonation patterns between individuals. It's a relational undertaking. You're not acting on yourself or other individuals separately. You're acting on them together, their togetherness, their field of belonging. The idea is that there are ways of acting upon the level of belonging itself, on the moving together and coming together of bodies *per se*. This would have to involve an evaluation of collective potential that would be ethical in the sense we were talking about before. It would be a *caring* for the relating of things *as such* – a politics of *belonging* instead of a politics of identity, of correlated emergence instead of separate domains of interest attracting each other or colliding in predictable ways. In Isabelle Stengers' terms, this kind of politics is an *ecology of practices*. It's a pragmatic politics of the in-between. It's an abductive politics that has to operate on the level of affect.

So what does this political ecology involve?

To move towards that kind of political ecology you have to get rid of the idea as power, or constraint as power *over*. It's always a power *to*. The true power of the law is the power to *form* us. Power doesn't just force us down certain paths, it puts the paths in us, so by the time we learn to follow its constraints we're following ourselves. The effects of power on us is our identity. That's what Michel Foucault taught us. If power just came at us from outside, if it was just an extrinsic relation, it would be simple. You'd just run away. In the 1960s and 1970s that's how a lot of people looked at it – including myself. Drop out, stop following the predictable, straight-and-narrow path, and things like sexism will just disappear. Well, they didn't. It's a lot more complicated than that. Power comes up with us from the field of potential. It '*in*forms' us, it's intrinsic to our formation, it's part of our emergence as individuals, and it emerges with us – we actualise it, as it in-forms us. So in a way it's as potentialising as what we call freedom, only what it potentialises is limited to a number of predictable paths. It's the calculable part of affect, the most probable next steps and eventual outcomes. As Foucault says, power is productive, and it produces not so much repressions as *regularities*. Which brings us to the 'society of control' and to capitalism...

I was just going to ask you about that...

It is very clear that capitalism has undergone a major reconfiguration since the Second World War, and it's been very difficult to think through what that has been. For me the most useful way of thinking about it comes from the post-Autonomia Italian Marxist movement, in particular the thought of Antonio Negri. The argument is that capitalist powers have pretty much abandoned control in the sense of 'power over'. That corresponds to the first flush of 'disciplinary' power in Michel Foucault's vocabulary. Disciplinary power starts by enclosing bodies in top-down institutions – prisons, asylums, hospitals, schools, and so on. It encloses in order to find ways of producing more regularity in behaviour. Its aim is to manufacture normality – good, healthy citizens. As top-down disciplinary power takes hold and spreads, it finds ways of doing the same thing without the enclosure. Prisons spawn half-way houses, hospitals spawn community clinics and home-care, educational institutions spawn the self-help and career retooling industries. It starts operating in an open field. After a certain point it starts paying more attention to the relays between the points in that field, the transitions between institutions, than to the institutions themselves. It's seeped into the in-between. At this point it starts to act directly on the kinds of interference and resonation effects I was just mentioning. It starts working directly on bodies' movements and momentum, *producing* momentums – the more varied, and even erratic, the better. Normalcy starts to lose its hold. The regularities start to loosen. This loosening of normalcy is part of capitalism's dynamic. It's not a simple liberation. It's capitalism's own form of power. It's no longer disciplinary institutional power that defines everything, it's capitalism's power to produce variety – because markets get saturated. Produce variety and you produce a niche market. The oddest of affective tendencies are okay – as long as they pay. Capitalism starts intensifying or diversifying affect, but only in order to extract surplus-value. It hijacks affect in order to intensify profit potential. It literally valorises affect. The capitalist logic of surplus-value production starts to take over the relational field that is also the domain of political ecology, the ethical field of resistance to identity and predictable paths. It's very troubling and confusing, because it seems to me that there's been a certain kind of convergence between the dynamic of capitalist power and the dynamic of resistance.

The flows of capitalism

For me, this raises a question about the way capitalism does capture potential and organises itself. There are two issues I want to address: firstly, in relationship to the question of hope – human aspirations and hopes are directly related to capitalism today. The natural or 'potential of hope' is seized upon and is tied very much to a monetary system, economic imperatives or questions of ownership. Secondly, the relationship between hope and fear in capitalism. I think that hope and fear are part of the same equation...

I think they definitely are. It would help to try to talk a little bit more about the change in capitalism and what that constitutes, and then go back to that question. Thinkers like Negri say that the products of capitalism have become more intangible; they've become more information- and service-based. Material objects and physical commodities that were once the engine of the economy are becoming more and more peripheral, in profit terms. For example, the cost of computers keeps plummeting. It's difficult to make a profit from their manufacture because there's a mass of basically identical versions from different companies, and they're all pretty interchangeable.

Is that mass production in the usual sense, or a different notion of mass production?

It is a mass production but it leads to a different kind of production, because what can someone sell if they can't make a profit from the object? What they can sell are services around the object and they can sell the *right* to do the things you can do through the object. That's why copyright is such a huge issue. The capitalist product is more and more an intellectual property that you buy a right to use, not an object you buy outright. If you buy a software package, often you're not supposed to even make copies of it for yourself, like one for your desktop and one for a laptop. If you buy a book, you own an object. You can resell it, or lend it, or rebind it, or photocopy it for your own use. If you buy a software package, you're not so much buying an object, you're buying a bundle of functions. You're buying the right to use those functions, with all sorts of strings attached. You're basically buying the right to be able to *do* things, ways of affecting and being affected – word-processing capacities, image-capture and processing capacities, printing capacities, calculation capacities... It's at the same time very potentialising, and controlled. The 'cutting edge' products are more and more multivalent. 'Convergence' is the buzzword. When you buy a computerised product, you can do a lot of different things with it – you use it to extend your affective capacities. It becomes a motor force of your life – like a turbo charge to your vitality. It enables you to go farther and to do more, to fit more in. The way even older-style products are sold has something to do with this. You don't just buy a car, the dealers tell us, you buy a lifestyle. When you consume, you're not just getting something to use for a particular use, you're getting yourself a life. All products become more intangible, sort of atmospheric, and marketing gets hinged more and more on style and branding...

More meaningless?

Possibly, possibly – but not necessarily, because, if you think of style or branding, it is an attempt to express what we were talking about before as the sense of vitality or liveliness. It is a selling of experience or lifestyles, and people put themselves together by what they buy and what they can do through what they can buy. So ownership is becoming less and less important *per se*. Accumulation for accumulation's sake, or just to signal the ability to accumulate – 'conspicuous consumption' – belongs to an earlier phase. It's this *enabling* of experience that is taking over. Now, that enablement of experience has to be tended. Companies work very hard to produce brand loyalty. 'Fidelity programs' involving things like rewards points are everywhere. The product becomes a long-term part of your life, you're brought into a *relationship* with the company through fidelity programs, service networks, promises of upgrades, etc. The way you use the product is also more and more oriented towards relationship – the most seductive products produce possibilities of *connection*. 'Connectibility' is another buzzword. When we buy a product, we're buying potential connections with other things and especially other people – for example, when a family buys a computer to keep in touch by email, or when you get a computer for work and end up joining online communities. What's being sold more and more is *experience*, social experience. The corporation, the capitalist company, is having to create social networks and cultural nodes that come together around the product, and the product gets used more and more to create social networks that radiate out from it. 'Networking' was the buzzword in the 1980s, when this new kind of capitalist power was just coming into its own.

Marketing itself is starting to operate along those lines. There is a new kind of marketing called 'viral marketing' where specialised companies will surf the web to find communities of interest that have spontaneously formed. It started in the music industry, around fan networks for bands. They find a group of people who have a very strong affective attachment to a band or a performer that is very central to how they see themselves and to what they perceive as the quality of their life. They will network with them, offer them tickets or inside information, or special access, and in return the members of the group will agree to take on certain marketing tasks. So the difference between marketing and consuming, and between living and buying, is becoming smaller and smaller, to the point that they are getting almost indistinguishable. On both the production side and the consumption side it is all about intangible, basically cultural products, or products of experience that invariably have a collective dimension to them.

So as consumers we are part of the new networks of global and collective exchange...

Individual consumers are being inducted into these collective processes, rather than being separated out and addressed as free agents who are supposed to make an informed consumer choice as rational individuals. This is a step beyond niche marketing, it's relational marketing. It works by contagion rather than by convincing, on affect rather than rational choice. It works at least as much on the level of our 'indeterminate sociality' as on the level of our identities. More and more, what it does is hitch a ride on movements afoot in the social field, on social stirrings, which it channels in profit-making directions. People like Negri talk about the 'social factory', a kind of socialisation of capitalism, where capitalism is more about scouting and capturing or producing and multiplying potentials for *doing* and *being* than it is about selling *things*. The kind of work that goes into this he calls 'immaterial labour'. The product, ultimately, is us. We are *in*-formed by capitalist powers of production. Our whole life becomes a 'capitalist tool' – our vitality, our affective capacities. It's to the point that our life potentials are indistinguishable from capitalist forces of production. In some of my essays I've called this the 'subsumption of life' under capitalism.

Jeremy Rifkin is a social critic who now teaches at one of the most prestigious business schools in the US (talk about the capture of resistance!). Rifkin has a description of capitalism that is actually surprisingly similar to Negri's. And he's teaching it to the next generation of capitalists. It centres on what he calls 'gatekeeping' functions. Here the figure of power is no longer the billy club of the policeman, it's the *barcode* or the *PIN number*. These are control mechanisms, but not in the old sense of 'power over'. It's control in Gilles Deleuze's sense, which is closer to 'check mechanism'. It's all about checkpoints. At the grocery store counter, the barcode on what you're buying checks the object out of the store. At the automatic bank teller, the PIN number on your card checks you into your account. The checks don't control you, they don't tell you where to go or what to be doing at any particular time. They don't lord it over you. They just lurk. They lie in wait for you at key points. You come to them, and they're activated by your arrival. You're free to move, but every few steps there's a checkpoint. They're everywhere, woven into the social landscape. To continue on your way you have to pass the checkpoint. What's being controlled is *right of passage* – access. It's about your enablement to go places and do things. When you pass the checkpoint you have to present something for detection, and when you do that something registers. Your bank account is debited, and you and your groceries pass. Or something fails to register, and that's what lets you pass, like at airport security or places where there's video surveillance. In either case what's being controlled is passage across thresholds.

Society becomes an open field composed of thresholds or gateways, it becomes a continuous space of passage. It's no longer rigidly structured by walled-in enclosures; there's all kinds of latitude. It's just that at key points along the way, at key thresholds, power is tripped into action. The exercise of the power bears on your movement – not so much you as a person. In the old disciplinary power formations, it was always about judging what sort of person you were, and the way power functioned was to make you fit a model, or else. If you weren't the model citizen, you were judged guilty and locked up as a candidate for 'reform'. That kind of power deals with big unities – the person as moral subject, right and wrong, social order. And everything was internalised – if you didn't think right you were in trouble. Now you're checked in passing, and instead of being judged innocent or guilty you're registered as liquid. The process is largely automatic, and it doesn't really matter what you think or who you are deep down. Machines do the detecting and 'judging'. The check just bears on a little detail – do you have enough in your bank account, do you not have a gun? It's a highly localised, *partial* exercise of power – a micro-power. That micro-power, though, feeds up to higher levels, bottom up.

And this power is more intangible because it has no 'real' origin...

In a way the real power starts after you've passed, in the feed, because you've left a trace. Something has registered. Those registrations can be gathered to piece together a profile of your movement, or they can be compared to other people's inputs. They can be processed *en masse* and systematised, synthesised – very convenient for surveillance or crime investigation, but even more valuable for marketing. In such a fluid economy, based so much on intangibles, the most valuable thing is information on people's patterns and tastes. The checkpoint system allows information to be gathered at every step you take. You're providing a continuous feed, which comes back to you in advertising pushing new products, new bundlings of potential. Think of how 'cookies' work on the Internet. Every time you click a link, you're registering your tastes and patterns, which are then processed and thrown back at you in the form of flip-up ads that try to get you to go to particular links and hopefully buy something. It's a feedback loop, and the object is to modulate your online movement. It's no exaggeration to say that every time you click a link you're doing somebody else's market research for them. You're contributing to their profit-making abilities. Your everyday movements and leisure activities have become a form of value-producing labour. You are generating surplus-value just by going about your daily life – your very ability to move is being capitalised on. Deleuze and Guattari call this kind of capitalising on movement 'surplus-value of flow', and what characterises the 'society of control' is that the economy and the way power functions come together around the generation of this surplus-value of flow. Life movements, capital and power become one continuous operation – check, register, feed-in, processing, feedback, purchase, profit, around and around.

So how do the more 'traditional' forms of power operate? I mean, they don't disappear – they seem to gather more momentum...

Yes, this situation doesn't mean that police functions and the other old disciplinary forms of power are over and done with. Disciplinary powers don't disappear. Far from it. In fact they tend to proliferate and often get more vehement in their application precisely because the field that they are in is no longer controlled overall by their kind of power, so they're in a situation of structural insecurity. There are no more top-down state apparatuses that can really claim effective control over their territory. Old-style sovereignty is a thing of the past. All borders have become porous, and capitalism is feeding off that porosity and pushing it further and further – that's what globalisation is all about. But there have to be mechanisms that check those movements, so policing functions start to proliferate, and as policing proliferates so do prisons. In the US they're being privatised and are now big business. Now policing works more and more in the way I was just describing, through gatekeeping – detection, registration and feedback. Police action, in the sense of an arrest, comes out of this movement-processing loop as a particular kind of feedback. Instead of passing through the gate, a gun is detected by the machine, and a police response is triggered, and someone gets arrested. Police power becomes a function of that other kind of power, that we were calling control, or movement-based power. It's a local stop-action that arises out of the flow and is aimed at safeguarding it. The boom in prison construction comes as an off-shoot of the policing, so you could consider the profits made by that new industry as a kind of surplus-value of flow. It's a vicious circle, and everyone knows it. No matter how many prisons there are, no matter how many people they lock up, the general insecurity won't be lessened. It just comes with the territory, because for capitalism to keep going, things have to keep flowing. Free trade and fluidity of labour markets is the name of the game. So no matter how many billions of dollars are poured into surveillance and prison building, the threat will still be there of something getting through that shouldn't. Terrorism is the perfect example.

Yes. In thinking about this now – after our initial conversation and in this revision of it, post-September 11 – it adds another dimension to this surveillance.

All the September 11 terrorists were in the US legally. They passed. How many others might have? With this stage of capitalism comes territorial insecurity, and with territorial insecurity comes fear, with fear comes more checkpoint policing, more processing, more bottom-up, fed-back 'control'. It becomes one big, self-propelling feedback machine. It turns into a kind of automatism, and we register collectively as individuals through the way we feed that automatism, by our participation in it, just by virtue of being alive and moving. Socially, that's what the individual is now: a checkpoint trigger and a co-producer of surplus-values of flow. Power is now distributed. It trickles down to the most local, most partial checkpoint. The profits that get generated from that don't necessarily trickle down, but the power does. There is no distance any more between us, our movements and the operations of power, or between the operations of power and the forces of capitalism. One big, continuous operation. Capital-power has become *operationalised*. Nothing so glorious as sovereign, just operational – a new modesty of power as it becomes ubiquitous.

At any rate, the hope that might come with the feeling of potentialisation and enablement we discussed is doubled by insecurity and fear. Increasingly, power functions by manipulating that affective dimension, rather than dictating proper or normal behaviour from on high. So power is no longer fundamentally normative, like it was in its disciplinary forms – it's *affective*. The mass media have an extremely important role to play in that. The legitimisation of political power, of state power, no longer goes through the reason of state and the correct application of governmental judgment. It goes through affective channels. For example, an American president can deploy troops overseas because it makes a population feel good about their country or feel secure, not because the leader is able to present well-honed arguments that convince the population that it is a justified use of force. So there is no longer political justification within a moral framework provided by the sovereign state. And the mass media are not mediating anymore – they become direct mechanisms of control by their ability to modulate the affective dimension.

This has all become painfully apparent after the World Trade Center attacks. You had to wait weeks after the event to hear the slightest analysis in the US media. It was all heart-rending human interest stories of fallen heroes, or scare stories about terrorists lurking around every corner. What the media produced wasn't information or analysis. It was affect modulation – affective pick-up from the mythical 'man in the street', followed by affective amplification through broadcast. Another feedback loop. It changes how people experience what potentials they have to go and to do. The constant security concerns insinuate themselves into our lives at such a basic, habitual level that you're barely aware how it's changing the tenor of everyday living. You start 'instinctively' to limit your movements and contact with people. It's affectively limiting. That affective limitation is expressed in emotional terms – remember we were making a distinction between affect and emotion, with emotion being the expression of affect in gesture and language, its conventional or coded expression. At the same time as the media helps produce this affective limitation, it works to overcome it in a certain way. The limitation can't go too far or it would slow down the dynamic of capitalism. One of the biggest fears after September

11 was that the economy would go into recession because of a crisis in consumer confidence. So everyone was called upon to keep spending, as a proud, patriotic act. So the media picks up òn fear and insecurity and feeds it back amplified, but in a way that somehow changes its quality into pride and patriotism – with the proof in the purchasing. A direct affective conversion of fear into confidence by means of an automatic image loop, running in real time, through continuous coverage, and spinning off profit. Does anyone really believe Bush stands for state reason? It doesn't matter – there are flags to wave and feel-good shopping to do. Once the loop gets going, you've got to feed it. You can only produce more pride and patriotism by producing more fear and insecurity to convert. At times it seemed as though US government officials were consciously drumming up fear, like when they repeatedly issued terrorist attack warnings and then would withdraw them – and the media was lapping it up.

Yes.

Affect is now much more important for understanding power, even state power narrowly defined, than concepts like ideology. Direct affect modulation takes the place of old-style ideology. This is not new. It didn't just happen around the September 11 events; it just sort of came out then, became impossible to ignore. In the early 1990s I put together a book called *The Politics of Everyday Fear.* It dealt with the same kind of mechanisms, but it was coming out of the experience of the 1980s, the Reagan years. This post-ideological media power has been around at least since television matured as a medium – which was about when it took power *literally*, with the election of Reagan, an old TV personality, as head of state. From that time on, the functions of head of state and commander in chief of the military fused with the role of the television personality. The American president is not a statesman anymore, like Woodrow Wilson or Franklin Roosevelt were. He's a visible personification of that affective media loop. He's the face of mass affect.

Transitions

It is really important to understand affect 'after a society of ideology'. Ideology is still around but it is not as embracing as it was, and in fact it does operate. But to really understand it you have to understand its materialisation, which goes through affect. That's a very different way of addressing the political, because it is having to say that there is a whole range of ideological structures in place. Then there is that point you were talking about, the transitional passages that you pass through that capitalism is part of and manipulating – but it does have the possibility of freedom within it. It seems to me that to express how those affective dimensions are mobilised is the main ethical concern now...

It seems to me that alternative political action does not have to fight against the idea that power has become affective, but rather has to learn to function itself on that same level – meet affective modulation with affective modulation. That requires, in some ways, a performative, theatrical or aesthetic approach to politics. For example, it is not possible for a dispossessed group to adequately communicate its needs and desires through the mass media. It just doesn't happen. It wasn't possible for marginal interest groups like the anti-globalisation movement, before the Seattle demonstration, to do that simply by arguing convincingly and broadcasting its message. The message doesn't get through, because the mass media doesn't function on that level of the rational weighing of choices. Unfortunately the kind of theatrical or performative intervention that is the easiest and has the most immediate effect is often a violent kind. If windows hadn't been broken and cars hadn't been overturned in Seattle, most people wouldn't have heard of the anti-globalisation movement by now. That outburst of anger actually helped create networks of people working around the world trying to address the increasing inequalities that accompany globalisation. It was able to shake the situation enough that people took notice. It was like everything was thrown up in the air for a moment and people came down after the shock in a slightly different order, and some were interconnected in ways that they hadn't been before. Dispossessed people like the Palestinians or the people in Irian Jaya just can't argue their cases effectively through the mass media, which is why they're driven to violent guerilla tactics or terrorism, out of desperation. And they're basically theatrical or spectacular actions, they're performative, because they don't do much in themselves except to get people's attention – and cause a lot of suffering in the process, which is why they spectacularly backfire, as often as not. They also work by amplifying fear and converting it into group pride or resolve. The resolve is for an in-group and the fear is for everybody else. It's as divisive as the oppression it's responding to, and it feeds right into the dominant state mechanisms.

The September 11 terrorists *made* Bush president, they created President Bush, they fed the massive military and surveillance machine he's now able to build. Before Bin Laden and Al-Qaïda, Bush wasn't a president; he was an embarrassment. Bin Laden and Bush are affective partners, like Bush Senior and Saddam Hussein, or Reagan and the Soviet leaders. In a way, they're in collusion or in symbiosis. They're like evil twins who feed off of each other's affective energies. It's a kind of vampiric politics. Everything starts happening between these opposite personifications of affect, leaving no room for other kinds of action. It's rare that protest violence has any of the positive organising power it did in Seattle. But in any case it had lost that power by the time the anti-globalisation movement reached Genoa, when people started to die. The violence was overused and under-strategised – it got predictable, it became a refrain, it lost its power.

The crucial political question for me is whether there are ways of practising a politics that takes stock of the affective way power operates now, but doesn't rely on violence and the hardening of divisions along identity lines that it usually brings. I'm not exactly sure what that kind of politics would look like, but it would still be performative. In some basic way it would be an *aesthetic* politics, because its aim would be to expand the range of affective potential – which is what aesthetic practice has always been about. It's also the way I talked about ethics earlier. Felix Guattari liked to hyphenate the two – towards an 'ethico-aesthetic politics'.

*

For me the relationship you were discussing earlier, between hope and fear in the political domain, is what gets mobilised by the Left and the Right. In some ways the problem of more Leftist or radical thinking is that it doesn't actually tap into those mobilisations of different kinds of affects, whether it be hope, fear, love or whatever. The Left are criticising the Right and the Right are mobilising hope and fear in more affective ways. The Right can capture the imagination of a population and produce nationalist feelings and tendencies, so there can be a real absence of hope to counter what's going on in everyday life, and I think the Left have a few more hurdles to jump...

The traditional Left was really left behind by the culturalisation or socialisation of capital and the new functioning of the mass media. It seems to me that in the US what's left of the Left has become extremely isolated, because there are fewer possibilities than in countries like Australia or Canada to break through into the broadcast media. So there is a sense of hopelessness and isolation that ends up rigidifying people's responses. They're left to stew in their own righteous juices. They fall back on rectitude and right judgment, which simply is not affective. Or rather, it's anti-affective affect – it's curtailing, punishing, disciplining. It's really just a sad holdover from the old regime – the dregs of disciplinary power. It seems to me that the Left has to relearn resistance, really taking to heart the changes that have happened recently in the way capitalism and power operate.

Connections – belief, faith, joy

In a way, this conversation makes me think about the relation of 'autonomy and connection' that you've written about. There are many ways of understanding autonomy, but I think with capitalism's changing face it is harder and harder to be autonomous. For instance, people who are unemployed have very intense reactions and feelings to that categorisation of themselves as unemployed. And, in my experience, I'm continually hounded by bureaucratic procedures that tend to restrict my autonomy and freedom – such as constant checks, meetings and forms to fill out. These procedures mark every step you take... So to find some way to affirm unemployment that allows you to create another life, or even to get a job, is increasingly more difficult and produces new forms of alienation and 'dis-connection'...

It is harder to feel like getting a job is making you autonomous, because there are so many mechanisms of control that come down on you when you do have a job. All aspects of your life involve these mechanisms – your daily schedules, your dress, and, in the US, it can even involve being tested for drugs on a regular basis. Even when you are not on the job, the insecurity that goes with having a job and wanting to keep it in a volatile economy – where there is little job security and the kind of jobs that are available change very quickly – requires you to constantly be thinking of your marketability and what the next job is going to be. So free time starts getting taken up by self-improvement or taking care of yourself so that you remain healthy and alert and can perform at your peak. The difference between your job life and off-job life collapses; there are no longer distinctions between your public and private functions. Being unemployed creates an entirely different set of constraints and controls, but it is not necessarily completely disempowering. For example, a lot of creative work gets done by people who are unemployed or underemployed.

Yes, but it is also the intensity of those experiences that get categorised in one particular way – you either work or don't work. But the way it's lived out isn't like that at all. I'm not just thinking of myself here and my experience of unemployment. The feeling of despair doesn't have a way of being expressed in our cultures, except with the feeling that you're not doing the right thing, or you're not part of the society. It is about the relationship to commodities, really, because in a sense you are no longer in a position to market yourself or consume.

There is definitely an imperative to have a job and to be able to consume more and *consume better*, to consume experiences that in-form you and increase your marketability for jobs. There's definitely an imperative to participate, and if you can't you're branded, you don't pass any more, you can't get by the most desirable checkpoints.

Yes, like getting a credit card – or simply having money in your bank account.

But what I was trying to say is that there is no such thing as autonomy and decisive control over one's life in any total sense, whether you have a job or whether you don't. There are different sets of constraints, and, like we were saying before, freedom always arises from constraint – it's a creative conversion of it, not some utopian escape from it. Wherever you are, there is still potential, there are openings, and the openings are in the grey areas, in the blur where you're susceptible to affective contagion, or capable of spreading it. It's never totally within your personal power to decide.

Is that what you mean by autonomy and connection?

Well, there's no such thing as autonomy in the sense of being entirely affectively separate. When you are unemployed you are branded as separate, unproductive and not part of society, but you still are connected because you are in touch with an enormous range of social services and policing functions that mean you are just as much in society – but you are in society in a certain relation of inequality and *impasse*. It's a fiction that there is any position within society that enables you to maintain yourself as a separate entity with complete control over your decisions – the idea of a free agent that somehow stands back from it all and chooses, like from a smorgasbord platter. I think there can be another notion of autonomy that has to do more with how you can connect to others and to other movements, how you can modulate those connections, to multiply and intensify them. So what you are, affectively, isn't a social classification – rich or poor, employed or unemployed – it's a set of potential connections and movements that you have, always in an open field of relations. What you can do, your potential, is defined by your connectedness, the way you're connected and how intensely – not your ability to separate off and decide by yourself. Autonomy is always connective; it's not being apart, it's being *in*, being in a situation of belonging that gives you certain degrees of freedom, or powers of becoming, powers of emergence. How many degrees of freedom there are, and where they can lead most directly, is certainly different depending on how you are socially classified – whether you are male or female, child or adult, rich or poor, employed or unemployed – but none of those conditions or definitions are boxes that completely undermine a person's potential. And having pity for someone who occupies a category that is not socially valorised, or expressing moral outrage on their behalf, is not necessarily helpful in the long run, because it maintains the category and simply inverts its value sign, from negative to positive. It's a kind of piety, a moralising approach. It's not affectively pragmatic. It doesn't challenge identity-based divisions.

Well, that is the problem of charity. When you have pity for someone it doesn't actually change the situation or give them much hope. But the other side of that is what you were talking about before, the idea of 'caring for belonging'. There is such a focus on self-interest and the privatised idea of the individual (although this is changing through the new fields of capitalism and the economy) – the valorisation of the individual against more collective struggles. This project has been trying to think about different notions of being, and collective life. In your ideas of autonomy and connection there is also another understanding or different notion of care – 'belonging' and our 'relations' to ourselves and others. It involves some other idea of being that is anti-capitalist, and also a different notion of caring...

Well, if you think of your life as an autonomous collectivity or a connective autonomy, it still makes sense to think in terms of self-interest at a certain level. Obviously a disadvantaged group has to assess their interests and fight for certain rights, certain rights of passage and access, certain resources – often survival itself is in the balance. But at the same time, if any group, disadvantaged or otherwise, identifies itself completely with its self-interests it's living the fiction that it is a separate autonomy. It is missing the potential that comes from taking the risk of making an *event* of the way you relate to other people, orienting it towards becoming-other. So in a way you are cutting yourself off from your own potential to change and intensify your life. If you think of it in terms of potential and intensified experience then too much self-interest is *against* your own interests. You have to constantly be balancing those two levels. Political action that only operates in terms of the self-interest of identified groups occupying recognisable social categories like male/female, unemployed/employed have limited usefulness. For me, if they are pursued to the exclusion of other forms of political activity they end up creating a sort of rigidity – a hardening of the arteries!

Which leads to a heart attack or death, doesn't it!

So it seems to me, there needs to be an ecology of practices that does have room for pursuing or defending rights based on an identification with a certain categorised social group, that asserts and defends a self-interest but doesn't just do that. If you do think of your life potential as coming from the ways you can connect with others, and are challenged by that connection in ways that might be outside your direct control, then, like you are saying, you have to employ a different kind of logic. You have to think of your *being* in a direct belonging. There are any number of practices that can be socially defined and assert their interest, but all of them interact in an open field. If you take them all together there is an in-betweenness of them all that is not just the one-to-one conflict between pairs, but snakes between them all and makes them belong to the same social field – an indeterminate or emergent 'sociality'. So I'm suggesting that there is a role for people who care for relation or belonging, as such, and try to direct attention towards it and inflect it, rather than denouncing or championing particular identities or positions. But to do that you have to abdicate your own self-interest up to a point, and this opens you to risk. You have to place yourself not in a position but in the middle, in a fairly indeterminate, fairly vague situation, where things meet at the edges and pass into each other.

That's the ethics, isn't it?

Yes, because you don't know what the outcome is going to be. So you have to take care, because an intervention that is too violent can create rebound effects that are unpredictable to such a degree that it can lead to things falling apart rather than reconfiguring. It can lead to great suffering. In a way I think it becomes an ethic of caring, caring for belonging, which has to be a non-violent ethic that involves thinking of your local actions as modulating a global state. A very small intervention might get amplified across the web of connections to produce large effects – the famous butterfly effect – you never know. So it takes a great deal of attention and care and abductive effort of understanding about how things are interrelating and how a perturbation, a little shove or a tweak, might change that.

Yes, and there is a relation between this ethics, hope and the idea of joy. If we take Spinoza and Nietzsche seriously, an ethic of joy and the cultivation of joy is an affirmation of life. In the sense of what you are saying, even a small thing can become amplified and can have a global effect which is life-affirming. What are your thoughts on this ethical relationship in everyday existence? And in intellectual practice – which is where we are coming from – what are the affirmations of joy and hope?

Well, I think that joy is not the same thing as happiness. Just like good for Nietzsche is not the opposite of evil, joy for Spinoza (or 'gaiety' in Nietzsche's vocabulary) is not the opposite of unhappy. It's on a different axis. Joy can be very disruptive, it can even be very painful. What I think Spinoza and Nietzsche are getting at is *joy as affirmation*, an assuming by the body of its potentials, its assuming of a posture that intensifies its powers of existence. The moment of joy is the co-presence of those potentials, in the context of a bodily becoming. That can be an experience that overcomes you. Take Antonin Artaud, for example. His artistic practice was all about intensifying bodily potential, trying to get outside or underneath the categories of language and affective containment by those categories, trying to pack vast potentials for movement and meaning in a single gesture, or in words that burst apart and lose their conventional meaning, becoming like a scream of possibility, a babble of becoming, the body bursting out through an opening in expression. It's liberating, but at the same time the charge of that potential can become unbearable and can actually destroy. Artaud himself was destroyed by it; he ended up mad, and so did Nietzsche. So it is not just simple opposition between happy and unhappy or pleasant or unpleasant.

I do think, though, that the practice of joy does imply some form of belief. It can't be a total scepticism or nihilism or cynicism, which are all mechanisms for holding oneself separate and being in a position to judge or deride. But, on the other hand, it's not a belief in the sense of a set of propositions to adhere to or a set of principles or moral dictates. There is a phrase of Deleuze's that I like very much, where he says that what we need is to be able to find a way to 'believe in the world' again. It's not at all a theological statement – or an anti-theological statement, for that matter. It's an ethical statement. What it is saying is that we have to live our immersion in the world, really experience our belonging to this world, which is the same thing as our belonging to each other, and live that so intensely together that there is no room to doubt the reality of it. The idea is that lived intensity is self-affirming. It doesn't need a god or judge or head of state to tell it that it has value. What it means, I think, is accept the embeddedness, go with it, live it out, and that's your reality, it's the only reality you have, and it's your *participation* that makes it real. That's what Deleuze is saying belief is about, a belief in the world. It's not a belief that's 'about' being in the world; it *is* a being in the world. Because it's all about being in *this* world, warts and all, and not some perfect world beyond, or a better world of the future, it's an empirical kind of belief. Ethical, empirical – and creative, because your participation in this world is part of a global becoming. So it's about taking joy in that process, wherever it leads, and I guess it's about having a kind of faith in the world which is simply the *hope* that it *continue*... But again, it is not a hope that has a particular content or end point – it's a desire for more life, or for more to life.

11
A 'Cosmo-Politics' – Risk, Hope, Change
A conversation with Isabelle Stengers

Every moment of life has a hopeful potential – if we can assume that our existence in the world is not dependent on guarantees but on situations or events that make them possible. Take, for instance, the risk you might take in a new relationship with a lover or friend – you cannot foresee the outcome but you have a certain trust that can sustain its possibility. Who knows if the friendship or love will last? But we can reflect on the experience and the feelings that allow us to take risks and to experiment – the laughter and joy in the face of uncertainty. These experiments move us towards a greater possibility in life, and the potential to live, feel and experience it. But what other risks can we take – in personal, critical or social terms – when we are confronted by a new relation, event or problem which requires creativity and invention? It is a hope and risk in thinking itself.

Building on her work in the field of science, and its connections with life and politics, Belgian philosopher Isabelle Stengers and I reflect on an 'ecology of practices', and the kinds of gratefulness in thinking, where action, freedom and invention create the possibility for transformation. This is a different kind of political ecology, where the 'cosmos' becomes a landscape for thinking and feeling – outside of individual ways of seeing the world, and in the potential *for connecting with others. This is about an adventure in life and thinking – the events and relationships that could emerge in scientific, cultural and political practices. And it is about where political actions and activities – unforeseen and unknown – can meet to create other kinds of questions and resistance in the rapid pace of our globalised world. Isabelle Stengers lives in Brussels, and her philosophical writings and reflections in science have revolutionised ideas of 'risk' and the adventures required in thinking. Her work evokes a radical politics for new kinds of critical and cultural dialogue.*

Adventures in thinking

Mary: There is an element of hope in all kinds of creative risks that we can take in life. I want to ask you about this hope, and how it connects to a 'political ecology' – your ideas on the relations between life, science and politics – the possibilities and risks we need to take to think, feel and live in this world.

Isabelle: I would say that the adventure of thinking is an adventure of hope. What I mean by 'adventure' is adventure as creative enterprise, in spite of the many reasons we have to despair. We have all the reasons we wish to despair – to think is to succeed in not following those reasons, one way or another. Thus I would say that hope is the difference between *probability* and *possibility*. If we follow probability there is no hope, just a calculated anticipation authorised by the world as it is. But to 'think' is to create possibility against probability. It doesn't mean hope for one or another thing or as a calculated attitude, but to try and feel and put into words a possibility for becoming. In my work, for instance, in the philosophy of science, what is obvious is the blindness of most scientists to what escapes their paradigms, and the fact that the whole scientific education and organisation of work enforces that blindness. I could describe that at length... and despair, because it accounts for a strong probability for scientists to be unable to participate in a transformation of the way sciences address common problems, or even understand its necessity. I will not deny it but describe it, starting from the point that the whole education and organisation of work are needed in order to enforce that blindness. It is not an essential property of scientific practices – they could possibly change, and they could change without a miracle. Hope is not about miracles. It is about trying to feel what lurks in the interstices. Alfred North Whitehead – a philosopher I love, the one who wrote about the adventure of reason itself as an adventure of hope – remarked that life is always lurking in the interstices, in what usually escapes description because our words refer to stabilised identities and functioning.

I think probability is often associated with the idea of chance – so do you mean something else here, not simply an encounter with chance?

The word 'chance' has many meanings. You may speak of chance when you calculate the chance *for* something to happen, and then it is probability. For instance, you can throw the dice and have a succession of nine and six – and you can calculate the probability of this particular succession. Probability is very interesting for all the people who spend time describing systems they can define, but the behaviour of which they are unable to predict. But it implies a closed definition, through a set of variables which will remain invariant. It is thus a static notion. I call *possibility* what cannot be calculated *a priori*, because it implies the fact that the very description of the system itself *can* change. And you cannot calculate that. Possibility is connected to what I call 'events'. Again, the term 'event' may have many meanings – the one I retain emphasises the difference an event makes between the past, which made it possible but which cannot explain it, and the future which, one way or another, takes it into account. Such a future may, and often will, include telling the past in such a way that it seems to explain the event. The philosopher Henri Bergson is the one who best described this 'retroactive power' of what happens.

So this creates the possibility of hope and the creativity to think and feel in life? You have written about the importance of the capacity to feel in critical practices, and that there needs to be a certain tenderness in understanding different traditions of thought (for instance, in revisiting thinkers like Karl Marx and Sigmund Freud). I am wondering about that – the capacity to feel and what that capacity enables, I mean it does enable a kind of hope, I think...

For me, feeling and thinking are closely connected, but their connection refers to experience as something which is not first 'my' experience, but which is forced by encounters which make me think and feel. It may be encounters with things or with people, or with ideas. When I read Whitehead I do not just examine his ideas; they oblige me to feel and think in a new way. They induce 'events'. Whitehead himself made the distinction between dead ideas and ideas which are alive – at school many ideas we try to transmit are dead. In the best case, students will learn them and then forget about them. They are devoid of any importance because they do not force you to think and feel. You cannot have *true thinking* without feeling – and what that means is that true thinking is about transforming yourself. But the very fact that we can be transformed by what we encounter, or what we participate in, is a matter of hope. It does not promise anything, but no-one has the right to say 'I know how things are, they are hopeless'.

This hope is an unknown quality, right, because you can't predict the outcome?

Yes. I think so. And you cannot tell someone else that he or she should have this experience, to think and feel. As a teacher I can only celebrate with a student the fact that I 'felt' it was happening for him or her, and hope the one for whom what I produced were dead ideas will encounter other opportunities. Again, the only thing which can be understood, explained and amply justified is *despair*. I think hope is itself an event, and you must just be grateful as long as you are able to hope or to think.

You mean as a form of discovery and creativity?

Creativity is everywhere, in each of our cells, in the very fact I am able to transform the sounds you made into a question I can understand. We usually take that as normal – you speak, I answer – but it is a quite extraordinary feat! Whitehead, like many philosophers, said that philosophy begins in wonder, and he adds, against many philosophers, that at the end, when philosophic thought has done its best, the wonder remains. To be grateful is a way of remembering wonder, and to wonder. That is, to be grateful is not because someone has given me something, it is a form of impersonal gratefulness, a gratefulness not for this factual, sorry world but for this world full of interstices where what may become possible is lurking. It is important to be grateful because it is a way to resist those who tell us to bow down in front of reality, of facts as they are, and those who will try to explain away events when something *did* happen which succeeded in producing open thinking and a change in direction. I am, for instance, grateful for all those people in Seattle who gave us a new sense of hope, and for the ones who now go on resisting in the US while everybody tells them to shut their mouths and accept the patriotic mobilisation. When I speak about what is happening now, I always try to keep alive and celebrate this powerful sense that something else is possible that was born, for so many people, in Seattle.

Yes, gratefulness in the sense of the appreciation of the gifts of thinking and living that provide us with some hope. For you, does that also mean the idea of event, as you explained before, the possibility of life which reveals itself through a situation? Is this related to your idea of risk?

Yes. In fact risk is something which I first learnt from scientists, because I saw that when they were *alive* with their practice it made them quite interesting, passionate and not arrogant. This is why I refuse denouncing science – it is a beautiful adventure, the centre of which is not power as such, but the passion of creating new possibility. I can struggle against the link between science and power, and I love scientists when their work cannot be dissociated from hope and the risks their hope entails. This risk is not associated with danger; it is their own ideas they then put at risk, and they do it because of the hope that something new could be produced. And the beauty of it, when and only when a scientific practice is alive, is that they certainly hope to have their ideas succeeding, but if, and only if, those ideas did indeed produce a new and reliable link with the world as they address it. The creation of such a link is always an event, something they hope for but cannot master or decide. I know it may appear as a somewhat romantic description, but again it is important not to deride it – because our world would be poorer and still more dangerous if we had still more scientists despairing and cynically submitting to bureaucratic, methodological norms, where the only risk you take is a colleague saying your statistics are wrong, and so on.

So risk is part of life – that adventure of thinking. But what about that in terms of faith – you've spoken about the problem of being a 'faithful witness' to something, for instance, in a scientific experiment?

I say a ' reliable witness'. Scientific experiments are not about faith, they demand that what is produced and observed can reliably testify for an interpretation against all others, that it can resist severe tests intended to show that what has been observed could be interpreted in another way. For instance, if we speak about the new kinds of beings science has produced, electrons for instance, we cannot say physicists have faith in the existence of the electron. They do not think that they can define the electron *as it is*, they just affirm that the electron has reliably testified for its own existence through their experiments. This is an event. If we can speak of faith, for the experimental scientist, it is the faith that if they try hard enough they should be able to get reliable witnesses, to produce those kinds of events again and again, and this faith is the very motor of experimental science. But it becomes very dangerous when you leave experimental science as such, and the term reliable *changes* to mean something which will satisfy methodological norms. For instance, you have reliable statistics in sociology, but this has nothing to do with an event, since you remain rather free to interpret those statistics as you wish.

But faith doesn't have to produce witnesses, right? The possibility of hope would be a different kind of faith?

If I were to use faith it would be more like what Spinoza has said, that we don't even yet know what the body is able to do – we simply don't know.

Yes, as a living, breathing and feeling body...

And I really think that we do not *know* what people are able to do together, and that is the adventure. I always close a book as soon as I find that the author says 'we now know' that something is impossible, because people are unable to do that... For instance, all those who defend the rules of the market will say there is no other possibility, history has shown what happens when you try to escape those rules. I do think it may well be that our human history will be cut short, and we will never know what could have been possible, but even if that happens it will not be the 'truth' of our history. Nobody may claim the final truth about what humans are capable of. Life is an adventure, and indeed some adventures have a bad end, but the end is not the moral of the adventure. So I have the faith that we cannot say, 'Sorry, we have learnt from our history and we can no longer hope this or that'. I am much more experimental than that. It may be that all the lessons of history are lessons about some kinds of simplification that failed, mistaken simplifications. We can certainly learn from our mistakes, as Karl Popper wrote, but in order to try again, not to hurry to definitive conclusions. For me, as a daughter to the Western tradition, it is very important to say that we are unable to produce any conclusion from our history, because it means resisting to the most obvious conclusion – we have won, we are the model for all people. We have only very timidly begun to face the fact that there are other populations and traditions that also exist and that we cannot ignore them, or define them as bound to become like us. We are only beginning to *feel* the kinds of problems which are *hopefully* waiting for us if we take seriously that we are not alone on the planet – that our traditions are not the 'thinking head of humanity'. Till now, in many presentations of an innovation, you could read the nice claim that 'since the dawn of humanity, man believed this or that, or hoped for this or that, or wondered if this or that, and now "we" can provide the answer'. So changing these kinds of ideas about ourselves demands a lot of imagination, because we have to work against all the words and stories which tell us we are the thinking head of humanity. We believe that others just believe and that we know.

Other kinds of dreaming – invention and hope

I'll come back to belief in a moment, but the idea of always being in a 'hurry' is important. You believe that life has to be 'slowed down', and that 'progress' is always about moving too fast. So, I think, that the idea of power having to be slowed down is interesting and, in terms of hope, it may be an anti-capitalist idea in a way – because what happens if we slow down the processes of rapid change?

Well, slowing down is truly an anti-capitalist idea, since the force of capitalism is an abstract motion forward, the ongoing invention of new abstractions and new definitions of what is a *resource*, what is to be exploited, and what profits can be made. Capitalism is terribly inventive and one of its conditions is that nobody can take the time to seriously ask about the consequences of what it invents, beyond profit-making. It is always a matter of speed, being faster than the others, claiming the right to be fast. I really think that what holds together the capitalist adventure is *speed*. Also capitalism is a process of mobilisation – a term which is originally a military one. The very problem when you mobilise an army is that nothing may slow down its motion – you have a binary judgment, what the army needs, and everything which may be an obstacle against this motion. You know all the *mots d'ordre* about nobody being able to arrest progress, which are used against everybody who wants to wonder about consequences. It is interesting to just imagine what would happen if we did slow down mobilisation. For instance, each time a government wanted to mobilise its army to go to war, what if they had to go to each village and explain to each mother, daughter and sister the reason why the war is needed, how come it could not be avoided, the reason why it is worth their men to go to their death. And then the village would discuss and decide. But now we have an army of professionals, and the US has invented the zero-death policy, so the problem is avoided.

But, perhaps because I am a woman, I cannot forget what women did probably feel, their impotence when the cry resounded, their despair at not being able to slow things down. But the same problem comes again and again with each capitalist invention, each new definition of what is a situation. My dreams and hopes are turned towards any process which would get people interested in the consequences coming together and becoming able to impose their questions, objections, counter-propositions. It is possible – but it would not be a miracle, because I deeply think that taking an active interest in what interests your life and your future may become a habit. If ever it did happen, people would truly wonder how we did accept so many things, telling us that 'they know best' or that 'we are unable to change things anyway'.

Do you think that the anti-globalisation movements would be part of this slowing down process?

Well, yes, I think so. I am surprised and happy when I remember that five years ago most people thought that there was nothing to be done. In Europe it began with the '*mouvement Attac*', in favour of the Tobin taxation of finance speculative operations. I am not among those who would say that such a taxation is the solution, but its success is in having many, many people beginning to think in terms of the possible slowing down, and imagining there is something which could be done... and thus learning about this world where people tell them it is not possible. But slowing down is not only about capitalism. It is about giving a chance to the event, to the encounters which have you feeling and thinking. For instance, at the university I work at, I am part of the creation of a small initiative which we call philosophical workshops. In these workshops we try to produce a collective process of thinking amongst us. In order to achieve this we have to produce games and rules, the aim and success of which is to slow down the questions/answers process in order for people not just to express what they were thinking anyway but to feel their thought becoming part of the collective adventure. When you go too fast you do not feel the possibility of new creations, new connections. The rules we invented are meant to make it impossible for anybody to be able to posit him or herself as 'I know what I think', in order for thought to emerge from a kind of collective stammering.

As for speed, I am impressed by the fact that capitalist speculation today needs young people and rejects them as soon as age makes their experience a bit more concrete, as soon as they slow down and start to think. I mean you have to be very young to play all those financial games without thinking for one minute what the stakes are and consequences of the game. Capitalism works like this – grabbing an opportunity and reacting as soon as possible to it. It is completely abstract thought and fits very, very nicely for young people, for whom it is fun. So, in a very strange way, a good part of our common future is in the hands of young people who are playing with it without a thought. It looks like science fiction, but we are *in* science fiction.

For me, slowing down is the condition for what I still call 'progress'. From that point of view, I would emphatically say I am not post-modern. What I mean by this is that the idea that we have to leave the ideas of progress behind is a too easy solution, much too easy. Because, as I said before, I think we still have the great challenge ahead, which is to learn that as Western people, including post-modern Western people, living in nice universities and publishing in sophisticated journals, we are not the only people in the world. We have to work in our own tradition, our own way of feeling, and not renounce progress – 'Sorry, we were wrong'. We cannot just leave the game, because the whole world is now poisoned by our games. But we should be cautious with progress, utterly disentangle it from mobilisation, when you quietly destroy what you define as an obstacle to progress. And this is a test for everybody. The idea of progress as authorising the destruction of what would slow it down has also infected anti-capitalist oppositional forces, for instance when they accepted that capitalist destructions, 'destroying the old world', did open the path to socialism. Maybe it is because I am a woman – again, I have always rejected this kind of abstraction, abstracting away the victims because they had no place in the socialist future anyway. I do not mean it as an essentialist view, but women have traditionally been outside of this abstract form of progress, but as soon as you slow down – and women have contributed to this process in different ways – many, many things become interesting.

I guess this is part of the anti-globalisation movements too. It is hard to know exactly where they'll go, and that's the interesting thing about slowing down, change and 'progress' in your sense of the word.

Politicians are furious because they are not 'serious', they refuse to play the game, to enter into calculations, to accept 'probabilities'. I am not overly optimistic but what they do is the only thing to be done, and they have already succeeded in a very important way – nothing has changed but the very description of the situation has changed, and this is the event. I have no real reason to be optimistic, but I would say that I do hope that people get *hope* and think they may succeed. The interstices of change are opening up. What will happen we don't know – new avenues can be closed down violently by many means – but the point is that they have opened and people are starting to think again.

And that's what is interesting too, because there are many political movements – it's not just one group, you know, the workers against the capitalist and so on; there are green groups, people for refugees – a diverse range of people under the banner of anti-globalisation movements. But maybe that's the wrong term to incorporate this diversity?

 Well, I think what the term means is rather clear. Now one says '*alter-mondialisation*' and that's right – the movement itself is at a planetary level. But what is interesting to me is that this diversity knows and values its own diversity. And I guess I am an anarchist in the sense that to *think* is to think against power which always demands we accept things as they are. But it is not sufficient to think 'against', or to try and define some fixed point around which to organise the opposition, a frontal opposition. I mean the older worker position understood itself in those terms, and they were cheated because, as soon as they took this static position, they were included in the capitalist definitions and played around. Thus the point now is to celebrate diversity and care for it. We need to recognise a strong difference between unity, as a condition for mobilisation, and convergence. Learning to converge is a new idea, and as such it is an 'event', and I try to think in those terms. I won't say at last we have found the right way to struggle against capitalism, but the older, more figural position is part of the past, and the new resistances are a matter of hope.

Hope in the sense of finding how different movements converge...

Well, not trying to find the principle which would force diversity to converge but *converging as a process* – as a real-time, demanding, creative process. For instance, there is now the problem of violence in protests, and I have received a text by the anti-globalisation protester and neo-pagan witch Starhawk, who has been involved in non-violent activism for decades now, and has been involved in training protesters well before Seattle onwards in non-violent actions. Some of her work comes in the form of fictional stories about how this form of non-violent activism could prevail even in an openly violent situation, but she is now struggling in order not to have the more violent forms of protest, the Black Block, being *ostracised*. She wrote that they are needed, that they should be welcome, even if it makes everything more complicated. Her writings are truly political texts in that sense and I feel happy to be alive at the same time as her.

In what way do you mean this violence not being ostracised?

Well, we know that it is the very strategy of power to divide non-violent and violent activism, to have them opposing each other. So we have to be smarter than that, be aware of the need for clever and intelligent co-existence. And always remember that the Black Block so-called violence is nothing compared to that of the cops. The matter is not to demand a unifying principle which would be stronger than the divergence, but to learn how to work together not in spite but through the divergence. As Starhawk wrote, this first needs feeling and the acknowledgement that the movement would be poorer without the Black Block, and then and only then can we start learning.

But all through the last century and into this new one it has been a learning process, and this learning process – for better or worse we don't know yet – is producing its effect... its tentative effect. And we should take it seriously, not just read the news and wonder if 'they' will achieve something. I accept and try to think with what Starhawk wrote: 'We don't know if we will succeed, but we know that if we fail now, maybe we will never have the force or resources to begin again'. Time is running against us.

*

Your idea of the 'event' and the more traditional Marxist positions we discussed earlier – of smashing the capitalist system, and the limitations of trying to find some 'true' or utopian change that will provide the end point for all struggles – offer possibility. The idea of slowing down and also of convergence is a new vision of time itself, which is not about hoping for something to come in the future, but hope in the present. You have written about the idea of a 'shameful present' and the need to open out the time we are living in. I want to explore that connection with the notion of time and hope.

The kind of hope I would associate with what I just said is that, while opposing capitalism, those people now do not accept 'hurry'; they pay attention to diversity, convergence and all those kinds of ethical issues about how to 'behave'. This stance takes on the true meaning of ethics, which is *how to behave*. Confrontation, we should accept now, after a century of it, is dangerous if it demands that we forget about what could slow us down, and asks us to accept an abstraction – that is, capitalism is responsible for everything, so the struggle should be the general solution for everything. Crushing capital or destroying capitalism or whatever is a dream, but as such it is not a very interesting dream, because nobody on earth is able to imagine what we would do if that suddenly happened. We live in a very complicated world; we have to learn and become able to dream other dreams, rather than the simplifying ones which are so useful for mobilisation.

So struggling is a learning process, as I suggested, and it is about empowering ourselves to *think together*, and to try not to postpone the 'good' for after the struggle – the two should be connected. I feel part of that struggle now and I don't feel part of the political opposition movements that I knew in Europe years ago. Perhaps, in the US, it was different because there were those connections between resisting the Vietnam War and cultural adventures. We did not know in Europe the story was going on, but for people like Starhawk it has gone on for more than 30 years. In Europe it was much more a confrontational politics, and I was unable to accept the way it demanded submission in the name of the cause. Here you have the difference between hope and faith that I try to make. I was not able to accept belonging to movements which – at least this is what I felt – would ask that in the name of a faith you become a bit less than what you could be and think that you keep silent your doubts and disagreements. It is not a matter of thinking that my freedom is above everything; I am just convinced that this way is wrong because it creates no concrete feeling of hope, knowing though experience that tomorrow could be different. For me what is important is the invention of practical and, I would say, spiritual ways of coming together that make you feel that because of the others you are becoming better, stronger, more free than what you would be alone. In contrast with faith, hope is not for a future in the name of which we should sacrifice ourselves. No, it must be born from the very collective process as it *happens*. We should never sacrifice anything in the name of tomorrow – because it is poison.

So where would something like individual freedom come in there – you don't aim for this idea of individual freedom, you work for it?

Yes, I think that individual freedom by itself is a rather empty word, because the individual as something in itself is a fictional construct and a dangerous one. Becoming, producing new thoughts and feelings, living new experiences did not have to wait for this strange idea – 'You are free'. Freedom, if we have to use this word, is not an individual property, an attribute of human being as such, but it is not an empty word either. You can crush somebody's freedom, we do it every day at school, everywhere, when you separate him or her from the process, personal or collective, through which he or she becomes able to think and feel. Becoming able is not a spontaneous activity— it comes in the connections that emerge through traditions and with others – we don't just exist 'freely'. Thus, you are never the owner of what you become. As a philosopher I am indebted to my tradition, to other philosophers and to many non-philosophers I did encounter, for what I did become, whatever the judgment one can produce about it. But I feel I am privileged because I was certainly wounded and diminished but not destroyed by my world. I was able to cultivate some interstices and not just despair and conform. Also I think that scientists, when their work makes them alive, give us a good example of individuals becoming able to live interesting thoughts because of the constraints enforced by the collective to which they belong. The idea of an isolated scientist, free to invent, to look for truth, is a poor idea. An isolated scientist is unhappy, he or she has failed and is in danger because of this failure, many of them become what can be technically described as 'mad scientists', claiming they have got a truth the nasty world refuses to accept. The scientists are alive because of their whole tradition, their colleagues and the possibility of producing something new in a concrete way – not in an absolute way – something which will make a difference for their colleagues. It is only when they address the public that they speak about what they did as if it was to interest to everybody, as if it was stemming from a universal source, rationality as opposed to opinion. Those kinds of statements are empty – the point is that they fear that if they speak about the very singular adventure they belong to, the public will conclude that it is just professional conventions, as with the legal system.

For me the political and spiritual practices associated with non-violent activism are the best example of practical freedom, which is about becoming able to participate with others and being indebted to others for this becoming. They understood that the activist non-violent stance was a very difficult one. The police would try and induce violence. It is rather easy because it is much harder *not to* throw stones than to throw them. So they needed a process of decision to go into action that would enable, empower them to resist provocation, to keep their stance when challenged directly by confrontation and violence. They created a decision-making process the aim of which was to empower eventual disagreements, to resist the temptation to conform. This is what I would call a 'spiritual' invention. And it has strong constraints. For instance, you should never tell anyone that his or her position is wrong – everyone is gathered around the problem, and it is in producing and creating the problem that people can also become. It is possible only because of the hope they share in a consensus-producing process. Such a consensus is what I call an event. It is important to celebrate such events, the demanding achievement they are. So I would say a consensus being created in this way is a cosmic event. It is something new in the cosmos.

The 'cosmos' meaning the very act of producing something new that resonates beyond a narcissistic or individual self-interest?

Well, yes, it has nothing to do with what physicists study and everything to do with hope. It is in fact very simple. As soon as we act in a way that implies we believe a contradiction could be solved – not ignored or forgotten but solved by creating a new understanding of the situation – we imply that we do not live in an arbitrary, blind world, that whatever the world is, our definitions must admit and affirm it. This includes the possibility and importance of relevant novelty – not blind novelty, relevant novelty. As soon as a mathematician starts thinking that a problem can be solved if she tries hard enough, she is presupposing a cosmos. So, to return to Starhawk, she is a thinker of hope, not faith. She wrote that there are many, many struggles to come and hard ones too, but that Seattle was a victory and that it is important to feel it, to tell about it, to celebrate it. We have the right to know about our own victories and to celebrate them because, whatever the end result, which nobody knows, the hope they create is empowering and is part of the process. They are cosmic events.

Cosmo-politics – believing in the world

Well, I would like to ask about your idea of the cosmos as a politics, and the idea of belief. You've written that 'we know that we can no longer believe' – so what is the relationship between a 'cosmo-politics' and this 'disbelief', in a way? For me, it is a problem of belief in terms of the Western tradition and how it imposes itself on other cultures...

Well, I cannot speak of belief in general terms, because it all depends on who is speaking. Belief often appears in rationalist and scientific thought as 'now we know' while before 'we did believe' or 'people did believe such and such'. This opposition between 'now we know' and 'before there was only belief' brings the idea that one way or an other belief is linked with illusion, or at least subjective convictions, as opposed to objective knowledge. It is then normal that objectivity destroys belief. For instance, people believed that the earth was the centre of the universe, and now we know that is not the case – or they believed that 'man' was the king of the animal kingdom, or that people were the master of their own mind. I am struggling against this kind of opposition.

You mean the idea that now we do know and so we discredit past traditions and other forms of belief?

Well, yes, but it is not to conclude that at the end of it everything is 'nothing but' belief. When you say 'forms' you allude to something which should be the most important point. It is not just a kind of indifferent diversity – you have your beliefs, I have mine. Just imagine a biologist saying that the different kinds of living beings are 'nothing but' different ways of increasing the production of entropy on earth... What I am struggling against is the opposition which puts every belief in the same basket, then discussing if the other basket is full of objective knowledge or, as some post-moderns would claim, just empty. This opposition, as Bruno Latour emphasised, leads us to destroy without even knowing what we destroy. We are at war, and present it as a 'pedagogical' operation – 'they' are to learn that what makes them different is only a matter of belief, which they are free to hold as long as they keep them private, as long as it does not interfere with universal 'civilisation'.

Thus I have to be prepared to face a scientist of good faith, who will say, 'I am sorry but it is true that the earth is orbiting the sun – it is the truth, and every other position is just belief'. Scientific practices certainly give the impression that we have truly produced a knowledge which is different, and can be opposed to other belief systems. My idea of cosmo-politics is part of this; it is trying to tell the story in another way, and a way which would emphasise that the scientist is not wrong, but that the kind of knowledge he or she claims is indeed a different knowledge – answering to different constraints. It is not superior; it is different – you cannot put into a hierarchy what you cannot compare. The very important differences – the knowledge that the earth is orbiting the sun – define what matters for scientists and for the technical processes of innovation which developed in symbiosis with sciences. But other things matter, and matter as much. And it is not only a question of respecting local traditions or human-centred perspectives. The physicist who tells about the laws of Newton will be proud to conclude that there is nothing special with the earth, and that it is the objective truth. But what he or she nicely forgets is that the questions this conclusion answers are very peculiar questions, which were produced on earth, at a given epoch in the history of mankind. We always forget that there is never an answer without a question, and that new questions never displace other questions; they are added to the others. The physicists' questions have a peculiar character: when they have the answer they are tempted to forget about the questions, to reduce the question to the occasion at which an objective knowledge was discovered. But for other forms of knowledge, not forgetting about the question is of a crucial importance. For me it is the case with philosophy: the answer matters less than the interest of the question – ancient questions already asked by Plato, or new questions our epoch obliges us to create.

In a way I've tried to work towards some kind positive pluralism, but it's an enigmatic pluralism because it is not a question of plural human point of view about the same reality – if it was only that, science would always have the last word, since what is specific with science is the demand that answers can be detached from human interests and questions. So scientific reality is not reality, but the selective grasping of those aspects of reality that are able to satisfy that demand. My hope is that scientists would be able to present themselves as representative of those aspects. It would not diminish their achievements but would produce a civilised version of what they achieve, a version which would not imply they are the only one to speak in the name of reality. I tried to show that it is possible to tell another story about scientific practices that are now associated with knowledge against belief, a story which is *at least as* interesting. I do not try to disenchant science but to enchant it in quite another way. It is my way of having 'life' lurking in the interstices, here the interstices of science.

When I worked with scientists I was never tempted to tell them how they should do what they are doing. I am much more interested in looking and trying to understand something about what they are doing and what they are producing. I do not think you can intervene directly inside scientific practices – or any other living practices, by the way. Where there is life there are boundaries. But I think that practices may change through their 'relation' with other practices, because a boundary is not a barrier; it connects the inside and the outside. If the outside changes so will the inside, but not as a function of the outside, in its own manner. So you cannot intervene *within* but you can try to produce a difference by struggling for scientists not to judge away, as mere opinion, what is outside their boundaries. The same for scientific fields. Many physicists and chemists judge away the question of life as some kind of complicated physico-chemical problem, the ideal understanding of which would refer to interactions among molecules, and biologists judge away human sciences as just waiting for a biological understanding of the functioning of the brain. A total lack of imagination is at the basis of scientific reductionism.

But they may become curious. When my science students begin taking interest in the diversity of scientific practices, *they get curious* and ask me lots and lots of questions. For instance, what is it to do psychology or sociology; how do they do it? So what they ignore and *do not even think could be interesting* is also part of what it is to be a disciplinary scientist. There is a cultivated lack of imagination for the outside which can and must be denounced without denouncing science. It is not needed for the scientific work; it is needed for getting disciplined scientists.

So this is what I call an 'ecology of practices' – it is about how different forms of knowledge and cultural practices work, but it is also the relation between what is happening and the way it defines itself in relation with others, or the way it represents those others. It is not concerned with individuals but with practitioners. I do not ask that scientists as people become better or more enlightened, I ask that practices stop ignoring each other, stop creating practitioners judging away what escapes their questions.

Now that is truly a collective, and it is also about the realm of non-judgmental forms of thinking. I mean, you are not imposing a judgment right from the beginning – you are open to the relation between often disparate knowledges? But what about belief and faith here, religious or otherwise... a belief that may not be an insult to ourselves and others...

Yes, well, this is a much more general problem. We are overfed with critical thought, thinking we have achieved something when demonstrating that belief or faith is addressed to something which is created by the believer. As Bruno Latour qualified it, we are professional anti-fetishists, and we feel quite rightful in destroying any fetish, both in the name of religion and in the name of scientific rationality. So, in fact, science and monotheistic religions are strongly correlated; they are part of the same story, a story of purification and destruction – our story.

What I see as possible, and hopeful, is if this story can be put at *risk* as systematically correlating truth and war. It is a fact that scientific truth may be presented as detached, and scientists would not achieve them if they were not practitioners, attached to their practices. As for religion, there is a beautiful sentence by Gilles Deleuze and Felix Guattari in their last book, *What is Philosophy?*, that says the problem has changed. It is no longer 'Does God exist?'; it is 'How to be for the world?' So the problem is no longer to believe in God, but to believe in the world.

I'm thinking about the connection between hope, belief and faith. What you are saying is that you have to believe to a certain extent in what is happening – in life and politics, as it is happening. In terms of your collective idea and the processes that come out of a real political event or a real situation, how does that come back to feeling, you know, in what makes us human? In some ways it has to have an element of faith that you can believe – which isn't about reliability, but is about believing in the world, don't you think?

Yes. I guess it is always so important to keep in mind that whenever we speak about what it is to be a human, what makes us human, we are always speaking as attached to our story, we do not speak in the name of all humankind. The question of what makes us human cannot have a unique answer, because it is the central question for many diverging traditions. More precisely, if I get one answer it would mean that 'we' have succeeded destroying all others. As I said before, we are not alone in the world, and other populations produce their own strength and faith by completely different means. And, you know, as a woman I feel this quite strongly. It has only been very recently that women have been allowed in universities, that they may be recognised as philosophers and all that. I am part of my tradition. I cannot get out of it; it would be an empty wish. But I am daughter of a tradition which till recently excluded its daughters from public thinking, and I am free to keep alive the souvenir of this, and thus belong to it in a slightly different way. This tradition has produced me, with my strengths and my weaknesses, with my imagination and my lack of imagination, and whatever I do will be what this tradition was able to produce. But as a woman I am part of an unknown produced by this tradition, and very often I think that we have just begun experimenting the differences that women, with their specific memories, will be able to do.

So taking a risk is learning how we embody our knowledges and learning to work with that?

I think new inventions or creations are not about replacing the old with the new, but adding to the old, producing new articulations. Again, it does not diminish the achievements of sciences but it directly puts into question what I call modernist science – not modern but modernist – those sciences that cannot be separated from the insulting way they define what they address. Because they want to mimic experimental sciences, and strictly separate the scientist who is asking questions and the 'object' which answers, many human sciences are insulting, defining what they address as 'weak', explainable through submission to opinion, social determination, irrational beliefs. That's why it is important to imagine what a 'human' science could be that would accept another link with experimental science that is being put at risk by what you address. The first consequence would be that there is no possible science when you address people as 'weak' – for instance, accepting to answer strange questions because they accept that you, as a scientist, must know better. Then the possibility for science and the political production, of empowered collectives being able to put at risk the way they are described, would become crucial. For instance, a feminist is someone that scientists can learn from, because she has been produced by a movement which enables her to recognise and deride any question which identifies her in a pejorative manner. The same with gays, and in the past with politically organised workers. The point is not that scientists have to accept whatever those empowered people tell them, the point is that learning from them is their chance to put their preconceived ideas at risk. I am quite interested by the way American Indians put to good use anthropological knowledge and turn it into a political weapon. They learned about us while we did think we were producing an objective knowledge about what defines them. The beautiful problem for human sciences, the problem for which we need a production of knowledge, is not what determines people or explains the way they think and feel, but the kinds of processes which may transform weak, isolated people into a collective able to invent its own position, its own strength. Again this is what I have called an 'event'. That is, we cannot think before something happens; if we anticipate it – if we claim we know beforehand what will take place and how – we destroy it, even by our goodwill. But this does not mean that we cannot learn from those processes, and also accept that we can learn from empowered people only. Again, I rejoin Bruno Latour, who wrote that trying to make a sociology of sciences may be a true starting point for sociology, because at last sociologists have to address people who are not impressed, who do not hesitate to tell them their questions are wrong and are beside the point.

But it comes back to what you said earlier, about a different type of consensus that comes out of real situation...

Yes, when an empowered group accepts your description as your own – it is not what interests them most, your interests are yours – but accepts it nevertheless as interesting and relevant, it is a kind of consensus. You did not put yourself in the place of the people you describe – it should never be done – but you succeeded in achieving a link between their interests and yours.

Is that where the relations come in?

Yes, the creation of such relations are events. I can never say to another person, 'Well, if you agree with that, *then you must*...' The 'then', if it must exist, must be created at each step, around each new problem that arises. The logic of the 'then' only rules when everybody agrees on everything. But our tradition gave a dangerous power to logic. We are the kings and queens of the 'then'. It leads us to claim we have the power to know what someone should do or think as if we were in his or her place.

*

I have been exploring the idea of revolution in relation to hope, political hope – as well as revolutions in thinking. And, in some ways, if you are working around problems that have come out of real events, that to me is a kind of revolution. I am thinking of your discussion of an 'ecology of practices' and the relation between different political spaces and movements, so where might revolution and hope fit in there?

Ah, revolution, well – it is a difficult word because in itself it is quite a modern invention. It is charged with the idea that we have to detach ourselves from the past for a new tomorrow, and this is a proposition that often communicates with a very strong and dangerous abstraction – for instance, the importance of getting a victory in struggles against capitalism or whatever, and then we will be free. We can't say once we get a victory then we will have time to learn how to coexist – no, we will never have time if we say it is for tomorrow. I think that the creation of new living habits is a constructive and positive process, and it is never too early to begin.

That's where the slowing down comes in?

That's where the slowing down comes in – you can create new habits only by slowing down, because new habits also mean new feelings, new interests, new possibilities. So the idea of revolution can be very dangerous if we think, for instance, that when we have gotten over this capitalist moment we will be able to turn to the Africans and say, 'Now that our common enemy is defeated, nothing should divide us'. If we keep our present habits, we will go on destroying them, destroying their 'absurd' beliefs which keep preventing them from becoming just like us... So I am a bit afraid of what revolution means, that it would mean that we have become the masters of our story, but I do think there is no possible peace as long as we frame the meaning of the world within the capitalist domain.

For me, one problem for today – if we do not wish what we call revolution to turn into a catastrophe, and if we wish to begin resisting today, not waiting for the revolution – is the problem of why did we resist so weakly the capitalist redefinition of our practices? Why were we so vulnerable to capitalism? For me, to struggle against capitalism cannot be separated from that problem. It was already Whitehead's position: why did so many people, good people, honourable people, who had no direct interests in capitalism, accept that those redefinitions were the very condition for progress? And he argues that the nineteenth century invented the 'professional', a new kind of people defined by the strange fact they glorify in their lack of imagination, in their ability to serve progress along one definite path, ignoring anything else. Just think of academics who sometimes seem to think that the whole fate of the world is suspended to their disagreement with their next colleagues, or to the biologists who are convinced that if they produce nice genetically modified organisms the problem of hunger will be solved. For Whitehead it was urgent that we try and change the habits of thinking and feeling which are stabilised already at school, then by the media, by the easy way, everywhere, you win an argument by freely judging away what does not interest you. I would say, nearly a century later, that it is still more important. When I read what they call 'thought experience', I must conclude that Anglo-Saxon philosophers have become true professionals. And I believe, as does Whitehead, that those habits of thought made and still make the way for capitalist redefinitions: indifference is the key; each may be the victim, but others do not care.

For me such habits will not disappear by themselves, but can be modified only through new appetites, new living interest. The problem is not to be worked through in a reflective way – reflection is only the opportunity for each academic to try and be more critical, more clever, more sophisticated than his, and unhappily her, colleagues.

So how do we work that through?

Well, working it out means changing the habits of thought.

Of thought and feeling? I mean, it is really about how we connect and relate to the world, since it is a world full of alienation and despair. And I suppose that would be the ethical responsibility of an intellectual?

The term 'intellectuals' was produced at the time of the Affaire Dreyfus in France, and it was meant as an insult against Dreyfusards, people defending Dreyfus – they were meddling in what did not concern them, they should leave the Dreyfus case to justice. If judges had concluded Dreyfus was guilty, he was guilty. In a way our world since Seattle is full of 'intellectuals' – people learning how to meddle into affairs which are decided at a superior level, higher than political or democratic decisions. People are judged away as 'fuzzy', because they do not have a well-defined program, by true professionals, by those who know that economic markets are too serious a business to be a matter of political discussion. I probably feel an ethical responsibility, but I most certainly feel the crucial importance of events which produce 'active passions' and appetites, becoming able to explore and feel in another way, to learn from other people who have become able to say 'no', who find ways to force us to think and feel in front of a situation we tolerate while we 'know' we should not. In my turn, I try to help those people to whom I feel indebted.

To open out the risk...

And never accept answering the question power people always ask so-called intellectuals: 'What would you do if you were in our place?' I am not in your place! And it is not by chance. A society where I would occupy any kind of power position and still think and feel as I do would be a completely different society, with different problems and different ways to solve them. Many people think that, since the problems are so urgent, nobody is entitled to intervene if she or he has not a ready-made, realistic counter-proposition. Part of me is not truly optimistic – there are indeed urgent problems, maybe still more urgent than we think. Indeed, the kind of processes which may induce or create hope are slow ones, while producing hate and despair is quick and rather easy. I cannot ignore the rate at which hate and despair are produced in our world; I can but understand it.

And maybe that is hope?

Well, if it is hope, it is, as I began, hope against probability. The difference between speed and slowness makes a pessimistic position the probable one. But in order to think, hope is technically required. Not hope for a miracle, against the sad truth about reality. There is no truth in speed – the fight is not against something which would be a reality, that of man or of history. Even if this history turns into a catastrophe, as is probable, it is not a question of its essence, of a fate, and thus it is not a matter of faith in something beyond our history. This is why hope and thinking are technically related, because it is not fighting against reality but against probability, which is something completely different.

Risk, laughter and joy

One of the other threads I have been working through in my conversations has been joy. For you, is there some connection between hope, joy and your idea of risk?

There is some connection between risk and intensity, but joy is still something else. I think there may be elation, and laughter, when you feel an 'event', and it makes you alive. Laughter is also part of what you can learn— learning not to be afraid, learning how to laugh in front of professionals who ask you what you would do in their place... But it is not joy in the sense we have come to understand it. I guess joy is part of our culture, and it is as near to a religious experience as we can go. It is also associated by some philosophers, like Spinoza, to wisdom, getting beyond the appearances, feeling free from the harm they do because they harm the unwise only. Joy then refers to feeling connected with the cosmos, whatever the cultural definition of the cosmos. We can certainly produce this connection through other means than religion, redemption and salvation, but it is quite another kind of event.

Yes, and we don't always 'need to suffer' or renounce life to experience joy. I think that life – in all its despair, difficulty and alienation – can be affirmative, and joyful. I mean, hope is about this joy...

For me, I keep associating joy with renunciation but it is not a suffering, a sacrificial renunciation. It is, again, renunciation as an event – you do not lose anything; in fact, you feel that what you had was some kind of an addiction... This is a most personal event. There are traditions which propose a path, but it is never an easy path, and it is full of advice – do not look too hard for your goal; do not take it as a goal you should achieve, take it as a gift which may happen but which you will never earn. In this way it can also be associated with love, because love is never easy, and it can quite easily turn into an addiction. Joy is, one way or another, the experience of being free from the many poisons we hold so dear. But you're never free yourself, you can help the process, you do not command the event.

Yes, I guess for me it is important to find other ways to love and experience joy. I mean we are all tied to habits of thought and thinking about love, and relations to the world which lead us into spirals of despair. But perhaps the real joy is to find new words, new languages, and new freedoms to love and be loved. And that is a real risk... And of course there is the love required in taking a risk in intellectual terms as well...

Yes. But risk should always refer to a concrete experience. For me it is extremely dangerous when one says, 'I am able to risk everything'. I guess nobody who has reached what I described through joy and wisdom would ever claim that. When a practitioner in any field of intellectual inquiry claims it, it is criminal. For instance, if a psychoanalyst says, 'I know about the unconscious, and thus I would not hesitate taking into analysis someone coming from another culture', this is a sheer professional statement. It means that what is important is my professional interest, which is relevant even for people who live in countries where gods, ancestors or spirits are part of life. In fact you do not take any risk, but you put the other at risk in the name of your professional certainty – you can even develop beautiful theories in order to legitimate your claims. Most theories in human sciences legitimise the possibility of judging others without even meeting them.

I have spoken of risk at length, but I would emphasise the strong relation between being able to take risks and belonging. If the risks you take are not related to what attaches you, they turn into the abstract power of 'deconstructing' everything, which is a kind of addiction. I would say that scientists take chances, take risks, but they can take these risks because they have roots in their community; they have togetherness and trust in the fact that their colleagues will evaluate what you did, accept a well-taken risk. It is a bit paradoxical because we usually identify risk and being detached, having nothing to lose, belonging to nothing. This is a romantic view and also a dangerous one. As I remarked, I never tell, or even feel like telling, a scientist what he or she should do. As a philosopher I do not risk anything; the risks are theirs. What I can understand with scientists is the way they are attached, the way they belong – that is, their fears, dreams, ambitions. What I cannot share is the kind of risk a scientist will be able to take, because I can understand the way they belong but I belong to something else. So it is the risk you cannot share, you see? You can understand the grounding for a risk, but you cannot say, 'In your place, I would take that risk'. That is what I mean about the relations between different practices, thoughts and traditions. If somebody takes a risk, you may be part of the reasons why she did it but the reasons are hers. You can only be grateful for the event.

And this is something that I link to the question of diplomacy – which is about the risks of war and peace. Diplomacy means that in such and such a situation war is the normal thing to do, but that it may be possible that peace has a chance. In other words, peace is possible not probable. When you have a police operation, peace is what you enforce. Today many wars are in fact police operations, pedagogical operations. 'They' will learn how to behave. It is easy to put yourself in the place of people having to face a zero-death war: stop fighting or you will be crushed. No place for diplomacy here, because diplomacy presupposes a peace to be invented, not the weak part bowing down in front of the strongest part. I think of the diplomat as a figure of inventing peace as an event. And a diplomat will never say to another diplomat, of the adverse camp, 'In your place I would do this or that'. They know they cannot share their risks because those risks are related with what the population they belong to will be able to accept, the risks this population will accept to take. If there is a practice where hope is important it is diplomacy – hope and not faith, because it is a matter of becoming able, not of 'seeing the truth'.

An important point here that makes diplomacy possible is the difference between sense and meaning. When you have a war situation, when 'This means war', there cannot logically be a place for peace – it is a matter of winning or being defeated. But the diplomats are the ones who can play between meaning and sense. You try and risk keeping the sense while a small modification of meaning may produce a possible articulation in the place of the contradiction from which war did follow, logically. But the population to which the diplomat belongs must accept this modification, must accept that sense has been preserved while meanings have been modified, and this is a risk for this population. If they refuse, the diplomat has failed; she can even be called a traitor. So the risks the diplomat is able to take depends on the trust she has in the population to which she belongs. Trust is always the condition of experimentation, of taking chance. Trust must be created for things to change.

Epilogue

The most interesting question I have been asked after writing this book is, 'Now that you've explored hope, are you more hopeful?' In some ways, I don't really know how to respond. This book emerged in one of the most despairing and 'hopeless' periods of my life – with the death of a close friend, the ending of a relationship, unemployment, and lack of faith in the political process. Looking at it now I realise that throughout these experiences the book has been a source of hope and inspiration for me. The conversations have encouraged me, and I thank all of my collaborators for their generosity and willingness to talk about hope. So, yes, I am more hopeful and I've learnt that in times of crisis, whether personal or global, change is possible. But I know there is still a lot of work that needs to be done.

I believe we have to have hope, and that to come to believe and trust during these uncertain times is about taking chances, about learning that the future cannot be predicted, and about realising that our hopes may not always mean obvious success (or failure, for that matter). Rather, hope may be that force which keeps us moving and changing – the renewal of life at each moment, or the 're-enchanting' of life and politics – so that the future may be about how we come to live and hope in the present. Hope may lie in our personal circumstances, or it may be in the call for different ways of thinking about political activity. Either way, I believe we have to find hope in new ways – to overcome the past, and to understand hope and despair in our lives. For our capacity to hope is shaped by the reality of our circumstances, which, depending on what those circumstances are, may not always provide the space to hope. This is why we need a sensitivity and an ability to have empathy and care towards others – which is about surrendering our prejudices, and this takes courage.

In the current world climate – post-September 11, with wars continually being fought, the treatment of refugees and asylum-seekers, and the cultural despair that shapes people's daily lives – hope should be about finding a way to move through mourning and despair. It seems to me our responsibility is to try and understand terror in all its forms, as it is only through traversing grief and mourning, and moving beyond despair, that we can have a hope for change. That is, we should try to cultivate a life built on joy rather than on hatred, fear or resentment – cultivate hopeful visions of the world that cherish life while understanding the grief, pain and suffering of others. This is about the responsibilities we have as individuals, and the connections we can make with other people. And to achieve this, empathy, care and understanding are essential.

I hope that the questions raised in this book encourage you to engage in further discussions on hope, change and the possibilities of life both now and the future, and that we will see the creation of new dialogues on what it means to hope and dream.

Appendix
Biographical Details
and Associated Readings

The conversationalists in this book are world-renowned writers and leading figures in contemporary philosophical, cultural and political thought. The conversations were recorded with equipment from *Radio Eye*, ABC Radio National, in Australia (and I thank them for their generous support and use of their facilities). The conversations took place over a three-year period from 1999 to March 2002. This included the first meetings, my research, writing and revisions, the subsequent follow-up conversations, and the translations required for this book. All the conversations involved face-to-face encounters, and in the follow-ups we met again in person, or *via* fax, email or telephone. I include below the full details of the conversational encounters – when and where we met, associated chapter readings, and some key texts for your further reading and enjoyment.

1. MURMURS OF LIFE

I met Alphonso Lingis at his home in State College, Pennsylvania, in October 2000. The conversation with Alphonso spanned over several days, and it was a continuation of the ongoing dialogue that has continued since we met in 1996. Alphonso has recently retired from his position as Professor of Philosophy at Pennsylvania State University.

Associated chapter readings and key books by Alphonso Lingis

(1989) Deathbound Subjectivity, Bloomington and Indianapolis: Indiana University Press.

(1994) The Community of Those Who Have Nothing in Common, Bloomington and Indianapolis: Indiana University Press.

(1994) Abuses, Berkeley and Los Angeles: University of California Press.

(1996) Sensation: Intelligibility in Sensibility, New Jersey: Humanities Press.

(2000) *Dangerous Emotions*, Berkeley and Los Angeles: University of California Press.

2. CARNIVAL OF THE SENSES

In early October 2000 I met Michael Taussig in New York. Our conversation was held in the corridors and in his office at Columbia University, where he is Professor of Anthropology. We continued our dialogue in the interim years and finalised the conversational journey in late 2001.

Associated chapter readings and key books by Michael Taussig

(1987) *Shamanism, Colonialism, and the Wild Man: A Study in Terror and Healing*, Chicago: Chicago University Press.

(1992) *The Nervous System*, New York and London: Routledge.

(1993) *Mimesis and Alterity: A Particular History of the Senses*, New York and London: Routledge.

(1997) *The Magic of the State*, New York and London: Routledge.

(1999) *Defacement – Public Secrecy and the Labor of the Negative*, California: Stanford University Press.

3. JOYFUL REVOLT

I met with Julia Kristeva at her Paris office in September 2000. In September 2001 we met again to follow up the ideas on 'hope'. I first met Julia in April 1996 when I was doing research for my book *Foreign Dialogues*, and since then we have maintained an ongoing dialogue. Julia is a practising psychoanalyst and is currently the Professor of Linguistics at the University of Paris VII.

Associated chapter readings and key books by Julia Kristeva

(1984) *Revolution in Poetic Language*, trans. Margaret Waller, New York: Columbia University Press.

(1987) *Tales of Love*, trans. Leon S. Roudiez, New York: Columbia University Press.

(1995) *New Maladies of the Soul*, trans. Ross Guberman, New York: Columbia University Press.

(1996) *Time and Sense: Proust and the Experience of Literature*, trans. Ross Guberman, New York: Columbia University Press.

(1998) *Contre la dépression nationale*, Paris: Les éditions Textuel.

(2000) *Sense and Non-Sense of Revolt*, trans. Jeanine Herman, New York: Columbia University Press.

(1999) *Le Génie féminin – Volume 1: Hannah Arendt*, Paris: Fayard.

(2002) *Le Génie féminin – Volume 3: Colette*, Paris: Fayard.

4. FAITH WITHOUT CERTITUDES

I travelled to Melbourne to meet Nikos Papastergiadis at his home in July 2000. Over many years we have discussed issues around exile and migration, and this dialogue gave us the opportunity to come together in a more formal sense. We met again in Melbourne to revise the conversation in March 2002. Nikos is Senior Lecturer at the Australian Centre, the University of Melbourne.

Associated chapter readings and key books by Nikos Papastergiadis

(1993) *Modernity as Exile: The Stranger in John Berger's Writing*, Manchester: Manchester University Press.

(1998) *Dialogues in the Diasporas*, London: Rivers Oram Press.

(2000) *The Turbulence of Migration*, Cambridge: Polity Press.

(2002) (Ed.) *What John Berger Saw*, Canberra: Canberra School of Arts.

5. ON BELIEVING

I met Christos Tsiolkas in July 2000 at the ABC radio studios in Melbourne, and travelled again to Melbourne to visit him at his home and discuss 'hope' in March 2002. We met early in 1999 and have worked together on numerous occasions producing his writings for radio. Christos is an Australian writer and has written several plays, film scripts, theoretical reflections and fictional works. His first book, *Loaded*, was adapted into the film *Head On*, and his collaborative work *Who's Afraid of the Working Class?* is currently being scripted for a major Australian film.

Associated chapter readings and key books by Christos Tsiolkas

(1995) *Loaded*, Sydney: Vintage.

(1999) *The Jesus Man*, Sydney: Vintage.

(1999) 'A capitalist faggot at the end of the millennium – musings on the disappointments of politics', in Dennis Glover and Glen Patmoore (Eds) *New Voices*, Sydney: Pluto Press.

6. HOPE, PASSION, POLITICS

I first met Ernesto Laclau and Chantal Mouffe in January 2000 at their home in London to discuss some preliminary ideas about 'hope'. We recorded the full conversation in August 2000 in Sydney and I had a follow-up discussion with Chantal in Paris in September 2001. Chantal is Professor of Political Theory at the University of Westminster, London, and Ernesto is Professor of Political Theory at the University of Essex.

Associated chapter readings and key books
Ernesto Laclau

(1979) *Politics and Ideology in Marxist Theory: Capitalism, Fascism, Populism*, London: Verso Editions.

(1996) *Emancipation(s)*, London and New York: Verso.

(1990) *New Reflections on the Revolution of Our Time*, London and New York: Verso.

(2000) (With Judith Butler and Slavoj Žižek) *Contingency, Hegemony, Universality: Contemporary Dialogues on the Left*, London: Verso.

Chantal Mouffe

(1992) (Ed.) *Dimensions of Radical Democracy: Pluralism, Citizenship, Community*, London: Verso.

(1993) *The Return of the Political*, London and New York: Verso.

(1994) 'Nomadic identity', in George Robertson et al., *Travellers' Tales – Narratives of Home and Displacement*, London and New York: Routledge.

(1996) (Ed.) *Deconstruction and Pragmatism*, London and New York: Routledge.

(2000) *The Democratic Paradox*, London and New York: Verso.

Laclau and Mouffe

(2001) *Hegemony and Socialist Strategy: Towards a Radical Democratic Politics* (2nd edn.), London and New York: Verso.

7. ON THE SIDE OF LIFE – JOY AND THE CAPACITY OF BEING

Ghassan Hage and I met to discuss hope in May 2000 at his home in Sydney, and we've had numerous formal and informal discussions about 'hope' over the last several years. We met again in March 2002 to finalise our conversation. Ghassan is Senior Lecturer in Anthropology at the University of Sydney.

Associated chapter readings and key books by Ghassan Hage

(1997) (With Helen Grace, Leslie Johnson, Julie Langsworth and Michael Symonds), *Home/World: Space and Marginality in Western Sydney*, Sydney: Pluto Press.

(1998) *White Nation: Fantasies of White Supremacy in a Multicultural Society*, Sydney: Pluto Press, and New York: Routledge (2000).

(2000) 'On the ethics of the pedestrian crossing, or why "mutual obligation" does not belong to the language of neo-liberal economics', *Meanjin*, December.

(2001) 'The incredible shrinking society: on ethics and hope in the era of global capitalism', *The Australian Financial Review*, 7 September.

(2001) 'Polluted memories: migration and colonial responsibility in Australia', *Traces*, Cornell University, No. 2.

(2002) (Ed.) *Arab-Australians Today: Citizenship and Belonging*, Melbourne: Melbourne University Press.

(Forthcoming 2002) *Phobic Dis/Orders: The Decline of Hope and the Rise of Paranoid Nationalism*, Sydney: Pluto Press.

8. THE REST OF THE WORLD

The conversation with Gayatri Spivak was recorded in Adelaide in February 2000. We met in her hotel room after a conference she was attending there, and we continued our dialogue by email during 2001. It was a dialogue that was a great learning experience for me – as a teacher, she took me on an unexpected journey. Gayatri is Avalon Foundation Professor in the Humanities at Columbia University, New York.

Associated chapter readings and key books by Gayatri Spivak

(1976) Translation of and introduction to *Of Grammatology*, Jacques

Derrida, Baltimore: Johns Hopkins University Press.

(1987) *In Other Worlds: Essays in Cultural Politics*, New York: Methuen.

(1993) *Outside in the Teaching Machine*, London and New York: Routledge.

(1999) *A Critique of Postcolonial Reason – Toward a History of the Vanishing Present*, London and Massachusetts: Harvard University Press.

(Forthcoming) 'Righting wrongs', in Nicholas Owen (Ed.) *Human Rights and Human Wrongs*, London and New York: Oxford University Press.

(Forthcoming) *Death of a Discipline*, New York: Columbia University Press.

9. THE ART OF LIVING

I've had a long interest in Michel Serres' writing and work on 'angels'. I was first introduced to his writing by a friend – to whom I am grateful. I met Michel at his home in Vincennes in September 2000. We continued to discuss 'hope' when I visited Paris again in September 2001, and revised the conversation later in that year. Michel has taught at Clermont-Ferrand, and the University of Paris VIII (Vincennes), he has served as a visiting Professor at Johns Hopkins University, and teaches part of the year at Stanford University in California. He was elected to the *Académie Française* in 1990.

Associated chapter readings and key books by Michel Serres

(1982) *Hermes: literature, science, philosophy*, Josué V. Harari and David F. Bell (Eds), Baltimore: Johns Hopkins University Press. (This English translation is selected essays from Michel Serres' *Hermès*, Vols 1-5)

(1982) *The Parasite*, trans. Lawrence Schehr, Baltimore: Johns Hopkins University Press.

(1995) *The Natural Contract*, trans. Elizabeth MacArthur and William Paulson, Ann Arbor: University of Michigan Press.

(1995) *Angels, A Modern Myth*, trans. Francis Cowper, Philippa Hurd (Ed.), Paris: Flammarion.

(1997) *The Troubadour of Knowledge*, trans. Sheila Faria Glaser with William Paulson, Ann Arbor: University of Michigan Press.

(1999) *Variations sur le corps*, Paris: Pommier-Fayard.

(2000) *Les cinq sens*, Paris: Hachette Littératures.

(2001) *Hominescence*, Paris: Les éditions le Pommier.

10. NAVIGATING MOVEMENTS

I met Brian Massumi in Sydney in December 2000. After our first encounter we began an extensive and ongoing dialogue on 'hope' which saw us come together at different times and in different cities (Sydney, Canberra, Vancouver) over the next two years, and we continued the conversation over the internet. Brian Massumi is Associate Professor in the Communication Department, Université de Montréal.

Associated chapter readings and key books by Brian Massumi

(1992) *A User's Guide to Capitalism and Schizophrenia – Deviations from Deleuze and Guattari*, London and Massachusetts: MIT Press.

(1993) (Ed.) *The Politics of Everyday Fear*, London and Minneapolis: University of Minnesota Press.

(1993) (With Kenneth Dean) *First and Last Emperors: The Body of the Despot and the Absolute State*, New York: Autonomedia.

(1998) 'Requiem for our prospective dead (toward a participatory critique of capitalist power)', in Eleanor Kaufaman and Kevin Jon Heller (Eds) *Deleuze and Guattari: New Mappings in Politics, Philosophy, and Culture*, Minneapolis: University of Minnesota Press.

(2002) *Parables for the Virtual: Movement, Affect, Sensation*, Durham: Duke University Press.

11. A 'COSMO-POLITICS' – RISK, HOPE, CHANGE

I caught the very fast train from Paris to Brussels in September 2001. Within the hour I had arrived in Brussels and later that day I met Isabelle Stengers at home. We did the conversation in English, which is not Stengers' native tongue, and with her care and willingness to continue to work in English, we revised the conversation in early 2002. She teaches philosophy at the Université Libre de Bruxelles.

Associated chapter readings and key books by Isabelle Stengers

(1992) (With Léon Chertok) *A Critique of Psychoanalytic Reason*, California: Stanford University Press.

(1996) (With Bernadette Bensaude Vincent) *A History of Chemistry*, London and Massachusetts: Harvard University Press.

(1996) *Cosmopolitiques, Vol. 1, La guerre des sciences*, Paris: La Découverte and Les Empêcheurs de Penser en Rond. (Her *Cosmopolitics* volumes are currently in translation).

(1997) *The Invention of the Modern Sciences*, trans. Daniel W. Smith, London and Minneapolis: University of Minnesota Press.

(1997) *Power and Invention: Situating Science*, trans. Paul Bains, London and Minneapolis: University of Minnesota Press.

INDEX